DVD edition

S/NVQ
Level
2

The Teaching Assistant's Handbook

Supporting teaching
and learning in schools

DVD
edition

WITHDRAWN

Louise Burnham

www.heinemann.co.uk

✓ Free online support
✓ Useful weblinks
✓ 24 hour online ordering

01865 888118

Heinemann
Part of Pearson

Heinemann is an imprint of Pearson Education Limited, a company incorporated in England and Wales, having its registered office at Edinburgh Gate, Harlow, Essex, CM20 2JE. Registered company number: 872828

www.pearsonschoolsandfecolleges.co.uk

Heinemann is a registered trademark of Pearson Education Limited

Text © Louise Burnham 2009

First published 2009

12 11 10 09
10 9 8 7 6 5 4 3 2 1

British Library Cataloguing in Publication Data
A catalogue record for this book is available from the British Library

ISBN 978 0 435468 91 0

Designed by Wooden Ark Studios
Typeset by Tek-Art, Crawley Down, West Sussex
Original illustrations © Pearson Education Ltd. 2008
Illustrated by Mark Beech and Tek-Art
Cover design by Siu Hang Wong
Cover photo © masterfile
Printed in the UK by Scotprint

Every effort has been made to contact copyright holders of material reproduced in this book. Any omissions will be rectified in subsequent printings if notice is given to the publishers.

Websites

The websites used in this book were correct and up-to-date at the time of publication. It is essential for tutors to preview each website before using it in class so as to ensure that the URL is still accurate, relevant and appropriate. We suggest that tutors bookmark useful websites and consider enabling students to access them through the school/college intranet.

Contents

Louise Burnham would like to thank the following people for their help and advice during the writing of this book:

Val Hughes and Sandhurst Junior School in Catford for a copy of their feedback form.

Lewisham Local Authority for a copy of a teaching assistant's job description.

Gina Kent from Lewisham LEA for looking through the chapter on ICT and for her suggestions.

Downderry Primary School in Downham for their example of a minor accident report form.

Catherine Baker for her motivational comments and Karen Hemingway for her attention to detail!

Elayne Gough from Stillness Junior School for her SHEEP acronym.

Graham Jameson, headteacher at Edmund Waller School in New Cross, for his example of a staffing structure.

Richard Rieser and Disability Equality in Education for their medical and social model of disability.

Yasmin Ahmad of Haberdashers' Aske's Knights Academy in Bromley for her literacy lesson plan.

Roy Leighton from Independent Thinking for his inspiring teaching ideas.

Carol Bird at Deptford Green School in New Cross for her help with the exams unit.

Anne Rae for her excellent work in checking the book's suitability for readers in Scotland.

All of the teaching assistant students at Lewisham College who continue to inspire with their hard work and commitment.

Photo acknowledgements

The author and the publishers would like to thank the following for permission to reproduce photographs:
page 41– © Pearson Education Ltd/Alexander Caminada
page 157– © Alamy/Sally & Richard Greenhill
page 226 – © iStockPhoto.com/Jeremy Voisey
page 235– © Masterfile/Pierre Tremblay
All other photographs © Pearson Education Ltd/Ian Wedgewood
Every effort has been made to contact copyright holders of material reproduced in this book. Any omissions will be rectified in subsequent printings if notice is given to publishers.

Dedication

In memory of Mary Burnham.

Introduction

Welcome to this handbook for the National Vocational Qualification (NVQ) or Scottish Vocational Qualification (SVQ) for Teaching Assistants at Level 2. If you are using this handbook, you will be setting out or have already begun to train for work as a Teaching Assistant. This handbook has been written for assistants in primary schools and secondary schools.

You may find yourself referred to under the general title of 'Teaching Assistant' within your school, but you may also be called a 'Classroom Assistant', 'School Assistant', 'Individual Support Assistant', 'Special Needs Assistant' or 'Learning Support Assistant'. These different titles have come about due to the different types of work which assistants are required to do within the classroom. At the time of writing, assistants are being increasingly required to take on a more leading role alongside teachers and are being given more responsibility. You may be one of a large team of assistants within a big urban primary school, or you may be part of a much smaller team of adults in a village school.

Some background information about the NVQ

The structure of the NVQ requires you to achieve **seven** units of competence from the national occupational standards. There are **five** mandatory units that each candidate must achieve. These mandatory units are longer than the optional units as they contain more information. In addition, each candidate must achieve **two** of the optional units.

Selection of optional units will be a matter of choice for the candidate in consultation with the school. Always bear in mind career aspirations and employment requirements.

Using the handbook

Each unit within this book has been written as a separate chapter. For each unit we have identified what you will need to know and understand and then given information and activities related to these items of learning. There are opportunities throughout the units to collect evidence for showing your competence. As each unit stands alone, this also means you will be able to use them in any order, although when collecting evidence remember that it may sometimes be used for more than one unit as they do overlap. When they do overlap, you will find cross references in the book.

For those taking the qualification in Scotland, the relevant Scottish terminology has also been placed alongside any non-Scottish terms.

Throughout the book you will need to think about how the theory fits in with your experiences in the classroom. As you gain experience and expertise in your work with children, you may also find it a useful reference, particularly with reference to specific issues, such as working with bilingual children.

There are some items of knowledge and understanding which are relevant to all the units. These are:

- awareness and appreciation of the rights of the child

- understanding of the need for confidentiality when working with children

- understanding for high standards of behaviour, commitment and reliability when working with children

- understanding your role and responsibilities towards children, their parents/carers, your colleagues and other professionals

- understanding and appreciation of the wide range of parenting styles, customs and cultures which co-exist in society.

You will need to consider all these in relation to all the work you undertake within a school.

Features in the book

What you need to know and understand
This section lists all the knowledge points that are contained in this unit. For points where the material has been covered in earlier units, this is clearly indicated in italic text and a cross-reference is supplied.

Case study
These are examples within real settings where you can apply what you have learned in particular situations.

Keys to good practice
These are checklists of the most importance aspects of what you have just learned.

Key terms
These explain clearly and concisely the crucial pieces of information found in the book.

Thinking point
These introduce new elements or further research you can undertake to explore topics.

Portfolio activity
These help you collect relevant information and experience for your portfolio. The knowledge points these apply to are clearly shown.

For your portfolio
These explain how best to produce and present evidence for this unit in your portfolio.

Activities to accompany DVD footage
This edition is accompanied by a DVD which contains short clips of teaching assistants working in a variety of activities in primary settings, and includes follow-up activities for your portfolio. Look out for the ⬤ symbol, which indicates that there is a clip you can view. You can find more guidance and the activity sheets on pages 245–260.

1 Provide Support for Learning Activities

This unit examines how you can most effectively support pupils and teachers when undertaking teaching and learning activities in school. This is one of the most important aspects of your role as a teaching assistant. All learning will take place under the direction of a teacher, but you may be asked to support both individuals and groups if you are working at Level 2. The unit identifies what you need to do in order to support and evaluate planned learning activities and applies not only to classroom activities but also to any setting where teaching and learning takes place, such as extended hours provision or educational visits.

The unit defines the type of support you may be asked to give in the presence or absence of the teacher. It will give you some idea of the kinds of problems you may encounter and how to deal with them. You will also need to look at the different ways in which you promote independent learning and the importance of doing this. This will include developing relationships with pupils to enable you to provide an appropriate level of assistance while encouraging them to make their own decisions about their learning.

What you need to know and understand

For this unit, you will need to know and understand:

- The relationship between your own role and the role of the teacher within the learning environment
- Your role and responsibilities for supporting pupils' learning and the implications of this for the sort of support you can provide
- The school policies for inclusion and equality of opportunity, and the implication of these for how you work with pupils
- Your experience and expertise in relation to supporting learning activities and how this relates to the planned activities
- The objectives of the learning activities to be supported
- The importance of planning and evaluation of learning activities
- The basic principles underlying child development and learning; the factors that promote effective learning; and the barriers to effective learning
- Strategies to use for supporting pupils' learning as individuals and in groups
- School policy on the use of praise, assistance, rewards and sanctions
- The sorts of problems that might occur when supporting learning activities and how to deal with these
- The importance of working within the boundaries of your role and competence and when you should refer to others
- How to give feedback in a constructive manner and in a way that ensures that working relationships are maintained

Relationship between your own role and the role of the teacher within the learning environment

Your role and the role of the teacher should both be very clear to you so that you are able to carry out your duties effectively. Although you are working as an adult within the classroom, what you do within the learning environment should be managed and led by the teacher. It is the teacher who has overall responsibility for pupils' learning and who needs to report back to others, such as parents and governors, about pupils' progress. Your role is to support what the teacher does: the two roles should therefore complement one another. For each teaching and learning activity, you should be aware what you are doing and what the teacher expects from you.

Some of the duties of a teacher and those of a teaching assistant around providing support for learning activities

Role of teacher	Role of teaching assistant
• To be responsible for planning and preparing learning activities to the National or Early Years Curriculum • To teach pupils according to their educational needs • To assess, record and report on the development, progress and attainment of pupils • To take responsibility for all other adults within the learning environment • To communicate and consult with the parents of pupils • To communicate and co-operate with persons or bodies outside the school • To participate in meetings arranged for any of the above purposes	• To plan and prepare work alongside the teacher • To support learning activities effectively as directed by the teacher • To assess or evaluate pupils' work as directed by the teacher • To report any problems or queries to the teacher • To give feedback to the teacher following planned activities

In England and Wales, many teachers also have responsibility for managing an area of the curriculum or an aspect of school life, for example, they may be the Science co-ordinator or the head of a year group. This will be included in their job description.

Portfolio activity K1

Identifying the difference between your role and the role of the teacher

Write a reflective account to show what you understand to be the difference between your role and the role of a teacher with whom you work closely.

Your role and responsibilities for supporting pupils' learning and the implications of this for the sort of support you can provide

In order to support pupils effectively you should have a very clear idea about exactly where you fit into the school structure and your role within it. If you are employed by the school, you should also have an up-to-date **job description** that is a realistic reflection of your duties. Your job description may divide your responsibilities under different headings such as:

- teaching and learning
- administrative duties
- standards and quality assurance
- other duties.

ⓘ Key terms

Learning activities – the learning activities planned by the teacher for individual pupils, groups of pupils or the whole class. The activities may relate to a single lesson or span several lessons, for example, as part of a topic, project or theme

Job description – a working definition of your roles and responsibilities

If you are working as a volunteer, you should have the opportunity to speak to a senior manager who will be able to tell you what the school expects of you while you are there. You may need to obtain a job description as a guideline, and it is likely that the school will also ask you what your course demands of you and about any specific experience you need to have while you are there. Ask to be involved in school life as much as possible and for the opportunity to work alongside teachers so that you can develop an understanding of the teaching assistant role.

Teaching assistants are likely to have different levels of responsibility within school, both in and outside the classroom, depending on their experience. These responsibilities may vary widely between schools and roles, although there will be many areas that overlap. However, in England and Wales, if you are being asked to support teaching and learning as one of the main aspects of your role, you should be working closely with teachers and have access to detailed plans. You should also have the opportunity to put forward your own ideas or thoughts about planned activities. If you are less experienced and feel that you are not trained to carry out some of the duties asked of you, you should be able to ask for additional support.

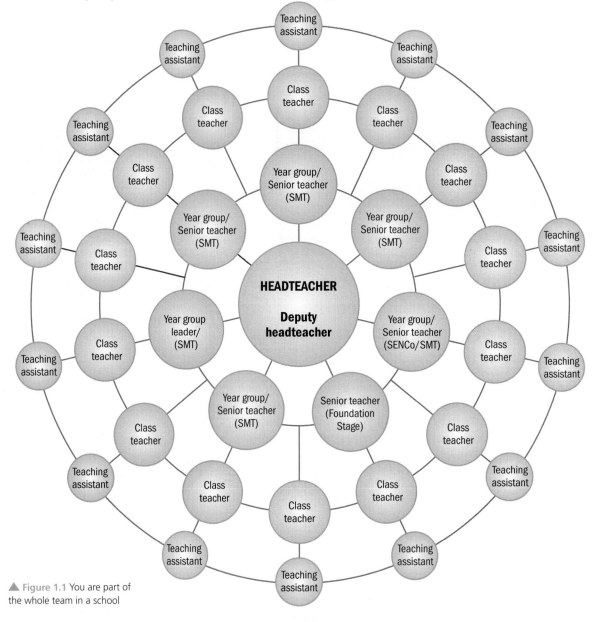

▲ Figure 1.1 You are part of the whole team in a school

Depending on your role within the classroom, the amount of support you are required to give individual pupils may vary. For example, a teaching assistant employed specifically to work with a pupil who has special educational (additional support for learning (ASL)) needs may have much more detailed information on the individual pupil than a teaching assistant who is supporting learning in the whole class. However, if you are new to a class you should ask the class teacher whether there is anything specific you should know about the pupils. (For more on special educational (ASL) needs, see Unit 12.)

When supporting learning you may be working with individuals, groups or the whole class. You may need to provide support using a variety of different strategies (see K8, page 14).

You will be supporting the class teacher and pupils in your class, but you will also be part of the whole school team. Teaching and learning activities will need to be planned and you may or may not be directly involved at the planning stage. However, you should have some advance notice of what you will be doing so that you can prepare yourself. This may involve discussing plans with the teacher before the class or having access to planned activities, for example, if they are displayed on the wall. You will also need to know about any groups within the class, for example pupils may be in set groups for different subjects depending on their abilities.

Case study K2

Recognising the boundaries of the support you can provide

You are working as a volunteer in a Year 1 (P2) class for two days a week and providing 'general' in-class support, which involves monitoring what the children are doing at any time and providing support where it is needed. You have not been working in the school for very long and are just getting to know the pupils. One day your class teacher is off sick and you are working with a supply teacher who asks you to take a group of pupils to the ICT suite. You do not feel very confident about doing this on your own.

- What would you say to the supply teacher?
- Should you say something if you are not confident about doing it? Why?

School policies for inclusion and equality of opportunity, and the implication of these for how you work with pupils

The principle that all pupils should be able to access all areas of the curriculum is high on the education agenda, especially in the light of the Every Child Matters framework and the focus on personalised learning in all sectors of education. The reasons for this are as follows.

Human rights
- All pupils have a right to learn and play together.
- Pupils should not be discriminated against for any reason.
- Inclusion is concerned with improving schools for staff as well as for pupils.

Equal opportunities in education

- Pupils do better in inclusive settings, both academically and socially.
- Pupils should not need to be separated to achieve adequate educational provision.
- Inclusive education is a more efficient use of educational resources.

Social opportunities

- Inclusion in education is one aspect of inclusion in society.
- Pupils need to be involved with all of their peers.

All schools should have information available about codes of practice concerning equal opportunities and inclusion. These will sometimes form part of the school policy for special educational (ASL) needs, but are usually separate. You should be familiar with your school's policies on inclusion and equal opportunities.

Always be aware of the needs of different pupils, whatever these may be. Remember that these may become more apparent as you get to know particular pupils. Those who may be vulnerable could include pupils:

- who have special educational (ASL) needs
- who speak English as an additional language
- who are new to the setting
- who are gifted and talented
- whose culture is different from the predominant culture of the setting
- who are in foster care
- whose parents' views are not consistent with those of the school.

K3 ## Portfolio activity

Identifying the impact of the equal opportunity or inclusion policy

Find a copy of your school's equal opportunity or inclusion policy. For your portfolio, you need to show what its implications are for how you support teaching and learning of pupils. You can do this by:

- highlighting the relevant parts of the text and putting this into your portfolio
- summarising the main points of the policy.

When supporting pupils for different activities, teaching assistants may find themselves in a variety of situations. For example, an individual teaching assistant may assist and support a particular pupil, and will usually work alongside or close to that pupil. As the pupil may have a Statement of Special Educational Needs (Co-ordinated Support Plan), they will need support from the teaching assistant to ensure that they have full access to the curriculum. However, when working with a group of pupils, it is vital that teaching assistants ensure that all individuals in the group are given the same opportunities to share their thoughts and opinions.

Your experience and expertise in relation to supporting learning activities and how this relates to the planned activities

All members of staff should be able to use their own experience to support learning activities. You may have a particular interest or strength that you would like to use when working with pupils; it might be in a subject area such as History or you may have your own ideas in relation to how activities are planned.

You should also have the chance to look at the planned activities and apply your own expertise to how you will carry them out. If you have been involved in planning, you will have been able to suggest to the teacher how certain pupils might work best together or what approach to take with pupils who might need additional guidance.

You should also be aware of your own areas of weakness. If you are not comfortable working on a particular area such as Maths or if you are asked to support pupils who you suspect know more about a particular subject than you, you should speak to the teacher. It is important that you feel confident about what you are doing when supporting pupils, as they may pick up on your anxiety if you are not. If you anticipate any other difficulties in carrying out the plan, which the teacher may not have foreseen, you should also point these out.

Case study K4

Using experience and expertise

Mohammad has been working as a teaching assistant in a primary school for a year and is based in Year 5 (P6), although he previously worked in a secondary school. The class teacher has been planning a Design Technology activity for the following day and he has asked Mohammad to take groups of pupils out to do it in a shared area of the school. Mohammad is experienced at the subject as he supported it for some time in secondary school and he has some ideas of his own that he would like to share with the teacher.

- Should Mohammad say something? Why?
- Think about the kinds of experience or expertise that you have and how these might be useful to you in your role.

Objectives of the learning activities to be supported

The learning objectives of a lesson define what we are hoping pupils will learn during that session and therefore what they will be assessed against. For example, the learning objectives of a Music activity might be to be able to recognise different styles of jazz (although some in the group may recognise more and some less at the end of the session).

Teaching assistants need to be clear on the learning objectives of the activities they will be supporting. Plans should be available and show a clear progression in the work pupils are being asked to do so that learning objectives build on each other. You should also have had at least some discussion with the teacher about the pupils and how you will be approaching the task, and you need to be clear on how what you are doing fits in with the overall plans. Usually teachers will put the learning objective on the smartboard or whiteboard at the beginning of the session so that all pupils are aware of what they will be learning.

Always make sure that you know in advance when your assessor will be coming into school to observe you working with pupils and that you are able to tell him/her what the objectives are for the sessions you are supporting.

Importance of planning and evaluation of learning activities

Planning and evaluation are important because they structure teaching and learning. We need to be able to look at what pupils have achieved so that we can help them to progress to the next stage. Planning, teaching and evaluating should form a cycle.

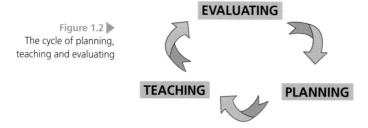

Figure 1.2 ▶
The cycle of planning, teaching and evaluating

ⓘ Key terms

Planning – deciding with the teacher what you will do, when, how and with which pupils, to ensure that planned learning activities are implemented effectively

Learning resources – materials, equipment (including ICT), software, books and other written materials, DVDs, etc. that are required to support teaching and learning

You need to know about the different types of planning that take place in schools. Usually, teachers plan for the long term (over a term or half term), then the medium term (over a week) and finally short term (for the day). You should have a copy of the long-term plans if you are working permanently in one class or department so that you know about the schemes of work that are to be carried out with pupils. Medium-term plans may be worked on at or before the start of term so that staff know in which week and order different areas of work will be covered. It is also important to know when different **learning resources** will be needed, including the use of additional adults, and to consider how to ensure that they are accessible.

You can plan in different ways. Time may be set aside for you to plan with the teacher or he/she may devise the plan and then work through it with you to ensure that you are happy with the activities you are asked to do and if you have anything to add. In some schools, particularly secondary, it is more difficult for teaching assistants to have time to plan with teachers, particularly if they are working in a number of different classes. Some teaching assistants in secondary schools are now attached to departments or curriculum areas so that they have the opportunity to become familiar with schemes of work and have more time to talk through plans with particular staff.

Plans should be accessible to all adults working with the class or group, so that they also have a clear understanding of the learning objectives and what they are expected to do. If you do not have time to look at plans, you should at least have a discussion with the teacher about learning activities. This may mean that you need to write things down so that you remember what you are going to be doing and what preparations you need to make. As you become more experienced, you will find that you become quicker at thinking of what you will need for an activity. You may also find that you have your own suggestions or ideas to add to teachers' plans. (See also K4 on page 7).

Through planning in advance with the teacher, you will be able to consider the activities you are going to work on with pupils and make preparations if required. If you are working as a cover supervisor, it is particularly important that you have access to teachers' plans in advance and are not given them at the last minute.

Figure 1.3 ▶
A lesson plan

Lesson Plan	YEAR 10 MIXED ABILITY
Objectives	Analysing exam questions Using marks to guide answers Finding answers in the text
Resources	GCSE AQA for English P 54-57 Activity Sheets Teacher 2 x T/A
Starter	Brainstorm around class around the aims - Elicit from pupils reasons for aims
Main Teaching	In differentiated groups Pairs → Pairs + group Pupils open envelope 1 - guided by teacher - Read the questions. (T. checks understanding) Pupils open envelope 2 - Working in groups answer first 4 questions. (Teacher checks answer as a class) Pupils now answer the questions proper after reading the text together - Answers in exercise books Teacher goes over answers as a group.

Development in groups or individually	(AA) Group	(A) Group	(BA) Group
	Working on activity sheets independently with some input from teacher	Working with T/A for less able pupils	Working with T/A for EAL pupils.
	All groups complete same activity		

Plenary	What skills have you learnt? Teacher recap on aims of lesson.
Homework	N/A.

Visual	Auditory	Tactile	Kinesthetic	Literacy	Numeracy	ICT
✓	✓	✓		✓		

▼ **Figure 1.4** Planning together

Sometimes changes need to be made to plans and this may happen at the last minute due to something unexpected happening. This is unavoidable and you need to be flexible and able to manage these situations. Any changes to pupils' routine or timetable may affect their behaviour and you also need to take this into consideration.

You also need to learn how to evaluate learning activities that you have undertaken with pupils. This is because you should have a chance to feed back to teachers (see also K12, page 19) on whether pupils have achieved learning objectives, so that they can plan effectively for next time. Evaluation means reflecting on how the activity has gone and why things may have gone a certain way. You may ask yourself the following types of questions to help you to evaluate activities.

- What went well? How do you know it went well? (For example, think about the resources, learning environment, pupils' reaction to the task and how much time was available.)
- What did not go so well? How do you know?
- Did you need to change any aspect of the activity as you were working? How?
- Would you change your approach if you carried out the activity again? How?

It is important to reflect on and evaluate what you do after each activity so that you become used to doing it as a matter of course. As you become more experienced, it will be easier for you to see why activities have or have not gone particularly well.

Keys to good practice

Planning and evaluation

✓ Try to set aside time to plan with teachers if possible.
✓ Ensure that you understand what you have been asked to do and are aware of learning objectives.
✓ Point out any queries you have or potential difficulties at the planning stage.
✓ Make sure you understand any differentiated activities and are aware of pupils' targets, particularly if you are supporting an individual child.
✓ Ensure that there is time for evaluation at the end of the task or use a feedback sheet to pass on information to the teacher.

K6 Case study

Finding time to plan and evaluate learning activities

Moira is working in Nursery and Reception at school. Her own two children are in Years 1 (P2) and 2 (P3). She finds it difficult to remember what is happening in each class and can sometimes muddle the topics. The teachers tend to plan together straight after school on a Thursday and Moira is unable to attend the meeting as she has to pick up her own children. As a result she feels that she is missing out and is not supporting the teaching and learning as well as she could.

- What could Moira do?
- Why is it important that she has time to discuss learning activities both before and after working with pupils?

Basic principles underlying child development and learning; the factors that promote effective learning; and the barriers to effective learning

Basic principles of child development and learning

These basic principles are based on how children learn, think and develop – often known as cognitive development. As professionals working in schools, teaching assistants need to know about and understand them. There have been a number of different theories about how children learn and are influenced as they develop, although most educationalists and practitioners believe that children learn best in a range of different ways.

Some theorists believe that children learn best when they observe other people. This is known as social learning theory and was developed by Albert Bandura. Bandura believed that children watch others, in particular adults, and copy what they do. This applies to both positive and negative behaviour. For example, if children see adults behaving violently or aggressively, they are much more likely to do the same. If they see adults who are considerate and caring towards others they are likely to copy this behaviour.

Another theory is that children pass through different stages of learning. Jean Piaget believed that the way children think and learn is governed by their age and stage of development, because learning is based on experience. As children's experiences change, they adapt what they believe; for example a child who only ever sees green apples will believe that all apples are green. Children need to extend their experiences in order to extend their learning.

Types of learning		
Age	**Stage of learning**	**Characteristics**
0–2 years	Sensory motor stage	Babies start to find out about the world around them and discover what things around them can do.
2–6 years	Pre-operational stage	Children start to develop thought processes and use symbolic play. They find it easier to learn when they can see and use practical examples.
6–11 years	Concrete operations stage	Children are able to think on a more abstract level. They can use more abstract concepts, e.g. a box can represent a car.
12+	Formal operations	Young people are able to apply what they have learned to new situations.

B.F. Skinner believed that children learn best through positive experiences. His theory is that we will repeat experiences that are enjoyable and avoid those that are not. This is as relevant for learning experiences as it is for behaviour. For example, a child who is praised for working at a particular task will want to work at it again. Skinner called this positive reinforcement.

Lev Vygotsky believed that children need adults to support them in their learning in order to extend their 'Zone of Proximal Development', which means where their learning might extend. He said that children cannot learn as much without adults and others helping them.

(For further references on theories of learning, see the end of this unit.)

Effective learning

Effective learning depends not only on effective teaching, but on the situation and aptitudes of the individual pupil. Learning is influenced by the pupil's age and stage of development, but is also dependent on the pupil's experiences and personality, influences that are different for each individual. You need to consider these factors when supporting learning in order to be able to understand the needs of each pupil.

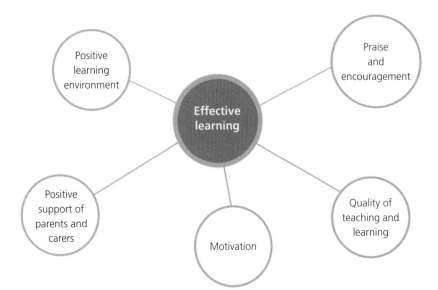

◀ **Figure 1.5** Factors that contribute to effective learning

◀ **Figure 1.6** An exhibition in praise of learning

Positive learning environment

The school should provide pupils with an environment that is positive and reflects the needs of all pupils. There should be a variety of stimulating areas within classrooms and around the school, and displays that reflect the work of all pupils, not just those who produce the best work.

Praise and encouragement

Adults need to give pupils as much praise and encouragement as possible in order to support their learning. Some pupils need more of this than others, particularly if they lack confidence (for more on this, see K9).

Good quality of teaching and learning

Pupils' learning is affected by the quality of teaching they receive and whether they are motivated. They need to know and understand the purpose of their learning and feel part of the learning process.

Positive support of parents and carers

The learning process is about more than what pupils gain while they are in school, although this is important. The support of parents and carers is vital to what school staff are doing and there should be a partnership between schools and families to ensure that lines of communication are always open, as this will benefit all parties.

Motivation

Pupils need to be able to identify that what they are doing is relevant and they need to want to do it. If they are finding it difficult to understand why they are doing something, they are less likely to be motivated to do it as it will not appear to have meaning to them. It is very important to involve pupils at all stages in the learning process so that they do not feel that learning is something which is being done to them; rather they should feel that they are part of the process.

The absence of any of the above factors can lead to barriers between pupils and their learning. Other barriers may be due to physical factors or the attitudes of those involved.

▼ Figure 1.7 Supporting the learning process

Physical barriers to effective learning might include not having access to the equipment or facilities to carry out a particular activity and this could particularly affect pupils with physical disabilities if special provision is not made for them.

The attitudes of staff, fellow pupils or the affected pupil may also present barriers to effective learning. We need to have high expectations of all pupils and avoid giving them 'labels' or assuming that they will not be able to achieve. Pupils may also have low self-esteem or expectations of their own abilities and be unwilling to try activities if they do not feel that they can do them. All of this can be very damaging as it leads to assumptions about what a pupil can or cannot do.

(See also K10, page 17 for problems when supporting learning activities and how to deal with them.)

Portfolio activity K7

Investigating learning theories

Find out a little more about the learning theories of Bandura, Piaget, Skinner and Vygotsky. How do the factors that promote effective learning relate to the theories? For example, Skinner's theory relates directly to the idea that children benefit from plenty of praise and encouragement during learning activities. Can you find other factors that relate to Piaget's, Vygotsky's and Bandura's theories?

Strategies to use for supporting pupils' learning as individuals and in groups

It is likely that as you become more experienced, you will develop a range of different strategies to help you support pupils more effectively. As well as encouraging them to carry out tasks as independently as possible, pupils may need you to challenge them further and motivate them to learn. Depending on the way that tasks have been set, you should offer as much encouragement as is needed while allowing pupils to develop their own self-help skills. There are different ways in which you can support pupil learning; the following list will give you some ideas, but it is likely that you will develop your own strategies as you grow in experience.

Before pupils start the task

Make sure pupils understand what they have to do and give them a starting point so that they are able to focus. Check their understanding of any specific vocabulary.

When the pupils are on task

Use open-ended questions (e.g. 'what', 'why' and 'who') with pupils rather than questions that prompt them to answer 'yes' or 'no'. Rephrase questions if necessary. Encourage pupils both by using praise and by involving them in discussion about what they are doing. Make sure you involve pupils in any further learning opportunities that become available as you are working. Modify or change the task if pupils are finding it hard to understand – they may be able to work better if it is presented differently.

When the pupils are finishing the task

Question the pupils to check on their understanding before you feed back to the teacher. Ask them to look again at the learning objectives to consider whether these have been met and to evaluate their own work against them. If they tell you that they have finished, it is always worth keeping an additional challenge or related task in mind for them to do.

If you are working with an individual pupil, it is likely that you will develop an understanding of their likes and dislikes as well as identify the kinds of strategies that will help to support and motivate them. Pupils will also have their own learning targets and both you and the pupil should be aware of these.

When working with groups, your main consideration must be involving all pupils and making sure that some individuals do not take over question and answer sessions. In particular you may need to discuss with the teacher additional strategies for supporting those children who are reticent about putting ideas forward, particularly if they lack confidence in larger groups.

Keys to good practice

Supporting pupils during learning activities

✓ Ensure that both you and the pupils understand what you are required to do.
✓ Use a range of questioning strategies.
✓ Remind pupils of the main teaching points.
✓ Model the correct vocabulary.
✓ Make sure you actively listen to all pupils.
✓ Encourage pupils to work together and listen to one another.
✓ Help pupils to use the relevant resources and ensure there are enough.
✓ Reassure those who are less confident about their ideas.
✓ Listen carefully.
✓ Give positive praise wherever possible.
✓ Have high expectations of all pupils.
✓ Adapt work where necessary.
✓ Inform the teacher of any problems that you have been unable to resolve.
✓ Provide a level of assistance that allows pupils to achieve without helping them too much.

Case study

K8

Supporting pupils' learning

You have been asked to work with a group of Year 9 (S3) pupils on an activity to find out how much they know about the First World War at the start of a History topic. You are finding it difficult to engage two of the pupils, who say they don't know anything about the war and do not seem to be motivated.

● What kinds of strategies might you use with these pupils?
● How could you help them develop independence in carrying out the task?

School policy on the use of praise, assistance, rewards and sanctions

You should be aware of your school's policy for the use of praise, assistance and rewards as they are all valuable tools when supporting pupils' learning and you will need to use them. They may be written down as part of your school's behaviour or inclusion policies, or it might be assumed that staff and volunteers just 'know' them. Make sure you are aware of which you can and cannot use when supporting learning.

Praise and encouragement

As you will be working with pupils who are learning all the time, it is vital that you use praise and encouragement to keep them on task and motivated. This kind of reward is very effective, although it must be clear to pupils why they are being praised. It is important, as you get to know pupils, to praise their efforts as well as their achievements. Pupils need to have recognition for what they do and this could take several forms:

- **Verbal praise** – This could be simple praise while pupils are working, for example by saying, 'well done, that's a great introduction' or by asking the pupil to show their work to the teacher at a convenient moment and so gain another adult's attention. Verbal praise can be a very powerful motivator as it gives the pupil instant recognition that they are doing well.
- **Stickers, charts and merit marks or house points** – You should be aware of any school policy on how these are used. Some schools leave it to the class teacher to use reward systems that they find the most beneficial, whereas others may not like the free use of stickers.
- **School recognition of a good effort** – If the pupil is rewarded during an assembly or gains a school certificate, this will offer motivation at all stages of learning.

Assistance

You need to be aware that your role is that of an enabler, rather than someone who does the task for pupils if they are having difficulties. It is important to remember to find different ways of encouraging pupils to arrive at the answer or complete the task themselves, for example through questioning and encouragement. If you need to give pupils too much support, they clearly do not understand the task and you need to inform the teacher.

K9 # Case study

Working within school policy on rewards

Femi is working in Year 1 (S2) and has recently started a new job. In her last school, she always kept a packet of stickers in her pocket to put on children's work if they had done well. She has continued to do this in her new school. In her group, Jack has just completed an activity for the first time this week and has tried very hard, so she gives him a sticker. She is surprised when the class teacher tells her that she is not allowed to do this because it is not school policy.

- Do you think that anyone is in the wrong?
- What might be Femi's next steps?
- How else might Femi encourage Jack if he has done well?

Problems that might occur when supporting learning activities and how to deal with these

You may encounter **problems** when supporting learning activities. They could take different forms, but could relate to any of the following factors.

> **ⓘ Key term**
>
> **Problems** – the barriers and hindrances to supporting planned learning activities

Learning resources

The task will usually require certain resources such as pencils, paper, worksheets or textbooks, Maths apparatus, paint pots, Science equipment and so on. If you have been asked to set up for the task, make sure that you have enough equipment and that it is accessible to all the pupils. Also, where you have equipment that needs to be in working order, check that you know how to use it, that it is functioning and that pupils will be able to use it. If the teacher or another adult has set up for your task, it is still worth doing a check to ensure that you have everything you need. In this way, you avoid potential problems before they arise.

Learning environment

This relates to the suitability of the area in which pupils are working. Problems may arise in the following circumstances.

Insufficient space to work

You should always ensure that you have sufficient space for people and equipment before you start. Check that there is enough space around the table or work area for the number of individuals that you have been asked to work with. If pupils are working on weighing, for example, and there is no room for them all to have access to the scales, they may quickly lose their focus on the task.

Too much noise

The pupils may be working with you in a corner of the classroom, but any other kind of noise will be a distraction whether it is from others in the room or an outside disturbance such as grass cutting or a nearby road. In this situation, it may be possible for you to investigate another area in the school that is available and free from this kind of noise. Alternatively, inform the teacher that the noise level in the classroom is preventing pupils from benefiting from the activity.

Disturbances from other pupils

This can often be a problem if you are working in the classroom because tasks with close adult supervision can often seem more interesting to pupils than what they are doing. They may be curious to find out what the guided group or individual is doing, and if there is a continual problem, the teacher should be informed.

Pupils' ability to learn

There may be a variety of reasons why pupils are not able to achieve.

Pupils' behaviour

If any pupils are not focused on the task due to poor behaviour, you need to intervene straightaway. If pupils are able to continue interrupting, they will do so and you will be unable to continue with the task. Always praise the good behaviour of any pupils who are doing what is required of them, as this sometimes makes the others try to gain your attention by behaving well. As a last resort, if one particular pupil is misbehaving and disturbing others, remove him/her from the group and work with them later.

Pupils' self-esteem

Sometimes a pupil with low self-esteem may think that they are not able to complete the task that has been set. Some pupils are quite difficult to motivate and you need to offer reassurance and praise wherever you can to improve their self-esteem. However, it is very important to remember that your role is one of a facilitator and that you are not there to complete the task for the pupil. Some may just need a little gentle reassurance and coaxing to 'have a go', while others may be more difficult to work with and require you to use your questioning skills.

Pupils' lack of concentration

There may be a few reasons for pupils finding it hard to concentrate on the task that has been set. A pupil may be unable to complete the work (the teacher has made the task too difficult) or complete the task quickly and need more stimulation. Some pupils, particularly younger ones, have a short concentration span and the task may be taking too long to complete. If this is the case, you need to stop the pupil and continue with the task later.

Pupils' range of ability

You may find that you are working with a class or group of pupils whose wide range of ability means that some of them are finished before others. If you are faced with a situation where one child has finished while others are still working, you may need to have something else ready for them to move on to. For example, if a group of Year 2 (P3) pupils are working on an activity to find words ending in '-ing', you could ask those who finish early to use their words in sentences of their own.

Unclear or incomplete information

Sometimes the teacher may set activities that are not suitable for the pupils involved or you may not have clear or complete information to support the activity. You may need to change the activity to make it more achievable for the pupils by going back and checking with the teacher.

Importance of working within the boundaries of your role and competence and when you should refer to others

As a teaching assistant you will be working under the direction of a teacher, even if you are working with a large group of pupils on your own. If you are working at NVQ Level 2, you will have some experience and may be able to resolve issues as they arise when supporting pupils' learning (for example, see the potential problems on page 17). However, even if you are more experienced, you are still working within the role of a teaching assistant so you should know the boundaries of your responsibilities and know when to refer to the class teacher or senior managers in the school.

Broadly speaking, you need to refer to others in situations that you cannot resolve or which:

- disrupt the learning of pupils working with you
- are indicators that a pupil does not understand the teaching points despite being approached in different ways
- show that a pupil has a very good understanding and is working at a higher level than others in his/her group
- are issues of which others need to be aware (e.g. child protection concerns or incidents that have happened at home)
- put others in danger.

Working within your role and referring to others

Cathy is working with a group of Year 7 (S1) pupils on recognising different verb endings in French. She has six pupils in the group, two of whom are upsetting one another. Cathy has already moved Ella, one of the pupils, but she is now distracting the whole group.

- What would you do in this situation?
- Give three reasons why it is important to resolve this as soon as possible.

How to give feedback in a constructive manner

You need to give **feedback** to teachers after you have carried out a learning activity with pupils so that he/she knows whether pupils have achieved the learning objectives and how much support was needed. Finding time to give feedback to teachers can be very difficult and you may need to make sure you give it at an appropriate moment. There is often little time to sit down in school and discuss pupils' work with teachers. Some teachers and teaching assistants will discuss each day's activities on the phone on a daily basis. Others will come into school early in order to plan and give feedback.

> **Key term**
>
> **Feedback** – providing the teacher with information about the pupils' responses to the learning activity, the materials involved and your contribution to supporting the activity

Another way in which feedback can be given if there is no time for verbal discussion is through the use of feedback forms. If these are planned and set out correctly, you will be able to show whether pupils have achieved learning objectives, how they responded to the activity and how much support they needed, which can be an effective time-saving device.

◀ Figure 1.8 Make sure you try to speak to the teacher about learning activities at an appropriate moment

Teacher/TA Feedback Sheet

Class: Year 7

To be filled in by teacher:
Teacher's name: J. Nakumura
TA's name: P. Wilkinson

Brief description of activity

Revision of Year 6 work on plotting different points and shapes using co-ordinates on x and y axes.
Follow up to revise reflecting shapes.

How session is linked to medium-term plans

Departmental schemes of work – Revision of work on shape carried out in Year 6

TA's role

To check understanding of how to plot co-ordinates.

Important vocabulary

axis, perimeter, shape, diagonal, co-ordinate, edge, corner
names of shapes

Key learning points

To be able to plot points using co-ordinates.
To identify and reflect shapes.

For use during group work: (TA to complete)

Pupils	D	H	Feedback/Assessment

D = Can do task
H = Help required to complete task

▲ Figure 1.9 A feedback form

You may need to be tactful when feeding back to teachers about learning activities. There may be a number of reasons why an activity has not gone well, for example, if the environment was not ideal for the task. However, if the problem is clearly due to planning or the pupils have not found the task engaging, it may be difficult to suggest this to the teacher. Depending on the personality and how well you get along with one another, this may or may not present problems. If you have a relationship that allows you both to give suggestions to one another and discuss any issues as they arise, you will find it easier. The most important thing to remember is that even if you are sure you are right, it is better to give your feedback in the form of suggestions.

Case study K12

Feeding back in a constructive manner

Mark has been working with a group of Year 10 (S4) pupils on a textiles activity. He has been asked to support them while they work on a project to design and make a leisure shirt. The project has been ongoing over a number of weeks and is progressing, but Mark feels that he has only had one opportunity to feed back to the teacher. This project forms part of the pupils' GCSE work and Mark is becoming progressively more frustrated by the fact that he is unable to speak to the teacher. Eventually he asks her how he is expected to support the pupils when he does not know what he is supposed to be doing.

- How might this approach be damaging?
- Are either Mark or the teacher acting appropriately in this instance?
- What might Mark say to the teacher in order to maintain a more positive relationship with her?

Which phrase from each pair would you use in these situations?

Situation A

'There is no way that group will only take half an hour to do that piece of work – it's just too hard for them.'

'Would you mind if, next time I did that activity, I made the introductory activity longer and the focused activity shorter? I don't think the next group will be able to go straight into the main task.'

Situation B

'I knew that those two could not work together.'

'What do you think about putting Charlie and Sam together, so that Charlie can guide Sam by reading the problems to him? Then I can swap some of the other pairs round too.'

Situation C

'Why don't we try it slightly differently with Kaleb so that he doesn't have to go straight into the abstract method?'

'Kaleb just won't be able to understand it if we do it that way.'

For your portfolio...

Write a reflective account of a learning activity you have undertaken with a group of pupils. Drawing closely on the knowledge base for this unit, include the following:

- information you had before the activity such as learning objectives, the needs of the pupils and any specific criteria you needed to follow
- whether you had any input or suggestions to make at the planning stage
- how you included all the pupils in the group and why you need to do this
- why it is important to plan and evaluate learning activities you have done with pupils
- any problems that have occurred and how you dealt with them.

Further reading

Donaldson, Margaret (1986) *Children's Minds* (New Ed edn) (HarperCollins: ISBN 978-0006861225)

Lindon, Jennie (2005) *Understanding Child Development Linking Theory and Practice* (Hodder Arnold: ISBN 978-0340886694)

Pound, Linda (2005) *How Children Learn: From Montessori to Vygotsky – Educational approaches and theories made easy* (Step Forward Publishing: ISBN 978-1904575092)

Wood, David (1997) *How Children Think and Learn: The social contexts of cognitive development* (2nd edn) (Understanding Children's Worlds series) (Blackwell Publishers: ISBN 978-0631200079)

National Curriculum documents

England: www.nc.uk.net

Northern Ireland: www.ccea.org.uk

Scotland: www.ltscotland.org.uk

Wales: www.old.accac.org.uk/eng/content.php?cID=5

Other websites

www.everychildmatters.gov.uk

www.support4learning.org.uk – (learning styles)

2 Support Children's Development

This unit requires you to have knowledge of the areas of development of children and young people in different age ranges. In particular, you will need to be competent in understanding the needs of the children and young people with whom you are working. The unit also requires you to have an understanding of the purpose and use of observations when working with children and young people.

What you need to know and understand

For this unit, you will need to know and understand

- The purpose of careful observation and noting what children/young people do and how they behave

- The importance of checking your observations of children/young people with others

- Where to refer concerns you may have about children's/young people's development

- The importance of confidentiality, data protection and sharing information, according to the procedures of your setting

- The role of play in development i.e. children and young people of all ages need to play in order to develop, learn and grow

- The kinds of influences that affect children's/young people's development, such as their background, health or environment

- Children's and young people's development is holistic and each area is interconnected

- That children and young people develop at widely different rates, but in broadly the same sequence

- A basic outline of the expected pattern of children's and young people's development. The pattern of development includes the order or sequence in which development takes place and the rate of development, to include:

  - a   physical development

  - b   communication and intellectual development

  - c   social, emotional and behavioural development

  in each of the age groups: birth–3 years, 3–7 years, 7–12 years, 12–16 years

Select one of the following age ranges covering the age range you currently work with and provide knowledge evidence for the points listed

- How to support children's development from birth to 3 years. You need to know why and how to:

  - a   provide a warm, safe, secure and encouraging environment in partnership with families

  - b   make sure all the children you work with can take part equally, including those with disabilities and special educational needs

  - c   develop a close and loving relationship with the child, including appropriate physical contact

  - d   help the child cope with their feelings, positively encouraging emotional well-being

  - e   support toilet training

  - f   be supportive in your responses to children's behaviour, following the policies of your setting

- g use everyday care routines and activities to support development

- h provide hands-on activities allowing children to explore and manipulate materials

- i identify activities and equipment to support children's play and early learning, including how these are used to best effect

- j support children's early interest in numbers, counting, sorting and matching

- k encourage children's creative play

- l play with and alongside the child, sensitively supporting their play

- m make sure children have quiet periods

- n use different ways of communicating, including verbal and non-verbal, listening/watching, talking, pausing and turn-taking in making sounds and 'conversations', making eye contact, singing, rhymes and stories

- o support children's early communication in bilingual or multilingual settings

- p support children's early interest in reading and mark-making

- q contribute to an environment that supports children's physical skills and confidence in movement

- How to support children's development from 3 to 7 years. You need to know why and how to:

  - a provide a safe, secure and encouraging environment

  - b make sure all the children you work with can take part equally, including those with disabilities and special educational needs

  - c develop close and consistent relationships

  - d support children's emotional well-being, confidence and resilience

  - e be realistic, consistent and supportive in your responses to children's behaviour

  - f allow children to assess and take risks without over or under protecting them

  - g use appropriate activities, materials and experiences to support learning and development

  - h *identify activities and equipment to support children's play, creativity and learning, including how these are used to best effect (see Unit 10, K24, page 172)*

  - i support children's interest in numbers, counting, sorting and matching

  - j play with and alongside the child, sensitively supporting their play

  - k use every opportunity to encourage children's communication and language development, such as talking, listening, making eye contact, singing, rhymes and stories

  - l support children's communication in bilingual or multilingual settings

  - m support children's interest in reading, mark-making and writing

  - n contribute to an environment that supports children's physical skills and confidence in movement

- How to support children's development from 7 to 12 years. You need to know why and how to:

  - a provide a safe and encouraging environment

  - b *make sure that all children you work with can take part equally, including those with disabilities and special educational needs (see K11, point 2, page 36)*

  - c *give meaningful praise and encouragement (see Unit 1, K9, page 16)*

CORNWALL COLLEGE
LEARNING CENTRE

- d   support emotional well-being, confidence and resilience

- e   be a listening ear when needed

- f   *stand back and allow children to assess, take risks and face challenges for themselves, according to their abilities, needs and stage of development (see K11, point 6, page 37)*

- g   provide opportunities for exploration and different experiences

- h   identify activities and equipment to support children's play, creativity and learning, including how these are used to best effect

- i   use every opportunity to encourage children's communication, literacy and language development

- j   contribute to an environment that supports children's physical skills and confidence in movement

- k   recognise and acknowledge children's particular needs as they enter puberty

- How to support young people's development from 12 to 16 years. You need to know why and how to:

  - a   provide an encouraging and safe environment that recognises approaching adulthood

  - b   *make sure that all young people you work with can take part equally, including those with disabilities and special educational needs (see page 36 and Unit 12, K5, pages 193–4)*

  - c   give meaningful praise and encouragement

  - d   support emotional well-being, confidence and resilience

  - e   support opportunities for young people to assess and take risks and face challenges, according to their abilities, needs and stage of development

  - f   *be a listening ear when needed (see K12, point 5, page 39)*

  - g   support young people's development and learning by encouraging exploration and different types of experience

  - h   encourage positive communication, being available to support, listen and encourage

  - i   encourage creativity

  - j   recognise and acknowledge young people's particular needs as they go through puberty and adolescence and become adults

  - k   contribute to an environment that supports young people's physical skills and confidence in movement

  - l   provide information for young people, when requested, about things that concern them

- Support children/young people through transitions in their lives, e.g.

  - a   children aged 0 to 3 years coming into day care, changing rooms, leaving parents

  - b   children aged 3 to 7 years as they move between different settings and into school

  - c   children aged 7 to 12 years as they move between different settings, such as moving to a new school

  - d   young people aged 12 to 16 years for change, personal growth and moving on

Purpose of careful observation

As you work with children and young people on a daily basis, you will be able to observe their development in different areas. Development is often divided into the following headings:

- physical development
- communication and intellectual development
- social, emotional and behavioural development.

It is important to understand the purpose of observations as part of your role because you will need to report back to the teacher, who will in turn report to parents and carers on pupil progress. Parents and teachers should share information about pupils to enable them to work together in the pupil's best interest. This may be carried out both formally and informally and there are advantages and disadvantages to each method.

Informal observations are those you carry out each day as you work with pupils. They may not seem particularly significant, but over time will enable you to build up a picture of each pupil. You may notice, for example, that an individual is able to understand new concepts very easily or that they are holding a pencil incorrectly. It is likely that you will discuss your observations with teachers as part of the feedback process after your session with pupils. A disadvantage to informal observations is that they may not be recorded and you might forget to pass on what you have seen to others.

You may also be asked to carry out formal observations on pupils to support the teacher in assessing pupils' levels of development. (See Unit 9, K10, page 155 for more on different types of pupil observation, including formal observation.)

Importance of checking your observations with others

If you carry out observations on pupils and have a cause for concern, make sure that you do not act on this without speaking to others. You should check what you have seen through observing the pupil on different occasions, ask other professionals to watch them seek further advice. (See also K3, page 28 for where to refer concerns.) It is important to remember that you are part of a team and that you cannot be an expert on all areas of pupil development. Others may be more experienced or have a more specific area of training and be able to guide you or help you to reach a conclusion.

Case study K2

You are working in Year 7 (S1) and have been there since the beginning of term six weeks ago. You have noticed a pupil who seems very withdrawn from the rest of the group on a regular basis. You have not mentioned it to anyone else who works with him, but have started to note down what he does and any interactions he has with others. You have tried to encourage him to join in, but he has not chosen to do so.

- Should you share this information? If so, with whom?
- Will it be useful that you have started to write things down or should you not have done this?

Where to refer concerns about children's/young people's development

If you have any concerns about pupils' **development** in any of the areas listed you should always share them with others. In the case of primary pupils, refer to the class teacher in the first instance, followed by the SENCo (Additional Support for Learning (ASL) teacher). In secondary schools you may wish to go straight to the latter. Even if concerns have already been noted by others in your school, it is still worth raising them as your observations will also be taken into consideration. You should give dates and examples, if possible, of the reasons for your concerns so that they can be backed up. It is also important to remember that if a school has concerns about a child, parents must always be informed.

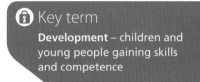

Key term

Development – children and young people gaining skills and competence

K3 Portfolio activity

Referring any concerns

Make a note of whom you would speak or refer to if you had concerns about a pupil with whom you are working.

Importance of confidentiality, data protection and sharing information, according to the procedures of your setting

If you are carrying out observations on pupils, your school should advise you on how to keep and store the information you have gathered. Remember that it is important that all pupil information is kept confidential and not left in places where others may find it. This applies to computer files as well as paper-based records of observation. One way in which you might protect pupils' identity is by using initials or first names only or by referring to pupils as pupil A, B and so on. However, staff need to be able to discuss and share information regarding pupils, including observations, so that pupil assessment and progress can be monitored. Make sure that if you are discussing pupil progress with other staff it is done in an appropriate environment, for example through meetings or in areas of the school where you are not likely to be overheard by others.

You should have read and understood your school's recording, reporting and record-keeping policy so that you know what the procedures are for keeping information safe. Although, working at Level 2, you are unlikely to have access to highly confidential material, you should still have an awareness of the principles of keeping information safe and secure.

Role of play in development

It is important to understand how play experiences support the development of children of all ages. Play can enhance all areas of development and can be directed specifically to address individual areas or used more generally to support all areas. Through play, children learn about themselves and others.

Children and young people need to have the opportunity to use play experiences in order to develop in all these areas. Although play is often spontaneous, it is important to plan the environment so that they are able to do this.

▼ Figure 2.1 Which of these areas of development have you seen children develop through play?

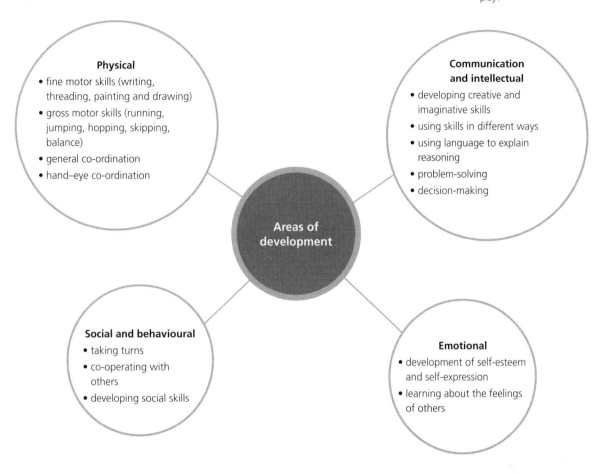

Physical
- fine motor skills (writing, threading, painting and drawing)
- gross motor skills (running, jumping, hopping, skipping, balance)
- general co-ordination
- hand–eye co-ordination

Communication and intellectual
- developing creative and imaginative skills
- using skills in different ways
- using language to explain reasoning
- problem-solving
- decision-making

Areas of development

Social and behavioural
- taking turns
- co-operating with others
- developing social skills

Emotional
- development of self-esteem and self-expression
- learning about the feelings of others

Portfolio activity K5

Recognising opportunities for play and their impact on development

Using an example from the age range with whom you are working, show what opportunities are made available to them for play activities and how these will affect different areas of their development.

Kinds of influences that affect development, such as background, health or environment

Pupils' development is influenced by a wide range of factors. Their background, health and the environment in which they are growing up have an impact on all areas of development. You need to have an awareness of some of these factors so that you know how pupils may be affected.

Pupils come from a range of different family environments, cultures and circumstances. This will affect the opportunities they are given and the breadth of experiences with which they come into contact.

If pupils suffer from poor health, this may restrict the opportunities available to them. For example, a pupil who has a medical condition or impairment may be less able to participate in some activities. This may initially affect physical development but may also restrict social activities, for example on the playground.

The different circumstances, or environment, to which pupils are exposed during their childhood and teens will also affect their development. Many families go through significant changes, such as illness, family break up, bereavement, moving house or changing country. These will all have an impact on the way pupils are able to respond in different situations.

Development is holistic and each area is interconnected

Although development is often divided into different 'headings', it is important to remember that these areas are interconnected and link with one another. For example, developing physically and refining physical skills also affects pupils' ability to become independent, socialise and grow in confidence (see also K5, page 28).

When planning or thinking about activities to carry out with pupils, you should try to think not only in 'subjects' but also in terms of the broader picture. Many activities will stimulate interest and encourage pupils to develop skills in different areas. For example, an activity such as cooking, or food technology for older pupils, will develop a range of skills.

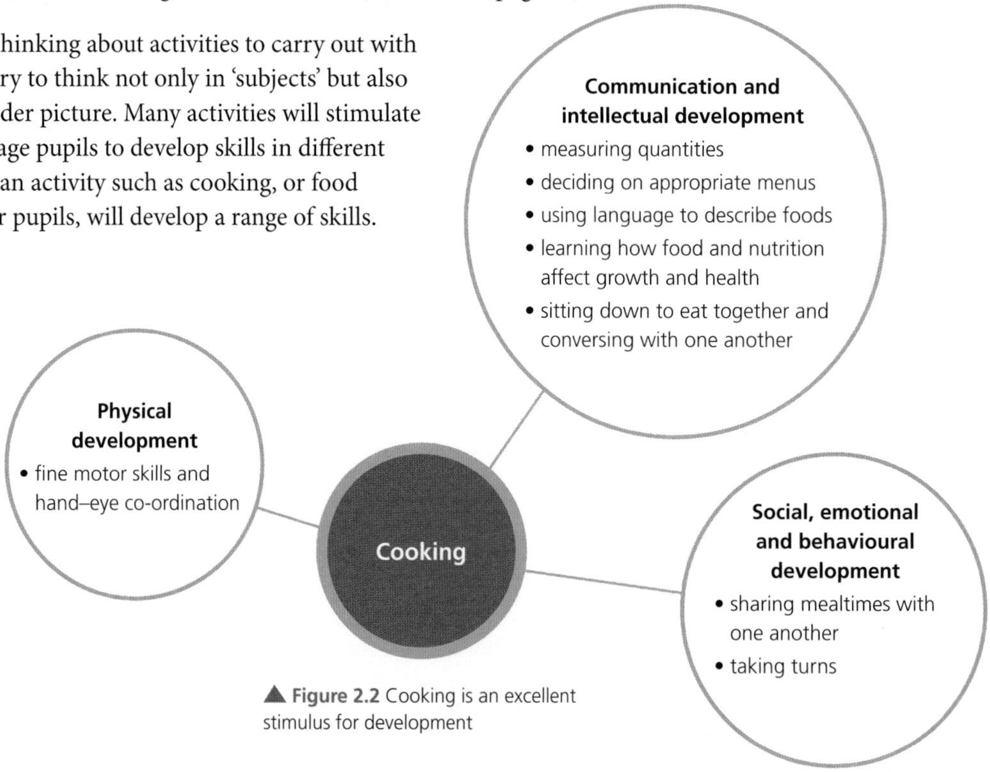

Communication and intellectual development
- measuring quantities
- deciding on appropriate menus
- using language to describe foods
- learning how food and nutrition affect growth and health
- sitting down to eat together and conversing with one another

Physical development
- fine motor skills and hand–eye co-ordination

Cooking

Social, emotional and behavioural development
- sharing mealtimes with one another
- taking turns

▲ Figure 2.2 Cooking is an excellent stimulus for development

Pupils develop at widely different rates, but in broadly the same sequence

Each child is unique and develops at their own rate. While children usually follow the same pattern of development, the ages at which they reach developmental milestones varies depending on the individual. Milestones of development are given as a broad average of when children may be expected to reach a particular stage. You may notice that in particular classes or year groups some pupils stand out because they have reached milestones in advance of or later than others. Sometimes, if a child's growth patterns are very different from their peers, this may have an effect on their behaviour. For example, in the last two years of primary school pupils may start to grow taller and develop some of the first signs of puberty. Girls, in particular, can become much taller than boys and this can put pressure on them to behave differently. Additional provision may be needed in this instance, for example, when pupils get changed for PE. There may also be pupils who are very tall or very small for their age and this can sometimes affect how they are treated by their peers and also their social and emotional development.

The **patterns of development** on the next few pages should therefore be seen as a guide to give you an overall idea of the different stages.

Basic outline of the expected pattern of development

Physical development
This is an important area of children's overall development and one which is often assumed to take place automatically as they grow and mature. Although children develop many skills naturally as they get older, it is imperative that they have opportunities to develop them in a variety of ways and they will need support to do this.

Key terms
Pattern of development – usual rate and sequence of development

Rate of development – usual time-frame in which development takes place

Sequence of development – usual order in which development occurs

0–3 years
This is a period of fast physical development. Newborn babies have very little control over their bodies. Their movements are dependent on a series of reflexes such as sucking and grasping, which they need in order to survive. In their first year, however, they gradually start to learn to have more control over their bodies so that by 12 months most babies have developed a degree of mobility such as crawling or rolling.

In their second year, babies continue to grow and develop quickly and it is at this stage that most children start to walk. Their ability to control their movements means that they can start using their hands for pointing, holding small objects, and dressing and feeding themselves. They will also be able to play with a ball and enjoy climbing, for example, on stairs or furniture.

3–7 years
At this stage, children are able to carry out more co-ordinated movements and grow in confidence as a result. They are refining the skills developed so far and have more control over fine motor skills such as cutting, writing and drawing. They are also more confident in activities such as running, hopping, kicking a ball and using larger equipment.

▶ **Figure 2.3** In their third year, children start to have more control over pencils and crayons and enjoy looking at and turning pages in books. They should be able to use cups and feed themselves. They will be starting to walk and run with more confidence and will be exploring using toys such as tricycles

7–12 years

Children continue to grow, develop and refine many of their skills through these years. They may start to have hobbies and interests, such as sport or dance, which mean that they are more practised in some areas. They may also be able to make very controlled fine movements such as those required for playing an instrument, sewing or drawing. Girls, in particular, start to show some of the early signs of puberty from the age of 10 or 11. In boys, puberty usually starts later, when there will be another period of rapid physical growth.

12–16 years

At this stage of development, young people are growing stronger. Boys are starting to go through puberty and many girls have completed the process and have regular periods. As a result, between these ages, there can be a great variety in height and strength. At the end of this stage, on average most boys are taller than most girls.

Communication and intellectual development

Communication skills and intellectual development are closely linked with one another as children need language in order to think and learn. If they have limited experiences and stimulation through social interaction with others, their learning and development may be affected. Where children have difficulties with speech and language, this may be due to a number of reasons and they may need support through alternative communication methods such as British Sign Language or visual aids.

Communication and language development

0–3 years

From the earliest stages, adults usually try to communicate with babies even though they cannot understand what is being said. It is important for babies to be stimulated and have an interest shown in them in this way. Children who were neglected and did not spend time with adults as babies find it very difficult to learn the skills of effective communication.

Babies listen to language from those around them and enjoy songs and games. Most start to try to speak at around 12 months, although pronunciation is not clear and words are usually used in isolation. Between 1 and 2 years, they start to put words together and their vocabulary increases fairly rapidly so that by 2 years old most children have about 200 words. Between 2 and 3 years, children start to use negatives and plurals in their speech. Although their vocabulary is increasing rapidly, they still make errors in grammar when speaking, for example 'I drawed it'.

3–7 years

As children become more social and have wider experiences, they start to use an increasing number of familiar phrases and expressions. They also ask a lot of questions and are able to talk about things in the past and future tenses with greater confidence.

7–12 years and upwards

By this stage, most children are fluent speakers of a language and are developing and refining their skills at reading and writing. Their language skills enable them to think about and discuss their ideas and learning in more abstract terms.

Intellectual development

Children's intellectual development depends to a great extent on their own experiences and the opportunities they are given from the earliest stages. It is also important to understand that children learn in a variety of ways and that some find particular tasks more or less difficult than others due to their own strengths and abilities. There have been a number of theories that outline the ways in which children learn (see Unit 1, K7, page 11) and it is important to bear these in mind when thinking about stages of learning.

0–3 years
Babies start to look at the world around them and enjoy repetitive activities in which they can predict the outcome. They start to understand that objects are still there even when hidden. They learn to identify different items and can point to them, and may also start to recognise colours.

3–7 years
This is the period of development in which children start to become skilled with aspects of numbers and writing, as well as continue to learn about their world. They still look for adult approval and are starting to learn to read.

7–12 years
Children start to develop ideas about activities or subjects they enjoy. They are still influenced by adults and are becoming fluent in reading and writing skills. They are developing their own thoughts and preferences and are able to transfer information and think in a more abstract way.

12–16 years
By this stage, young people usually have a clear idea about their favourite subjects and activities, and are usually motivated in these areas. They will be selecting GCSEs (in Scotland National Qualifications) in which they are able to achieve. They may lack confidence or avoid situations in which they have to do less popular subjects, to the extent that they may truant. It is particularly important to teenagers that they feel good about themselves and they want to belong.

Social, emotional and behavioural development
This area of development is about how children and young people feel about themselves and relate to others. They must learn to have the confidence to become independent of adults as they grow older and start to make their way in the world.

0–3 years
Babies need to form strong attachments, the earliest of which will be with parents and carers. From the age of 2, children start to find out about their own identities. In nursery, children are usually given a keyworker to be their main contact. At this stage of development, children may start to have tantrums through frustration and will want and need to start doing things for themselves.

3–7 years
Children are still developing their identities and are starting to play with their peers and socialise, using imaginative play. This helps them to develop their concept of different roles in their lives. It is important that they understand the importance of boundaries and why they are necessary. They also respond well to being given responsibility, for example as class helpers, and need adult approval.

7–12 years
Children's friendships become more settled and they have groups of friends. They need to have the chance to solve problems and carry out activities that require more independence. They continue to need praise and encouragement and are increasingly aware of what others think of them.

12–16 years

At this stage, the self-esteem of children and young people can be very vulnerable. Their bodies are taking on the outer signs of adulthood, but they still need guidance in many different ways. They want to be independent of adults and spend more time with friends of their own age, but often display childish behaviour. They can find that they feel the pressures of growing up and increasing expectations, and may be unsure how to behave in different situations.

Keys to good practice

Supporting pupils' social, emotional and behavioural development

✓ Make sure you are approachable and give pupils your time.
✓ Give fair but firm boundaries and explain the reasons for them.
✓ Ensure pupils feel valued and are given praise and encouragement.
✓ Give pupils the chance to develop their independence.
✓ Be sensitive to pupils' needs.
✓ Act as a good role model.

K9 Portfolio activity

Understanding the stages of development

You may have to use a range of methods to show that you know and understand the stages of development for each age group. You can do this in a variety of ways, such as:

- write a reflective account, making sure that you include all ages and all areas of development
- have a professional discussion with your assessor to show that you know and understand the milestones of each particular age and stage
- complete an assignment from your assessment centre to cover the knowledge points.

Supporting pupils' development in different age ranges

You need to select the age group with which you work from the following age ranges, given that you are supporting teaching and learning in schools: 3–7, 7–12 or 12–16 years (birth to 3 years does not apply for this award). The sections below give an overview of the main factors you need to consider in providing evidence for your assessor.

In order to gather evidence for these age-related knowledge points, see 'For your portfolio' at the end of the unit.

How to support children's development from birth to 3 years

This age group does not apply for this S/NVQ. However, if you would like to find out about this age group and how to support the development of very young children, Beith *et al* (2005) is a good reference as it forms part of the guidance for the Children's Care, Learning and Development S/NVQ.

How to support children's development from 3 to 7 years

Providing a safe, secure and encouraging environment

Young children need to feel that they are in an environment that is safe and allows them to develop to the best of their ability. In nurseries and Early Years classes, children need to play and enjoy their learning in different environments. If they are not happy and settled, it is unlikely that they will gain confidence and develop their skills.

Adults need to ensure that the surroundings help to develop pupils' independence as well as provide a safe environment. This includes developing pupils' understanding of danger and supervising them appropriately in different environments. Also remember to provide plenty of praise and encouragement as this will build pupils' confidence.

▼ **Figure 2.4** There can be plenty of stimulus for development from children's environment

Making sure all the pupils you work with can take part equally

When planning and carrying out different activities, you need to make sure that all pupils in this and all age ranges are given equal opportunities. It is important that any pupils with disabilities or special educational (ASL) needs are not disadvantaged in the activities you have planned. It is also important to develop pupils' understanding of the need to respect others through showing positive aspects of diversity.

Developing close and consistent relationships and supporting children's well-being

As you are supporting pupils' learning and seeing them on a daily basis, you will be developing relationships with them. Pupils should feel that they have someone to talk to about what is happening in their day-to-day lives and someone to go to if they are feeling happy or sad, or need to talk about a problem. It is important for them not to feel isolated and for adults to support them in forming positive relationships by being friendly and supportive themselves and acting as good role models.

Being realistic, consistent and supportive in your responses to children's behaviour

This age group are learning why it is important to have boundaries and to have an understanding of the reasons for them. They need you to be realistic in what you ask of them and not expect too much of them for their age (see also K9, page 33). This works best when there is a consistent whole school behaviour management policy of which all staff are aware. Where pupils have learned to manage their behaviour and developed self-control, they respond well to praise and recognition of their achievements. It is important that adults take time to notice when pupils have made a particular effort. Often, with this age range, we can encourage good behaviour by noticing and praising those who are doing as they are asked.

◀ **Figure 2.5** Always be supportive of good behaviour in order to reinforce it

Allowing children to assess and take risks

Children of this age are starting to need more independence and this should be encouraged within a supervised environment. For example, they need to be encouraged to think about the risks that may arise and to act accordingly. Although you are making sure learning environments in which pupils can work and play are safe places, you can also encourage them to think about why certain courses of action, such as playing football or using ride-on toys too close to other pupils, may not be sensible. As pupils grow older, you should give them opportunities to discuss potential problems with each other and adults. It is through allowing pupils to assess their own needs that they will grow in confidence. Overprotecting them will result in their not learning to take risks, which can make them overanxious or unable to act on their own initiative.

Using appropriate activities, materials and experiences to support learning and development

Working with the teacher and with careful planning, you can support the needs of all pupils through a range of activities that stimulate and engage them, and develop their skills in different areas. It is important to evaluate whether what you are doing is supporting the learning and development of all pupils and whether the kinds of experiences you are providing need to be modified so that individuals are able to achieve.

Supporting children's interest in numbers, counting, sorting and matching

Young children enjoy numbers and counting, and at this age should be encouraged to take part in a variety of activities that consolidate and build on their knowledge. Singing, games and rhymes should be offered regularly as these are a fun and enjoyable way of reinforcing pupils' knowledge of numbers. They should also be carrying out activities that enable them to sort and match items by particular criteria and can be encouraged to decide on these themselves (see also Unit 10, K19, page 169 and K20, page 170).

Playing with and alongside the child, sensitively supporting their play

While pupils need to have opportunities to play independently of adults and to gain confidence, you may sometimes need to check on their learning or encourage them to extend themselves. This should not be over intrusive (see Unit 10, page 164), but should take the form of participation and sensitive questioning. Pupils need to feel that they have ownership of the play activity and it is important that adults do not try to take over what is happening.

Encouraging children's communication and language development

Pupils need to be encouraged to develop language and communication skills as much as possible as this is a key area of their development. Adults need to give all pupils opportunities to take part in speaking and listening for different purposes and in different situations. It is important that they use language both in whole class and small group activities and that you encourage them by asking them to talk about their own ideas.

Supporting children's communication in bilingual or multilingual settings

When working in bilingual or multilingual settings, you need to be aware of specific issues that may affect pupils' learning. These may be linked to their background, language needs and general self-esteem (see also Unit 11, page 182).

It is very important for bilingual/multilingual pupils that they have opportunities to develop their language skills and that adults check their understanding in each language. For very young children, it is important to encourage their communication skills as much as possible, whether this is verbal or non-verbal. As they get older, pupils who are learning more than one language may need to focus on specific vocabulary in order to develop their knowledge and understanding of different concepts.

There may also be cultural differences that make the school environment more difficult for bilingual/multilingual pupils to settle, particularly when they have been used to speaking another language or to having different routines. In Early Years environments it is particularly important to make sure that these pupils feel included and welcomed from the outset.

Keys to good practice

Supporting play and communication development in bilingual and multilingual settings

✓ Provide opportunities for all pupils to experience a variety of situations.
✓ Encourage the involvement and participation of parents.
✓ Make sure the learning environment reflects the cultures of the community.

Supporting children's interest in reading, mark-making and writing

You should always support pupils' interest in the development of their reading and writing skills (see also Unit 10, K8, page 162). This is because reading and writing are key areas of their learning and they need to be given as many opportunities as possible to develop these skills. There should be areas in the classroom for pupils to write without any adult intervention. There should also be opportunities to use reading and writing in many different forms, including making signs for the home corner and labels for displays, and checking off lists as they complete activities.

Contributing to an environment that supports children's physical skills and confidence in movement

Pupils need a range of opportunities to develop their physical skills, both indoor and outdoor (see also Unit 10, K16, page 167). They should have a varied and stimulating routine and curriculum, which provides them with the chance to develop their confidence in different ways and allows them to assess risk.

How to support children's development from 7 to 12 years

Providing a safe and encouraging environment

As children grow older, they need to start to take more responsibility for safety in their environment and look at different ways in which they can do this. Adults should continue to support their learning in a range of environments in which pupils feel secure and settled.

▲ **Figure 2.6** A safe and fun environment will stimulate emotional and physical development

Supporting emotional well-being, confidence and resilience

Children of this age continue to need the positive encouragement and reassurance of adults. They are developing their own ideas and learning about themselves and others. It is important that pupils learn to face challenges and about success and failure so that they are able to manage their emotions in different situations.

Being a listening ear when needed

As a teaching assistant, pupils may come to you to ask questions or when they need a listening ear. They may need information or advice and you need to handle questions sensitively. If you are approached by a pupil who needs to confide in you, it is important that you give them time and actively listen to what they have to say. If pupils ask you not to tell anyone, it is important to tell them that you cannot keep secrets as you may need to pass on information if it is in the best interest of the pupil.

Providing opportunities for exploration and different experiences

All children and young people need to be given opportunities to experience a range of learning experiences and situations in order to fulfil their potential. Pupils of this age are becoming increasingly aware of what they perceive they can and cannot do. They need adults to encourage them to take part in activities about which they feel less confident in order to develop their self-esteem. They should also be enabled to experience new activities such as attempting to play a musical instrument or taking part in an unfamiliar hobby. This may be through activities within school or trips and excursions through clubs.

Identifying activities and equipment to support children's play, creativity and learning

As they grow older, pupils still need to be given the chance to enjoy activities and equipment to support their play, creativity and learning across the curriculum. It is important that they are given opportunities to use their own initiative, work with others and develop in all areas. These can often be used to best effect when pupils are introduced to new ideas in practical, imaginative and stimulating ways. Giving pupils a project or getting them to decide in a group how they are going to solve a problem can be very beneficial. For example, you might ask them to come up with a design for a house for a well-known fictional character. They would then need to justify what features it might need and why, and present this to their class.

Encouraging children's communication, literacy and language development

At this stage, pupils should be learning to communicate in different ways and with increasing confidence with a variety of people. They should have the skills to adapt their method of communication in different contexts. You need to model appropriate communication methods and use of language to support their development (see also page 32).

Contributing to an environment that supports children's physical skills and confidence in movement)

As pupils grow older they need to be given increasing independence when developing physical skills and encouraged to take more responsibility for assessing risk (see also page 37). They should still be in a managed environment, but be able to make more decisions about when adult intervention is needed.

▼ **Figure 2.7** Encouraging children to talk to people from different backgrounds and ages can be a great help to their development

Recognising and acknowledging children's particular needs as they enter puberty

Pupils of this age may be starting to go through physical and emotional changes. They may need the support and reassurance of adults as this happens, because they could lose confidence. Some primary age pupils remain physically very small towards the end of this stage, while others are showing the outward signs of approaching adulthood. Pupils may be particularly vulnerable as they pass from primary to secondary. You may need to handle any questions sensitively and give them support where needed.

How to support young people's development from 12 to 16 years

Providing an encouraging and safe environment that recognises approaching adulthood

It is important for young people of this age to feel confident in their environment while recognising that they still need some support in unfamiliar situations. You should ensure that any pupils in your care are able to work in an environment that supports them and recognises their needs while remaining safe and allowing them to set their own boundaries in some, but not all, situations.

Giving meaningful praise and encouragement

It is important for all individuals, whatever their age, to be given meaningful praise and encouragement. If young people feel that their contributions are not valued, they may lose confidence. At this age in particular, pupils need adults to encourage them to participate and enjoy a variety of activities, as well as giving them opportunities to make their own decisions (see also Unit 1, K9, page 16).

▼ **Figure 2.8** Giving clear encouragement to young people will empower them to make decisions

Supporting emotional well-being, confidence and resilience

Pupils of this age are entering puberty and undergoing physical changes. They are likely to need some sensitive support from adults in managing their emotions at times and maintaining confidence in different situations. You should do this through remaining approachable and facilitating opportunities for pupils to discuss any issues as they arise.

Supporting opportunities for young people to assess and take risks and face challenges, according to their abilities, needs and stage of development

Pupils of this age are rapidly learning about life in the adult world. They need to have the chance to think about and discuss risks that may affect them, such as those from drugs and alcohol or from socialising with those who may have a negative influence on them. They should have both curricular and extra-curricular opportunities to discuss and evaluate how the decisions they make will affect them both now and in later life.

Supporting young people's development and learning by encouraging exploration and different types of experience

At this age, young people need to develop their independence and confidence by taking part in activities that allow them to do this. As well as clubs and school trips, many secondary schools encourage pupils to work towards awards such as the Duke of Edinburgh Award. This allows pupils to work together, solve problems and develop confidence in a different environment, as well as having their initiative recognised and awarded. Your school may also encourage pupils who take part in sport or musical activities to travel to other areas and broaden their experience (see also K12, point 7, page 39).

Encouraging positive communication

This is a time of great changes for teenagers and is very important that as an adult you encourage them through positive communication. This means taking time to listen, giving them opportunities to express their thoughts and feelings, and acting as a good role model in your communication with others. You should also ensure that you give them information relevant to them and their situation as it becomes available. (See also point 12, page 43.)

Encouraging creativity

It is important to remember that creativity does not just mean art or 'messy' activities. Young people need to be given opportunities to be creative in a range of different situations. These may be through the more obvious 'design and make' situations, but should also be in other areas of the curriculum, through activities which encourage pupils to solve problems, think about how to approach a project or find their own way to tackle particular learning activities.

Recognising and acknowledging young people's particular needs as they go through puberty and adolescence and become adults

This is an age when pupils need to come to terms with a number of changes. They need you to offer them support depending on their own particular needs and you need to get to know individuals so that you are able to do this. It may be that some pupils have particularly challenging or difficult circumstances to face up to. It is important that you remain able to take a balanced view and give pupils advice and support.

Contributing to an environment that supports young people's physical skills and confidence in movement

It is important for young people to continue to be involved in activities that provide a physical outlet. This is a good opportunity for them to participate in both team and individual sporting activities, which will also support their confidence in movement. They should be given the chance to devise and organise their own activities to develop their independence and decision-making skills.

Providing information for young people, when requested, about things that concern them

You may be involved with others, both within and outside school, who give young people information about different services and facilities available to them as they approach school-leaving age. This may take the form of career information and guidance, counselling services, youth services such as Connexions or health advice. Make sure that you find out what is available if you are asked so that you can support pupils and provide appropriate information.

Support pupils through transitions in their lives

Whatever age group you are supporting, at some stage you will be working with pupils who are going through a transition phase. This may be because they are moving between key stages or need to change settings, for example, from nursery to school or primary to secondary. Examples of support may be home visits for pupils who are moving to nursery or opportunities to meet teachers and pupils in secondary school before transferring to Year 7 (S1).

Transitions may also take place between year groups within one school, which, if not handled well, can be traumatic for some pupils. As you get to know the pupils in the age range in which you work, you will find out about routines that the school uses to familiarise pupils with new environments before they move to them.

When managing the needs of older pupils, you should have opportunities to discuss with them the kinds of choices they need to make. This may be their selection of GCSE or A-level subjects (in Scotland, National Qualifications), but can also be career decisions they may need to be thinking about at this age. Opportunities to take part in external activities, such as work experience or voluntary work, can be very beneficial as they give young people inside knowledge about different careers and also develop their confidence.

Keys to good practice
Supporting transitions

✓ Give pupils the opportunity to visit their new school.
✓ Liaise with pupils already in the year group in order to build relationships and facilitate questions from pupils who are moving on.
✓ Familiarise pupils with routines and procedures in their new school and the teachers with whom they will be working.
✓ If possible, encourage projects between pupils so that they have the opportunity to work together.
✓ Give older children the opportunity to try out different experiences to develop their confidence.

Portfolio activity

Supporting pupils through transitions

Using examples from your own school, write a reflective account to show what provision the school makes for supporting pupils who are going through transitions.

For your portfolio

You need to show your assessor that you understand the stages of development for all ages, but in particular that you can support the age range with which you are working.

Your assessor will be able to observe you carrying out activities with pupils that demonstrate how you cover most of these points. They should see you working in different situations and in a range of curriculum areas. However, make sure you also show the reasons behind what you are doing. One way of doing this would be to produce a table for your age range such as the one started below.

Age range: 3–7 years	How	Why
Provide a safe, secure and encouraging environment	Ensure all environments (indoor and outdoor) are safety checked before use. Make sure the environment is stimulating and offers a range of activities that give pupils the opportunity to develop in all areas. Make sure pupils are given plenty of praise and encouragement for effort and achievement.	Children need to feel secure and settled so that they can explore their surroundings. If they are anxious, they are less likely to feel able to take part. Praise is important as it motivates children.
Make sure all pupils are included	Check the involvement of all pupils when working in groups. In classrooms where there is free choice, ensure that individual pupils do not dominate particular activities and all pupils have the opportunity to take part, especially those with special educational (ASL) needs.	Equal opportunities should be given to all pupils. If they are not given the chance to try out activities and develop their skills at this age, pupils may decide they are 'not good at' particular types of activities or ways of working and lose confidence.

References

Beith, K., Tassoni, P., Bulman, K., and Robinson, M. (2005) *Children's Care, Learning and Development S/NVQ Level 2* (Oxford, Heinemann)

Websites and further information

www.connexions-direct.com

www.opsi.gov.uk/ACTS/acts1998/19980029 – Data Protection Act

Most local authorities have youth services, which are also a good source of help and information.

3 Help to Keep Children Safe

This unit requires you to know about procedures that exist in your school for the safeguarding of children, both from a health and safety point of view and with regard to child protection. The Every Child Matters framework has brought to the forefront the importance of keeping children safe and healthy and having an awareness of different ways in which, as professionals, we should work together to do this. You will need to have a clear understanding of the expectations of your role and what you should do in different situations, and you will need to show that you assist with the safety and protection of children. You should know and understand your responsibilities for maintaining a safe environment and ensuring that risks and hazards are dealt with appropriately.

What you need to know and understand

For this unit, you will need to know and understand:

- Setting's safety, safeguarding and protection and emergency procedures, what these are and why they must be followed, including controls on substances harmful to health and other key aspects of health and safety

- The laws governing safety in your home country, including the general responsibility for health and safety that applies to all colleagues and to employers

- The duty of all within the sector to safeguard children, including the difficulties in situations where your concerns may not be seen to be taken seriously or followed through when following normal procedures

- Regulations covering manual handling and the risks associated with lifting and carrying children

- Safety factors and recognised standards of equipment and materials for children. Importance of using equipment that is appropriate for the age, needs and abilities of the child. The importance of following manufacturers' guidelines

- Routine safety checking and maintenance of equipment. Safe storage of hazardous materials and disposal of waste

- Safe layout and organisation of rooms, equipment, materials and outdoor spaces

- How to adapt the environment to ensure safety for children and young people, according to their age, needs and abilities and taking into account disabilities or special educational needs, e.g. keeping the floor tidy to limit hazards for children/young people with visual difficulties

- When and how to use safety equipment such as safety gates, socket covers, window and drawer catches, cooker guards, safety harnesses. Safety in respect of animals, plants, sand pits and outdoor spaces

- Good hygiene practice: avoiding of cross-infection, disposal of waste, food handling, handling body fluids. Issues concerning spread of HIV/AIDS virus and hepatitis

- Familiarity with adult/child ratio requirements, according to regulatory and setting requirements

- How to supervise children/young people safely, modifying your approach according to their age, needs and abilities. The balances between safety and risk, and challenge and protection for children and young people

- Policies and procedures of setting for responding to and recording accidents and emergencies. Basic first aid required in an emergency and how to apply it, recognition of and response to choking, unconsciousness, breathing difficulties, bleeding, anaphylactic shock, burns. Awareness of location and contents of first aid box. How to treat common minor injuries that may be dealt with on site, such as minor skin abrasions, cuts, bumps

- The importance of following instructions about children's diets carefully to avoid known allergic reactions. How you would recognise allergic reactions

- Policies and procedures of setting to deal with children/young people's illness. How to recognise when children/young people are ill, including when they cannot communicate, e.g. fever, rashes, headache, crying and breathlessness

- The emergency procedures within settings and the types of possible emergency. This must include:
  - a   procedures for fires
  - b   security incidents
  - c   missing children or persons

- Types and possible signs and indicators of child abuse: physical, emotional, sexual abuse, bullying and harassment, neglect and failure to thrive not based on illness. This must include:
  - a   behavioural changes such as regression, withdrawal, excessive attention seeking, aggression and negative behaviour
  - b   physical indicators such as unlikely bruising, burns, marks, genital irritation or damage, hunger, being dirty, lack of health care

- Recognition that social factors, e.g. substance abuse, may increase a child's vulnerability to abuse

- Safe working practices that protect children/young people and adults who work with them

- Ways to encourage children/young people to be aware of their own bodies and understand their right not to be abused, according to their age, needs and abilities. These may include:
  - a   use of appropriate descriptive language
  - b   activities involving discussion about their own bodies

- The importance of consistently and fairly applied boundaries and rules for children/young people's behaviour, according to their age, needs and abilities, and the avoidance of stereotyping

- How to respond to children/young people's challenging behaviour, according to their age, needs and abilities, and in line with the policies and procedures of the setting

- The importance of encouraging and rewarding positive behaviour

- Safety issues and concerns when taking children/young people out of the setting

- The legislation, guidelines and policies which form the basis for action to safeguard children and young people

The setting's safety, protection and emergency procedures

All schools need to ensure that they take measures to protect all adults and pupils while they are on school premises. This means that there will be procedures in place for a number of situations that may arise, including the following.

Accidents and first aid
There should be enough first aiders in the school at any time to deal with accidents. First aid boxes should be regularly checked and replenished. (See also K13, page 58.)

School security and strangers

This includes making sure that all those who are in school have been signed in and identified. Schools may have different methods for doing this, for example, visitors may be issued with badges. If staff notice any unidentified people in the school, they should challenge them immediately. If you are on playground duty and notice anything suspicious, you should also send for help. Schools may also have secure entry and exit points, which may make it more difficult for individuals to enter the premises. (See also K16, page 65.)

Fire procedures

There should be clear procedures in place so that everyone on the premises knows what to do in case of fire. (See also K16, page 65.)

Emergencies

These do sometimes occur and schools should have procedures in place to deal with them. (See also K13, page 58.)

Personal hygiene

Pupils should develop routines and good practice for general personal hygiene and understand its importance.

General health and safety

Health and safety should be a regular topic at staff meetings and during assemblies, so that everyone's attention is drawn to the fact that it is a shared responsibility.

Controls on substances harmful to health (COSHH)

Anything that may be harmful should be stored out of pupils' reach or locked in a cupboard, for example, cleaning materials or medicines. COSHH legislation gives a step-by-step list of precautions that need to be taken to prevent any risk or injury.

▲ **Figure 3.1** Fire procedure notice

K1 Portfolio activity

Investigating safety, protection and emergency procedures

Using a copy of your school's health and safety policy, highlight the procedures your school has in place for the areas above. If a particular area is not documented in the policy, find out whether it is recorded elsewhere. If you are unable to find the information recorded anywhere, you will need to speak to your headteacher or health and safety representative in order to find out about it. Then write a reflective account under each heading.

Laws governing safety

The Health and Safety at Work Act 1974 was designed to protect everyone at work through procedures for preventing accidents. The procedures everyone in the workplace is expected to observe are described below.

Reporting any hazards

Everyone should be alert to any hazards in school that are likely to cause injury to themselves or others. The school is required to carry out an annual risk assessment to determine which areas and activities are most likely to be hazardous, the likelihood of specific hazards occurring and those who are at risk. Pupils and staff need to be vigilant and immediately report any hazards that they notice to the appropriate person. This may be the school's health and safety representative, the headteacher or another member of staff. You should be aware of the designated person to whom you should report health and safety matters.

▼ Figure 3.2 How can you encourage pupils to assess and manage risks?

Following the school's safety policy

The school has an obligation to have a safety policy, which should give information to all staff about procedures that the school has in place for ensuring that it is as safe as possible. All new staff joining the school should be given induction training in safety procedures and what to do in case of emergencies. Safety should be a regular topic at staff meetings.

Making sure that their actions do not harm themselves or others

Staff must also ensure that any actions they take are not likely to harm or cause a danger to others in the school. This includes tidying up and putting things away after use. You must also consider the effects of not taking action. For example, if you discover a potential danger, it is your responsibility not to ignore it but to report it as appropriate.

Using any safety equipment provided

Staff need to ensure that safety equipment that is provided for use when carrying out activities is always used. This includes the safe use of tools used for subjects such as Design Technology or the use of gloves when handling materials in Science activities. There should be guidelines in the school's policy for the safe use and storage of equipment.

All staff working in a school have a responsibility to ensure that pupils are cared for and safe. The Children Act 1989 also requires that staff protect children as far as possible when they are in their care. This includes preventing any risks that may occur.

K2 # Portfolio activity

Investigating legal requirements for safety

Find out about and briefly describe the requirements of the following:

- Health and Safety at Work Act 1974
- Children Act 1989
- Every Child Matters.

The duty of all within the sector to safeguard children

Under the Health and Safety at Work Act, it is the responsibility of everyone in the school to ensure that safety is maintained and in particular that vulnerable groups such as children are safeguarded. Standards for safety are also set by the Department for Education for each country and are monitored by the body responsible for school inspections, for example, Ofsted in England and HMIE in Scotland. As well as having an awareness of health and safety, all routines should be planned carefully with safety in mind so that incidents are less likely to occur. Pupils should also be encouraged to think about safety when they are in the learning environment, so that they develop their own awareness.

If you notice and report something, which you consider needs to be addressed through the correct channels but which is not subsequently followed through, you should take the matter further. You should approach the headteacher or governing body, who should have a committee that manages general facilities and should be able to advise you on what the next steps should be.

Pursuing safety issues

Carrie has been concerned about a safety issue in her Year 4 (P5) class. The desks are much too small for the pupils and there is barely enough space in the room for the thirty pupils and two adults to move around. She has spoken to various senior managers about it as some of the pupils who are slightly taller are really struggling to sit and write comfortably. It is November and behaviour in the class has deteriorated noticeably since the start of the academic year.

Carrie has been told that there is no funding for new furniture and the room is too small to accommodate it, so nothing can be done.

- Should Carrie continue to be concerned or has she passed the responsibility on?
- Is there anything else she could do?

Regulations covering manual handling and the risks associated with lifting and carrying children

If you are asked to lift and carry pupils or equipment as part of your job, you should receive appropriate training. By the time a child is of primary age, it will be difficult for you to lift them on your own and it is unlikely that you will be asked to. However, if you are working with pupils who have special educational (additional support for learning (ASL)) needs, lifting them with hoists or other equipment may be part of your daily routine. You should be aware of the risk of spine and back muscle injury and should make sure that you follow the correct procedures. A quarter of all accidents involving staff in schools are caused by moving heavy objects.

As part of the Manual Handling Operations Regulations 1992, your employer should make sure that you always follow correct guidelines when lifting pupils or equipment. You should also be aware of the dangers of bending over small desks or tables as this can also lead to problems – always better to crouch down and keep a straight back. Under the Health and Safety at Work Act, all adults have a duty to look after themselves.

▼ Figure 3.3 To lift a child, two adults grasp each other's wrists to make a four-handed seat. The child then puts an arm around each of the adult's shoulders. The adults then stand up together.

Keys to good practice

Lifting and carrying

✓ Only lift if absolutely necessary.
✓ Check the weight of the object or pupil before you start to lift.
✓ If necessary, share the load with another person.
✓ Make sure you are holding the pupil or object securely.
✓ Bend your knees and keep your back straight as you lift.
✓ If the pupil or object is too heavy, put it down again slowly and do not attempt to continue.

Safety factors and recognised standards of equipment and materials for children

All materials and equipment used in schools must fulfil recognised standards of safety. The most widely used, although not legally required, safety symbol is the Kitemark, which shows that an item has been tested by the British Safety Institute. In addition, before items can be offered for sale within the European Union, they must carry a CE symbol to show that they meet European regulations.

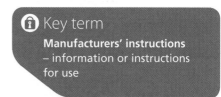

◀ **Figure 3.4** How many of these safety symbols do you recognise?

Always make sure that any equipment to used by pupils is age and ability appropriate. The **manufacturers' instructions** or guidelines are intended to be a realistic means of checking that equipment is not misused. A child who is too young or too old may be unable to use the equipment safely and may hurt themselves and others as a result.

> **ⓘ Key term**
>
> **Manufacturers' instructions** – information or instructions for use

K5 Portfolio activity

Considering the suitability of materials and equipment

Find and list as many items in your classroom that display the Kitemark as you can. How have the age and needs of the pupils you work with been taken into consideration when choosing materials and equipment? Show one way in which manufacturers' guidelines are followed.

Routine safety checking and maintenance of equipment

The person responsible for health and safety in your school should routinely carry out safety checks or make sure that these take place on a regular basis. There should be regular walkabouts or other means of making sure that hazards are not being left unreported. Where hazards are discovered, for example, items stored on top of cupboards, which could fall down when the cupboard is opened, these should be recorded immediately. Safety checks should also be made on all equipment that could be hazardous if neglected. All electrical items used in school should have annual checks, carried out by a qualified electrician. Equipment such as fire extinguishers should also be checked annually and checks recorded on the outside of the extinguisher.

Hazardous materials should always be locked away (see K1, page 48). (For disposal of waste, see K10, page 56.)

▲ **Figure 3.5** Pupils need to be sitting properly in order to be able to write correctly

Safe layout and organisation of rooms, equipment, materials and outdoor spaces

Safe layout and organisation of rooms

Rooms should be organised safely and there should be adequate space to move around comfortably for the number of people using them. Everyone should be able to access materials and equipment as required. The furniture should be an appropriate size for the age of pupils, so that they are able to sit comfortably when working.

Preparing learning materials and equipment

All primary schools use a variety of materials that need to be prepared daily. Some, such as putting out glue and scissors, will be easily achieved, but others, for example where children are using different materials to make a collage, may take longer to organise. If there is more than one class in a year group, there may be several classes needing to use similar materials in the same week and it is important to check that there are enough to go around.

You will often have to make sure that there are sufficient general classroom resources. This includes getting out items such as Maths equipment, puzzles, and resources for role play and other classroom activities. If you or other adults are working in other areas in the school, it should be made clear to you exactly what resources to use and where to find them. It should also be made clear to you where particular items are stored and whether you have access to storage areas and store cupboards. Teachers should ensure that items that are needed will be available at the time and that other classes will not be using the same resource area. Some schools may have rotas and procedures in place for ensuring that all classes have equal access to resources and facilities.

▲ **Figure 3.6** There are many potential hazards that can be caused by a messy workplace

Outdoor spaces

Outdoor areas used by pupils should be safe and boundaries should be inspected regularly to ensure that they are secure. Outdoor areas should be checked before pupils go into them to ensure that they are tidy and that any litter, broken glass or animal mess has been cleared up. If you are responsible for putting out toys and equipment, make sure that pupils are aware how they should be used and reinforce rules wherever possible to remind them how to behave.

How to adapt the environment to ensure safety for children and young people

All children should be given equal opportunities and this should be remembered in the learning environment. All pupils, including those with special needs, should be considered when planning and setting out materials and resources. The environment may often need to be adapted for the needs of particular children within the class.

Factors to be considered, include the following:

- **Light** – This may need to be adjusted or teaching areas changed if a visually impaired pupil's eyes are light sensitive.
- **Accessibility** – A pupil in a wheelchair needs to have as much access to classroom facilities as others. Furniture and resources may need to be moved to allow for this.
- **Sound** – Some pupils may be sensitive to sounds, for example an autistic child who is disturbed by loud or unusual noises. It is not always possible for such noises to be avoided, but teaching assistants need to be aware of the effect that they can have on pupils.

Demonstrating outdoor and indoor safety

Show your assessor how the learning environment in which you work fulfils safety requirements. You will need to look at a variety of indoor and outdoor spaces and equipment, and include a description of how you make safety checks before use.

Next, look at and evaluate a classroom in your school and assess whether its layout takes the following into account:

- accessibility for all pupils, particularly those with special needs
- maximum use of space
- good use of storage areas
- safety issues
- accessibility of materials.

When and how to use safety equipment; safety in respect of animals and outdoor spaces

This kind of safety equipment is more likely to be used where there are very young children, for example in nurseries and other Early Years settings. However, if you are working in a special school or in a setting where pupils need additional supervision, you may be required to use this type of safety equipment. Safety gates are sometimes used in schools to deter young children from entering a particular area such as a kitchen. You should always use manufacturers' guidelines when setting up equipment and it should be checked regularly. Any broken or incomplete equipment should be removed and disposed of.

Keeping animals

You may keep animals in school or there may be opportunities for staff or pupils to bring them into school as part of a topic or activity. Children can learn a great deal from contact with and caring for animals. However, animals should always be handled carefully and pupils should be taught to treat them with respect and be mindful of heath and safety issues. Tadpoles, for example, can die if they are kept in very warm classrooms. You must make sure that whenever animals are kept in school, health and safety requirements are carefully considered and that there is adult supervision at all times.

▲ **Figure 3.7** When would you use this type of equipment?

Keys to good practice

When animals are in school
- ✓ Make sure pupils wash their hands after handling animals.
- ✓ Always supervise pupils' contact with animals.
- ✓ Keep animal cages, tanks and other areas clean.
- ✓ Ensure that there are rotas and routines for feeding animals.

Safety in outdoor environments and spaces

Pupils should be encouraged to use the outside environment as much as possible. However, there can be dangers if outside areas are not monitored carefully. Ponds and sandpits should be covered when not in use, as both can be hazardous if children are unattended and uncovered sandpits can attract foxes and dogs. Toys or equipment should always be appropriate to the space available and should be put away safely. Plants can also be dangerous – thorns or nettles should be kept back and any poisonous plants noted and/or removed.

K9 Portfolio activity

Procedures for checking and maintaining safety of equipment and outdoor spaces

Can you think of any other safety equipment, which is used in your school? What are the procedures for checking and maintaining it? How are outdoor spaces monitored and maintained?

Good hygiene practice

You should be a good role model for pupils and always follow good practice yourself with regards to hygiene. This includes washing your hands before any activity involving foodstuffs, such as lunchtime or cooking activities. If you are giving first aid, you must make sure you follow the appropriate procedures.

Principles of cross-infection

When working with children you are vulnerable to picking up and also to carrying infection, so you should keep up to date with your own immunisations for diseases such as mumps, flu and meningitis. However, most childhood illnesses are most infectious before the symptoms occur and many pupils come to school with coughs and colds. Your school may have its own policy for these circumstances. For example, some children seem to have a permanent cold during winter and it would not be practical for them to be out of school for long periods. You should be aware of the signs of the common illnesses (see page 64).

Appropriate systems for disposing of waste and for handling body fluids

Your school will have a policy that follows local and national guidelines for handling body fluids and disposing of **waste**. When dealing with body fluids, you should always wear latex gloves, disposing of them after use. There should be special bins for first-aid waste, which should be disposed of appropriately.

> **❶ Key term**
> **Waste** – unwanted materials, soiled clothing, body fluids, dressings, cleaning cloths

Issues concerning the spread of HIV/AIDS virus and hepatitis

The virus that causes AIDS is called the HIV virus. It is only spread through body fluids (i.e. blood, semen, breast milk and vaginal fluids). The most common ways of HIV being passed from one person to another are through unprotected sex, sharing of needles or from mother to child during pregnancy, birth or breastfeeding. HIV cannot be spread through casual contact, or tears or sweat as these body fluids are not infectious.

Although there are different forms of hepatitis, it is caused by a virus that attacks the liver. It is also transmitted through blood-to-blood contact, sharing needles and general poor hygiene.

Adult/child ratio requirements

Adult to child ratios will vary according to the setting and the age group of the children. In school, it may vary according to local authority requirements within and outside school hours, whereas in nurseries and early years settings there are specific legal requirements (see Table 3.1).

Table 3.1 Adult/child ratios for different ages

Age	Adult/child ratio (legal requirements)
0–2 years	1 adult for every 3 children in early years group
2–3 years	1 adult for every 4 children in early years group
3–5 years	1 adult for every 8 children in early years group or outside the school day; 1 for every 13 if a registered teacher is present
4 years and over	1 teacher for every 30 pupils in Reception classes in maintained schools; 1 adult for every 5 children on school trips and during out of hours activities

How to supervise children safely

When supervising pupils, you should be aware of the kinds of risks to which they are exposed and how likely these are to happen bearing in mind the age and/or needs of the child. Pre-school children, particularly those under 3 years, are more likely to have

▼ **Figure 3.8** Pupils will need supervision for a variety of tasks

accidents as they are less likely to have an understanding of risk or danger. If you are working with pupils who have learning difficulties, they may also be less likely to have a fully developed awareness of danger: you need to modify your supervision according to the needs of the children and their level of awareness.

You may be involved in risk assessment activities, in particular if you are taking pupils off school premises. Always encourage pupils to talk and think about any risks when they are working with you, so that they develop their own awareness of danger.

Most activities carry some element of risk. Many educationalists now believe that the current tendency for many parents to keep their children indoors and take them everywhere by car is detrimental and overprotective, as it does not allow them to explore and discover the world for themselves. Therefore, it is important for all children to have the opportunity to take some risks.

(See also K24, page 72.)

K12 Portfolio activity

Balancing learning experiences against the risks involved

Think about the areas of risk for the following groups. How does the risk involved balance with the learning experience?

- Taking a group of pupils with learning difficulties to the park
- Working with a Reception group in the outside classroom
- Going on a Maths walk to local shops with Year 1 (P2)
- Working with Year 2 (P3) on a Design Technology activity, using hot glue guns and hacksaws
- Doing a traffic survey with Year 4 (P5)
- Taking Year 6 (P7) swimming each week

Policies and procedures for responding to and recording accidents and emergencies

In any environment where children are being supervised it is likely that there will be incidents or injuries at some time. You may find that you are first on the scene in the case of an accident or emergency and need to take action. If you are the only adult in the vicinity, you must make sure you follow the correct procedures until help arrives. It is vital to send for help as soon as possible. This should be the school's qualified first aider and, if necessary, an ambulance.

You will also need to support and reassure not only the casualty but also other children who may be present. Children quickly become distressed and, depending on what they have witnessed, may be in shock themselves. Make sure that you and any others on the scene are not put at unnecessary risk.

Warning! If not trained in first aid, and if at all unsure about what to do, you should only take action to avert any further danger to the casualty and others.

Resuscitation

If you are the first on the scene and find a casualty is not breathing, you may need to attempt resuscitation. This is known as Cardio Pulmonary Resuscitation (CPR). In all cases you should call for an ambulance immediately. Before carrying out CPR, check that there is no further risk to the casualty or to others.

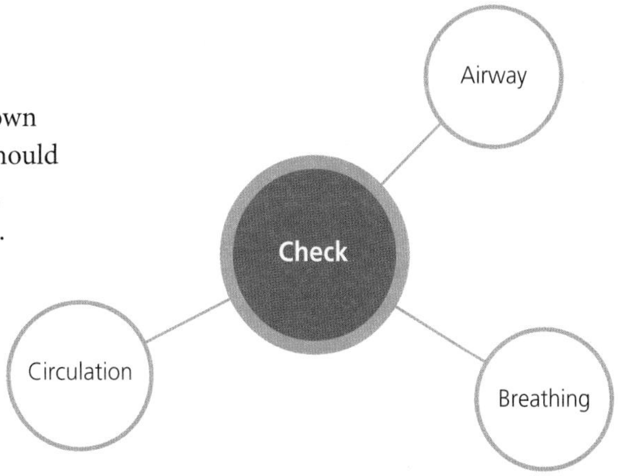

▲ **Figure 3.9** The three key elements to check when giving first aid

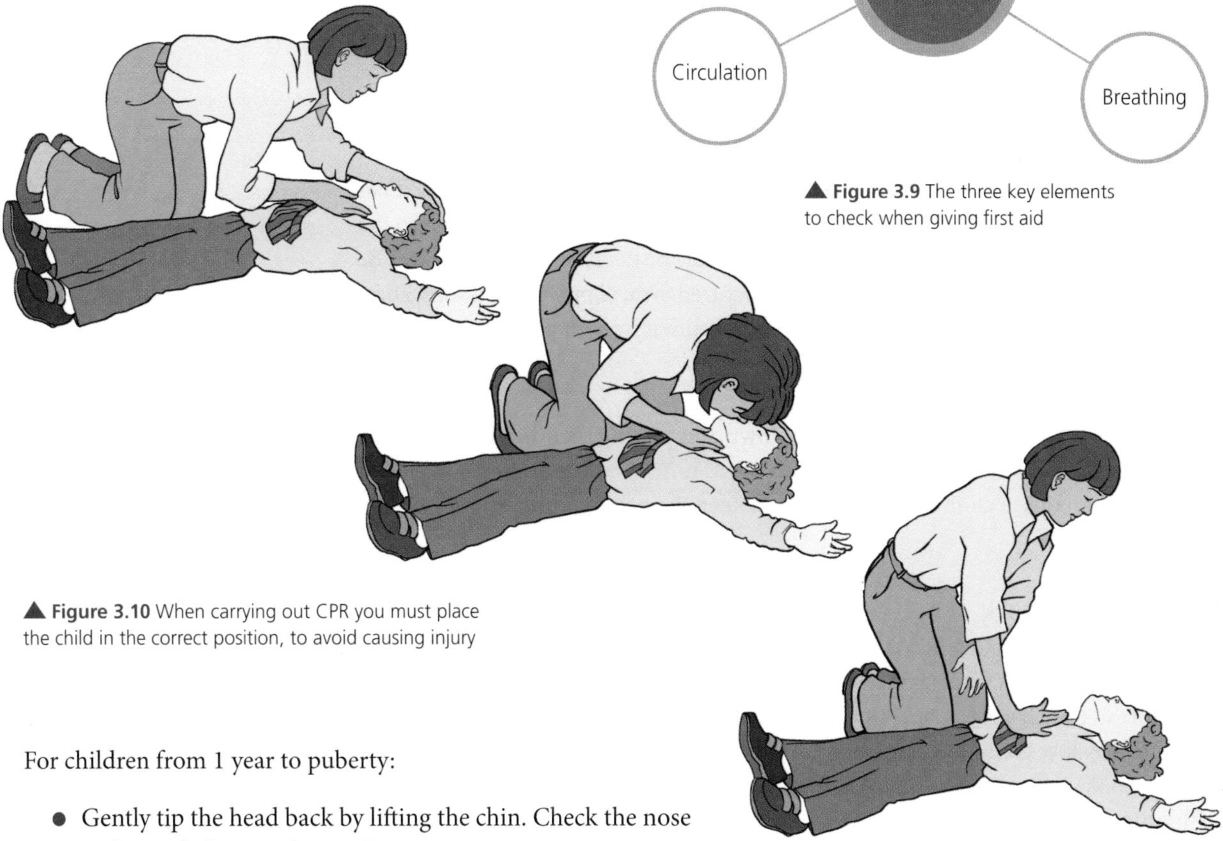

▲ **Figure 3.10** When carrying out CPR you must place the child in the correct position, to avoid causing injury

For children from 1 year to puberty:

● Gently tip the head back by lifting the chin. Check the nose and mouth for any obstructions.
● Pinch the child's nose, place your mouth over the child's mouth and give five rescue breaths.
● Give chest compressions using the heel of your hand in the centre of the child's chest. After 30 compressions, give two further breaths.
● Continue until emergency help arrives.

(For procedures for administering CPR to other age groups, see www.redcross.org.uk)

Different emergencies and what you should do

Burns and scalds

Cool the affected area immediately using cold water. Do not remove any clothes that are stuck to the burn.

Electrocution

Cut off the source of electricity by removing the plug. If there is no way to do this, stand on dry insulating material, such as newspaper or a wooden box, and push the victim away from the source using something wooden, such as a chair. Do not touch the victim until the electricity has been switched off. Then, place the victim in the recovery position (see page 60).

Choking or difficulty with breathing

Encourage the victim to cough to dislodge the blockage. Bend the casualty over with the head lower than the chest and slap between the shoulder blades five times using the heel of the hand.

Poisoning

If possible, find out what the child has taken or swallowed. Stay with the child and if they become unconscious, call an ambulance and put the child in the recovery position. Do not try to give the child anything to drink. Take the suspected poison to hospital with you.

Falls: fractures

Treat all cases as actual fractures. Do not attempt to move the casualty. You will need a qualified first aider to come to the scene. Support a fractured leg by tying it to the other leg, using a wide piece of fabric such as a scarf or tie. If the knee is broken, do not try to force it straight. If you suspect a fractured arm, support it in a sling and secure it to the chest. If the arm will not bend, secure it by strapping it to the body.

Faints or loss of consciousness

Treat those who feel faint by sitting them down and putting their head between their knees. If they do faint, lie them on their back and raise their legs to increase blood flow to the brain. Loosen clothing at the neck and keep the patient quiet after regaining consciousness.

Anaphylactic shock

This is a severe allergic reaction and can be due to ingestion of a particular food, such as nuts, or caused by insect stings. It may cause constriction of air passages and can be fatal. Sit the casualty up and find out if they have any medication. Seek emergency help. If they lose consciousness, open the airway and start resuscitation.

Bleeding

Reassure the child and keep them calm if distressed. Elevate the wound if necessary and put a dressing on it. If there is a foreign body in the wound, do not attempt to remove it. Press on or around the wound to stop the bleeding.

Breathing difficulties or asthma attack

Ensure that the child has nothing in their mouth. Make sure they have their inhaler and encourage them to breath slowly. Keep them away from others in a quiet area. Call for help if there is no improvement.

Putting a casualty into the recovery position

If you are dealing with an unconscious person, you will need to place them in the recovery position. This will prevent any blood, vomit or saliva from blocking the windpipe. You should always do this unless you suspect that the victim has a fracture of the spine or neck.

1. Kneel beside the victim and turn their head towards you, lifting it back to open the airway.

2. Place the victim's nearest arm straight down their side and the other arm across their chest. Place the far ankle over the near ankle.

3. While holding the head with one hand, hold the victim at the hip by their clothing and turn them onto their front by pulling towards you, supporting them with your knees.

4. Lift the chin forward to keep the airway open.

5. Bend the arm and leg nearest to you, and pull out the other arm from under the body, palm up.

If you are treating a casualty, you should be aware of the dangers of contamination from blood and other body fluids. If possible, always wear protective gloves when treating an open wound or when in contact with other body fluids. Many infections such as HIV and hepatitis can be passed on through contact with these fluids.

You should always stay with the casualty and give support by your physical presence, as well as giving as much care as you are able. If you feel that you are not able to deal with the situation, you should always do what you can and reassure the patient as much as possible while sending for help. Where a child has been injured badly, their parents or carers should be notified immediately. They will need to know exactly what is happening and if the child is being taken to hospital they will need to know where.

How to treat common minor injuries such as minor skin abrasions, cuts, bumps

Minor injuries such as cuts and grazes will usually be dealt with as they occur by a first aider. It is unlikely that creams and lotions will be applied; most school first aiders will clean minor injuries with cold water. A note should be sent home stating what has happened so that the parent is informed. It is particularly important that parents are aware if their child has had a bump on the head.

Figure 3.11 ▶
A minor accident report form

Remember that following all injuries or emergencies, even minor accidents, a record should be made of what has happened and the steps taken by the staff present.

Sunnymead Secondary School
Accident report form

Name of casualty ....

Exact location of incident ....

Date of incident ....

What was the injured person doing? ....

How did the accident happen? ....

What injuries occurred? ....

Treatment given ....

Medical aid sought ....

Name of person dealing with incident ....

Name of witness ....

If the casualty was a child, what time were parents informed? ....

Was hospital attended? ....

Was the accident investigated? .... By whom? ....

Signed .... Position ....

▲ **Figure 3.12** An accident report form

Awareness of location and contents of first aid box

The appropriate contents of a first aid kit

You should know the location of safety equipment in school and the identity of trained first aiders. It is strongly recommended that there are first aiders in all educational establishments. They need to have completed a training course approved by the Health and Safety Executive (HSE), which is valid for three years. You should also be aware of the location of first aid boxes in the school. The school's trained first aider should be responsible for ensuring adequate supply and regular restocking of the first aid box. Supplies should be date stamped when they are received as they have a five-year shelf life. If you find that there is not sufficient equipment, you must report that to the health and safety officer.

There is no mandatory requirement for the contents of first aid boxes but they should include certain items, as listed in Figure 3.13.

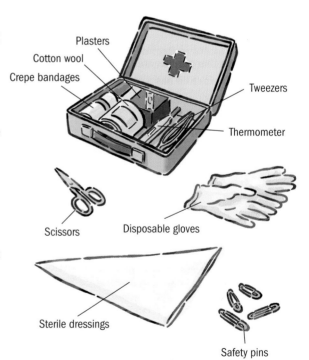

▲ **Figure 3.13** Contents of a first aid box

How to recognise and avoid allergic reactions

There are an increasing number of children who have allergic reactions to foods such as nuts or intolerances to foods such as wheat. All school staff should be aware of the identities of pupils who have these reactions and clear instructions on how to deal with each case must be readily available. In particular, lunchtime supervisors need to be kept informed. There may be a book containing photographs of relevant pupils, information about their condition and contact telephone numbers. In some schools, photographs and information may be displayed on staffroom walls. Care must always be taken to keep such information as confidential as possible.

Case study K14

Maintaining awareness of pupils' allergies

Jemma is supervising at lunchtime. A new pupil starts to have difficulty breathing and his friend calls Jemma over. She finds out that the pupil has a nut allergy and is sitting close to a pupil who has peanut butter in her sandwiches.

- What should Jemma do first?
- What should have happened to avoid this situation from occurring?

Policies and procedures to deal with children's illness

Signs and symptoms of some common illnesses

All staff should be aware of the types of illnesses that may occur in children and also be alert to physical signs that show children may be incubating illness. Incubation periods can vary between illnesses, from one day to three weeks in some cases. Remember that young children may not be able to communicate exactly what is wrong. General signs that children are 'off colour' may include:

- pale skin
- flushed cheeks
- rashes
- different (quiet, clingy, irritable) behaviour
- rings around the eyes.

The Department of Health has issued a useful poster, 'Guidance on infection control in schools and nurseries', to schools, which could be displayed in the first aid area as a quick reference. It clearly sets out some common illnesses and their characteristics. Some of these are listed in the table below, although the list is not exhaustive. Staff must be alert to the signs and symptoms of these common illnesses and notice changes in behaviour that indicate that children may be unwell.

Children often develop symptoms more quickly than adults, as they may have less resistance to infection. Most schools will call parents and carers straight away if their child is showing signs or symptoms of illnesses. If children are on antibiotics, most schools will recommend that they stay off school until they have completed the course.

Illness and symptoms	Recommended time to keep off school and treatment	Comments
Chickenpox – patches of itchy red spots with white centres	For five days from onset of rash. Treat with calomine lotion to relieve itching.	It is not necessary to keep at home until all the spots have disappeared.
German measles (rubella) – pink rash on head, trunk and limbs; slight fever, sore throat	For five days from onset of rash. Treat by resting.	The child is most infectious before diagnosis. Keep away from pregnant women.
Impetigo – small red pimples on the skin, which break down and weep	Until lesions are crusted and healed. Treat with antibiotic cream or medicine.	Antibiotic treatment may speed up healing. Wash hands well after touching the child's skin.
Ringworm – contagious fungal infection of the skin; shows as circular flaky patches	None. Treat with anti-fungal ointment; it may require antibiotics.	It needs treatment by the GP.
Diarrhoea and vomiting	Until diarrhoea and vomiting has settled and for 24 hours after. No specific diagnosis or treatment, although keep giving clear fluids and no milk.	
Conjunctivitis – inflammation or irritation of the membranes lining the eyelids	None (although schools may have different policies on this). Wash with warm water on cotton wool swab. GP may prescribe cream.	
Measles – fever, runny eyes, sore throat, cough; red rash, which often starts from the head, spreading downwards	Give rest, plenty of fluids and paracetamol for fever.	This is now more likely with some parents refusing MMR inoculation.
Meningitis – fever, headache, stiff neck and blotchy skin; dislike of light; symptoms may develop very quickly	Get urgent medical attention. It is treated with antibiotics.	It can have severe complications and be fatal.
Tonsillitis – inflammation of the tonsils by infection. Very sore throat, fever, earache, enlarged red tonsils, which may have white spots.	Treat with antibiotics and rest.	It can also cause ear infection.

K15 # Portfolio activity

Dealing with ill pupils appropriately

Either write a reflective account detailing how you have dealt with an incident when a pupil was ill or ask your assessor to speak to a first aider or other staff member who can confirm that you acted appropriately and in compliance with school policy.

Emergency procedures

Procedures for fires

Schools may need to be evacuated for different reasons, for example, in the case of fire, bomb scare or other emergency. Your school is required to have a health and safety policy, which gives guidelines for emergency procedures and you should make sure that you are aware of these. Fire notices should be displayed at various points around the school, showing what to do in case of a fire and where to assemble in case of building evacuation. All adults should know what their role requires them to do and where to assemble pupils.

The school should have regular fire drills – around once a term – at different times of the day (not just before playtime for convenience!) so that all adults and pupils are aware what to do wherever they are on the premises. Fire drills should also be practised at lunchtime or during after-school or breakfast club, when there are different staff on site and when pupils are in different environments. Records should be kept of all fire drills, any issues that occur and the action taken.

Security incidents

It is important that all staff are vigilant and make sure that unidentified people are challenged immediately. Do this by simply asking whether you can help the person or by asking to see their visitor's badge.

Missing children

Fortunately it is extremely rare for children to go missing, particularly if the school follows health and safety guidelines and procedures. On school trips you should periodically check the group for whom you are responsible, as well as keeping an eye on pupils supervised by helpers. If for some reason a pupil does go missing, raise the alarm straightaway and make sure that you follow school policy.

Keys to good practice

Health, safety and security arrangements

✓ Always be vigilant.
✓ Use and store equipment safely.
✓ Check both indoor and outdoor environments and equipment regularly and report anything that is unsafe, following the correct procedures.
✓ Challenge unidentified persons.
✓ Check adult–child ratios in all situations.
✓ Ensure you are aware of procedures at the beginning and end of the day.
✓ Make sure you are thoroughly prepared when carrying out unusual activities or when going on trips.
✓ Use correct procedures for clearing up blood, vomit, urine or faeces.

Types and possible signs and indicators of child abuse

As an adult working with children, you need to have an understanding of the different signs that may indicate that a child is being abused. Although you will do your best to ensure a child's safety while they are in your care, you also need to look out for any signs that they are being mistreated when they are out of school. The signs may include both physical and behavioural changes. There are four main types of abuse.

Physical abuse

This involves being physically hurt or injured. Physical abuse may take a variety of forms and be either spasmodic or persistent. Injuries may come from children being hit, kicked, shaken, punched or beaten.

The signs of physical abuse are often quite straightforward to spot and can include bruises, cuts, burns and other injuries. However, you should be aware that such injuries can also be caused by genuine accidents. If you notice frequent signs of injury or if there appear to be other signs of abuse, it is important to take action. Less obvious signs of physical abuse may include fear of physical contact with others, reluctance to get changed for PE, wanting to stay covered up, even in hot weather, and aggression.

Emotional abuse

This involves the child being continually 'put down' and criticised, or not given love or approval at a time when they need it the most. It includes bullying, discrimination and racism, which may also take place outside school. This could take the form of name calling, humiliation or teasing. Increasingly, it can also take place through mobile phones and the Internet.

The signs of emotional abuse are that the child is withdrawn and lacks confidence, shows regression or is 'clingy' towards adults, and has low self-esteem. Children who suffer from emotional abuse are likely to be anxious about new situations and may show extremes of behaviour or appear distracted and unable to concentrate.

Sexual abuse

Sexual abuse involves an adult or young person using a child sexually, for example, by touching their bodies inappropriately or by forcing them to look at sexual images or have sex.

The signs of sexual abuse may include sexual behaviour inappropriate to the child's age, genital irritation, clinginess or changes in behaviour, regression and lack of trust of adults. Sexual abuse can be almost impossible to identify and its signs can be caused by other kinds of abuse. It is therefore important that any signs are seen as possible, rather than probable, indicators.

Neglect

This means that the child is not being properly cared for and not having its basic needs met by parents or carers. Basic needs include shelter, food, love, general hygiene and medical care. The signs of neglect may include being dirty, tired, hungry, seeking attention and generally failing to thrive.

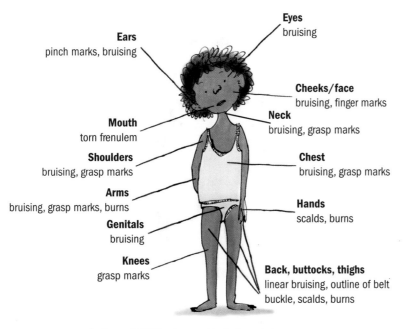

Eyes
bruising

Ears
pinch marks, bruising

Cheeks/face
bruising, finger marks

Neck
bruising, grasp marks

Mouth
torn frenulem

Shoulders
bruising, grasp marks

Chest
bruising, grasp marks

Arms
bruising, grasp marks, burns

Hands
scalds, burns

Genitals
bruising

Knees
grasp marks

Back, buttocks, thighs
linear bruising, outline of belt
buckle, scalds, burns

▲ **Figure 3.14** The signs and indicators of abuse

As a teaching assistant you are in a good position to notice changes in pupils' behaviour and other signs of possible abuse. You should always look out for the indicators above and, if you are at all concerned, speak to either your class teacher or the school's Child Protection Officer (usually the headteacher). They will follow the school's child protection policy and, if necessary, follow local authority guidelines for informing social services. Always keep a note of what happened, what you reported and who you told.

◀ **Figure 3.15** You may need to report to others about possible cases of abuse

Case study

Identifying and acting on signs of possible abuse

Marie has been working in Francesca's class for six months. Recently she has noticed that Francesca, who is usually happy and settled, has become very withdrawn and less involved with her friends. She appears very reluctant to join in during class activities and at playtimes, and her clothing does not appear to have been washed. She has not had her PE kit in school for two weeks. Marie knows that Francesca's mother has been treated for alcoholism in the past, but as far as she knows this is not currently an issue. She speaks to the class teacher and tells her about her concerns.

- What signs is Francesca showing that may be indicators of abuse?
- How should Marie and the class teacher proceed?

Recognition that social factors may increase a child's vulnerability to abuse

If you know that a pupil comes from a home background where there are likely to be pressures on the family, for example if there is a parent or older sibling who misuses drugs or alcohol, it is possible that the pupil is more vulnerable to abuse. However, it is very important that you do not jump to any conclusions or assume that abuse has definitely taken place.

Safe working practices that protect children and adults who work with them

It is important to follow safe working practices to ensure that pupils are protected from abuse. Child protection is the responsibility of all who work with children and you need to be aware of your school's policy for recording and reporting suspected abuse. Records will need to be kept of what pupils have said and when they said it, as well as notes, dates and times of any meetings that have taken place between the school and social services. If a pupil reports anything that is a cause for concern, the school needs to make sure it is followed up.

Adults who work with children also need to protect themselves by making sure that they are never on their own with individual children for any length of time or, if they have to be, that they are in an area that is open to others.

Portfolio activity

Investigating protection and behaviour policies

List the different ways in which your school protects both children and adults through the use of safe working practices. You may need to look at your school's child protection and behaviour policies.

How to encourage children to be aware of their own bodies and understand their right not to be abused

All children have a right to be safe and feel protected. The UN Convention on the Rights of the Child, which was signed by the UK in 1989, sets out the rights of all children to be treated equally and fairly. These include:

- the right of all children to grow up in an atmosphere of happiness, love and understanding
- the right to be as healthy as possible
- the right to grow and develop to the best of their ability
- the right to live in a safe environment.

Children must be protected from things that threaten to infringe these rights. This means that forms of abuse or abduction, taking them out of school without cause or making them work on activities harmful to their health must be prevented.

Children need to be taught how to keep safe in a number of different ways. As well as encouraging their awareness of health and safety issues, you should support their development by helping them to have a positive self-image. Children need to have plenty of opportunities and encouragement as they grow up in order to develop their independence and learn about their likes and dislikes. They should also be aware that they have a right to be safe and know what to do if they do not feel safe. If you are talking to pupils about their bodies, using activities you have planned with the teacher, be aware that people use different terms to describe body parts and functions, such as going to the toilet, when speaking to children. If pupils confide in you and tell you what has happened to them, they may need time or additional help to use the right language or to draw what has happened. The curriculum should include giving pupils information about organisations that exist to protect them, such as the NSPCC, Childline and Kidscape.

Keys to good practice

Keeping pupils safe

✓ Ensure that pupils are taught to keep themselves safe.
✓ Encourage pupils to talk about their worries and speak to others.
✓ Use age-appropriate language when speaking to pupils.
✓ Never promise not to tell others if a pupil discloses that they have been abused.
✓ Set an example by encouraging co-operation and positive behaviour.

Portfolio activity K20

Supporting positive self-image and awareness of rights

How does your school encourage positive self-images in pupils? What kinds of activities or discussions might staff encourage in order to develop pupils' awareness of their rights? Investigate the different forms of support that might be available through outside organisations to help with this.

The importance of consistently and fairly applied boundaries and rules for children's behaviour

It is important that all staff are consistent when managing pupils' behaviour. Children need to have boundaries that they can understand and are regularly reinforced by adults. If it is not clear to them how they are expected to behave or if adults give them conflicting messages, children become confused and upset, and find it hard to know how to behave next time. Although all children will test boundaries for behaviour, if they are met with the same response each time they will be less likely to repeat it. Rules should be appropriate for the age or ability of the child and the language used should make the expectations of adults clear.

When managing pupils' behaviour, be careful of stereotyping or making assumptions about how they will behave. If pupils are expected to behave well or badly, they will usually live up to the expectation.

K21 Case study

Applying boundaries and rules

Barbara is working in Reception as a teaching assistant. There is also a work experience student and a parent helper, as well as the class teacher. This afternoon, Barbara notices that the student, who is watching pupils in the outside area with her, is allowing five pupils in the sand and water when the rule is for four. When Barbara asks her about it, she replies that the pupils were upset when she had told them only four at a time and wanted to be together. She also tells Barbara that she has not allowed James and Hanif to use the bikes because 'they always terrorise the others'.

- Should Barbara say anything to the student about what she has told the pupils?
- Why is it important that the adults in the class give pupils the same messages?
- What might have been a more appropriate way of managing James and Hanif?

How to respond to children's challenging behaviour

Children who display challenging behaviour need to know what will happen if they regularly and persistently do this. As well as consistent boundaries, managed by all staff and agreed through school policies, there should also be age-appropriate sanctions. Be aware that what may deter younger children may not always work for older ones.

K22 Portfolio activity

Managing inappropriate behaviour in different age groups

Consider the sanctions used in your school for managing inappropriate behaviour. Do they vary in line with different age groups? If not, are some more effective than others at deterring pupils of different ages? Give reasons for your answer.

Importance of encouraging and rewarding positive behaviour

It is important for all pupils, but especially for those who tend to be 'told off' more than others, that we recognise and reward positive behaviour. Even as adults we like to be noticed for something good that we do. Research has shown that we need to be given six positives for every negative in order to balance this out. It is always much easier for us to focus on negative aspects of a pupil's behaviour and react to this. When recognising and rewarding positive behaviour, however, you must not forget to notice those pupils who always behave appropriately.

Pupils also attempt to gain attention through undesirable behaviour, so be aware of this and try to ignore it where possible, instead giving attention to those pupils who are behaving well.

Modelling the correct behaviour

You need to demonstrate that you are a good role model in all areas of behaviour within the school. Pupils take their lead from adults and need to see that they too are behaving appropriately and responsibly. This is also true for good manners! Be careful when speaking to others that you are showing the same respect that we are asking pupils to show.

Notice when pupils are behaving well or trying hard

This is important because it helps to build positive relationships and shows that you care about the individual.

Use positive recognition such as merit marks

Most schools use these kinds of systems and have assemblies and evenings to celebrate work and behaviour.

Follow up on important issues

Always make sure you follow up, particularly if you have said that you will. There is little point in saying to a pupil that you will tell their teacher how impressed you are with their behaviour if you then forget to do so. The pupil will think that you do not really think it is important.

Build trust with all pupils to maintain positive relationships

Do all you can to show pupils that you are interested in and value them. As you get to know them, you will remember particular things about them. Giving your trust to pupils encourages them to take more responsibility, for example taking the register down to the school office.

Ensure pupils know why they are being rewarded

You must be clear on exactly what you are praising or rewarding, for example 'I am giving you this merit mark because you have been so helpful to others this morning.'

Making sure directions are unambiguous

Make sure that you communicate clearly to pupils so that they understand what you are asking. Young children may find directions confusing, especially if there are too many instructions at once or if they are occupied doing something else. If you communicate through questioning, for example 'Is it nearly home time?', pupils may think that there is some choice involved. If we want pupils to do as we ask, we need to say things as though we mean them!

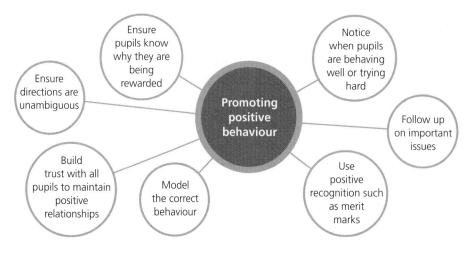

▲ **Figure 3.16** Ways to promote positive behaviour

Case study

Monitoring negative behaviour

Matt is in Year 7 (S1) and although he has not been in the school for long he is already getting a reputation for being a troublemaker. You are allocated to his form group and work with Matt for the majority of the time at present. The SENCo (ASL teacher) has asked you to keep an eye on Matt and let him know when there are any issues so that he can keep track of how often his disruptive behaviour is occurring and whether there are any triggers. You notice that Matt is being spoken to about negative behaviour at least once in every lesson.

● Why will this constant negative attention be bad for Matt?
● Can you think of any suggestions you could make to the SENCo (ASL teacher) about how you could help with Matt's behaviour?

Safety issues and concerns when taking children out of the setting

You need to be aware of safety issues when taking pupils out of school. If you are taking a large number of pupils on an outing or residential trip, a member of staff should undertake a risk assessment beforehand. This means that they will check what kinds of risks there might be and the likelihood of the risk occurring. The level of risk may be dependent on a number of factors:

● the adult/child ratio
● where you are going
● how you will get there
● your planned activities on arrival.

The facilities will need to be checked to make sure they are adequate for the needs of the pupils, for example, if you are taking a disabled child. As well as a risk assessment, preparations need to include other considerations. A trip must always be planned thoroughly so that the adults are prepared for whatever happens. Preparations include the need to:

- seek and gain parental consent
- arrange for suitable safe transport
- take first aid kit and a first aider with you
- take appropriate clothing for the activity or weather
- make lists of adults and the pupils for whom they will be responsible
- give information sheets to all helpers, including timings and any safety information
- make sure that pupils you have concerns about are in your group rather than with a parent.

Portfolio activity K24

Identifying safety issues for trips

Outline the different safety issues you need to be prepared for when undertaking each of the following:

- a Reception class trip to the farm
- a Year 2 (P3) trip by train to a local museum
- a Year 4 (P5) visit to a Tudor castle and gardens
- a Year 6 (P7) five-day trip to the Isle of Wight.

Legislation, guidelines and policies which form the basis for action to safeguard children

The Every Child Matters guidelines, which led to the Children Act 2004, came about as a direct result of the Laming Report following death of Victoria Climbié. The report was highly critical of the way in which the Climbié case was handled and made 108 recommendations to overhaul child protection in the UK. The main points that emerged were that:

- there should be a much closer working relationship between agencies such as health professionals, schools and welfare services
- there should be a central database containing records of all children and whether they are known to different services
- there should be an independent children's commissioner for England to protect children and young people's rights
- there should be a children and families board, which is chaired by a senior government minister
- Ofsted will set a framework that will monitor children's services.

The Children's Act 2004 required that these recommendations became a legal requirement and as a result the Every Child Matters framework was introduced to implement the Act and the wider reform programme.

(For a full outline of the Laming Report, see www.victoria-climbie-inquiry.org.uk. For more on Every Child Matters, see Unit 12, page 191.)

For your portfolio...

A good way of producing evidence for this unit is to go for a health and safety walkabout with your assessor. You can point out any hazards and carry out your own safety check of facilities and equipment in all areas of your school. This could include fire extinguishers and exits, first aid kits, access to first aid, how the school routinely checks equipment and stores hazardous materials, and any accidents you have recorded. You could record the walkabout, include it as evidence in your portfolio and ask your assessor to use it as part of the assessment process. They might ask witnesses in school whether you always follow health, safety and security procedures yourself and encourage pupils to do the same. For the school's policies for dealing with health emergencies, including allergic reactions, you could carry out a simulated activity showing how you would respond to different symptoms.

For the child abuse section of the unit, you may need to have a professional discussion with your assessor to show that you know and understand the different indicators of abuse and how you should respond to any concerns you may have.

Websites

www.barnardos.org.uk

www.bbc.co.uk/health/firstaid

www.hse.gov.uk – Health and Safety Executive

www.kidscape.org.uk – a charity to prevent bullying and child abuse

www.nch.org.uk – The Children's Charity

www.redcross.org

www.sja.org.uk – St John Ambulance

www.teachernet.gov.uk – gives a list of charities that work together with schools

www.unicef.org.uk

Contact details

helpline@nspcc.org.uk

nspcc helpline: 0808 800 5000

4 Contribute to Positive Relationships

This unit is about showing how you contribute effectively to the relationships you have with others in school, whether with adults or children and young people. Positive relationships will benefit all the pupils and adults in the school and enhance their ability to participate in school life.

Children and young people should have the opportunity to put forward their ideas and express themselves in their own time and using their own words. You also need to demonstrate that you support the care, learning and development of children and young people through your communication skills and the way in which you relate to them.

When developing positive relationships with adults, you need to show that you are sympathetic to their needs and make time to listen to them. You should show that you have understood them and clarified any points that are ambiguous. You should also show that you are able to give your own suggestions and pass on any information required as soon as possible to the appropriate person.

What you need to know and understand

For this unit, you need to know and understand:

- The importance of giving children and young people full attention when listening to them and how you demonstrate this through body language, facial expression, speech and gesture

- Why it is important to give all children and young people the opportunity to be heard and how you do this in a group

- An outline of how children and young people's communication skills develop within the age range 0–16 years

- Why it is important to give children and young people sufficient time to express themselves in their own words

- Why it is important to help children and young people make choices and how you can assist them to do this

- The key features of effective communication and why it is important to model this when interacting with adults, children and young people

- The main differences between communicating with adults and communicating with children and young people

- How to demonstrate that you value adults' views and opinions and why it is important to the development of positive relationships

- Communication difficulties that may exist and how these can be overcome

- How to cope with disagreements with adults

- Why it is important to reassure adults of the confidentiality of shared information and the limits of this

- Organisational policy regarding information exchange

- The importance of communicating positively with children, young people and families

- How children and young people's ability to communicate can affect their behaviour

Importance of giving children and young people full attention when listening to them and how you demonstrate this

Although this may be difficult at times if you are busy or have other demands on your time, it is very important to give pupils your full attention when communicating with them. This is because pupils will be able to tell if you are not 'tuned in' to what they are saying and may learn over time not to try to communicate with adults who do not seem interested in what they have to say. This can also have an effect on pupils' self-esteem and perception of how others see them. As part of the development of positive relationships, good communication is vital.

As part of your role in a school, you may be required to work with individual pupils. This may be because they have a Statement of Special Educational Needs (Co-ordinated Support Plan) or have learning requirements that mean that they will benefit from occasional one-to-one support. As part of this role you need to show that you are interested in the pupil by **listening** to what they say and having time for them. There are a number of ways in which you can do this.

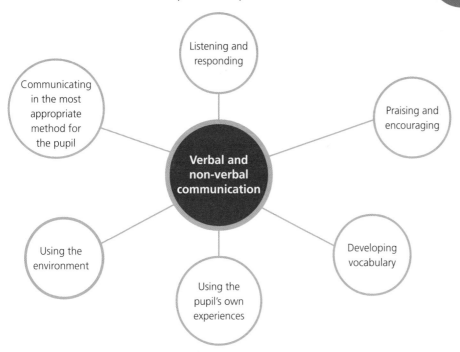

▲ **Figure 4.1** Communicating with pupils effectively

Your communication with pupils may be verbal or non-verbal and take place on a number of different levels.

Verbal communication

This interactive part of the communication process involves listening and responding to what others are saying. In schools it is often referred to as 'speaking and listening'. For it to be effective, you need to have time to hear, think and respond. Pupils, especially younger ones, usually find it easier to speak than to listen and many of them need to learn to wait and listen to others. You therefore need to show them how to do this and model good verbal communication skills.

▲ **Figure 4.2** The importance of non-verbal communication

Non-verbal communication

Body language can be a very powerful communicator. Through it we can often tell how someone is feeling without speaking to them. We can also use it to communicate with others in different ways, through:

- **Facial expressions, eye contact and gestures** – These can be very useful in a classroom. You may only need to look at a pupil to show approval or disapproval. When the teacher is speaking to the class or when pupils are working, you can often show that you are aware of what they are doing and encourage or discourage them to continue. Gestures can also be very effective across a busy classroom.
- **Body stance** – You may find that you need to bend down to speak to younger pupils. Always try to be at their level if you are supporting their work as constantly standing over them can feel threatening, even intimidating. With older pupils, make sure that you are not intimidated by them if they are taller than you or use defensive body language such as crossed arms, which can be seen as a barrier.

During school visits, your assessor should be able to observe you demonstrating that you are aware of the importance of showing your full attention to pupils, so other evidence for this K point is not necessary.

For more on effective communication see K6, page 83.

Why it is important to give all children and young people the opportunity to be heard and how you do this in a group

In order to build relationships with pupils, you need to adapt your behaviour and communication skills. Pupils of all ages, cultures and abilities need to feel secure and valued, and your interactions with them should demonstrate this. Through positive communication and involvement with them, you can show them that they are part of the school community. However, this is not the same as giving all pupils attention whenever they demand it!

When you are working with groups of pupils, you may find it difficult to balance the needs of individuals with those of the group. This will be because often individuals seem to require different levels of attention: some may be able to work and organise themselves independently, whereas others may need the reassurance of an adult. When speaking and listening, some may be constantly trying to contribute their ideas, while others may be very quiet. Make sure you give all pupils the opportunity to contribute to discussions. Part of the reason for this is that you will not be able to assess what they know or be able to challenge their ideas unless you know what they are. You can give pupils opportunities to contribute in different ways:

- by aiming your questioning at different pupils to ensure that all have the chance to contribute
- by asking the group a question or giving them a task and then inviting them to discuss it with a talk partner or buddy before seeking a response
- by giving pupils 'thinking time' and then asking the group so that they are more confident before responding; this also avoids the more enthusiastic pupils having opportunities to call out
- by giving the group small whiteboards and pens, and asking them to write down the answer and then hold these up at the same time
- by asking the group a question and then telling them all to find out the answer, if they do not know it, from someone who does. You will need to give them a little time to do this. You can then ask the group the question again and be sure that everyone knows the answer. This is very effective in helping those pupils who do not have the confidence to answer questions in a group situation.

Case study K2

Giving pupils the opportunity to be heard

Myra is working with a Year 7 (S1) class in a mixed ability Geography lesson. The class are finding out about their local area and have been asked to discuss in their groups their likes and dislikes about their neighbourhood. Myra is working with a group of six, two of whom are not engaged at all in the discussion.

- How might you approach this situation?
- Why is it important to ensure that all of the group have a chance to contribute?

An outline of how children and young people's communication skills develop within the age range 0–16 years

Communication skills are an important aspect of how children learn to use language and to relate to others. As they learn and develop these skills, they will be able to understand their own identities and to develop relationships with others better. You need to have an awareness of the different stages of communication development in order to support this process. However, you should also know that all children are individuals and do not develop at the same rate – the information below shows the average age for each stage.

In addition, it is likely that children who speak English as an additional language will take longer to develop their vocabulary and, as a result, their patterns of speech. Learning more than one language should not mean that they are hindered, but it needs to be handled in a sensitive way so that children's identities are valued. Your school should support the development of children's home languages through the involvement of families, the inclusion of different cultures and the celebration of pupils' individuality. (See also Unit 11.)

Before children learn to speak, they are known as being in the pre-linguistic stage.

Age	Pre-linguistic skills
0–6 months	Babies communicate by crying when hungry or tired. At this stage they are learning to differentiate between tones of voice. They start to establish eye contact with adults and smile.
6–12 months	Babies start to babble and form individual sounds. They start to recognise and point to objects. They start to enjoy repetitive and predictable games such as peek-a-boo.

▲ **Figure 4.3** The linguistic stage begins when the first recognisable words appear

Age	Linguistic skills
12–18 months	The first recognisable words are formed. By 18 months, children's main carers will be able to identify about ten words.
18 months – 2 years	Vocabulary develops rapidly and by 2 years children know about 200 words. They start to use phrases such as 'want drink'.
2–3 years	Children are still learning new words, quickly although they will still be making some errors in how they string words together. They may start to use questions more.
3–4 years	Children use questions and negatives, and take their lead from adults, copying what they say. Their vocabulary continues to expand and their social circle widens.
4–8 years	Children use language to develop relationships with others and use more and more vocabulary. They use more methods of communication, e.g. writing and reading, and use language to socialise.
8–16 years	Children and young people use more complex sentences and start to develop their confidence in a variety of situations, e.g. in discussions and negotiations.

Figure 4.5 Complex sentences are used by teenage years

Portfolio activity

Identifying communication skills

For this K point, you need to show that you know an outline of the stages of children's communication development. Using the information above as a basis, give examples of the kind of language and interactions you might expect from children and young people at each of these stages.

Why it is important to give children and young people sufficient time to express themselves in their own words

People take different lengths of time to organise their ideas and put them into words. Some may be able to verbalise what they are thinking straightaway, whereas others need to take time to be sure about what they are going to say. You should not put pressure on pupils to give you a response if it is clear that they are thinking about it, in particular if they have communication difficulties. Pressure will make them more anxious about communicating and therefore make it more difficult for them to concentrate on what they want to say. Pupils may benefit from having thinking time or discussion time with a partner so that they can decide how they are going to respond. This technique also prevents pupils who are more enthusiastic and always have their hands up from automatically having their say.

Case study

Allowing young people time to express themselves

Matthew is in Year 1 (P2) and has a stutter. It is not severe, but he occasionally needs a little longer to put forward his ideas. You are working with him in a group situation and have asked the pupils a question. Matthew has started to reply, but is finding it difficult to speak. One of the others in the group has anticipated what Matthew is trying to say.

- What would you do in this situation?
- Why is it important to allow Matthew the time to express himself?

Why it is important to help children and young people make choices and how you can assist them to do this

Making choices for themselves is an important part of pupils' learning. In the earliest stages of school, making choices is part of the curriculum and pupils are given opportunities to practise it in their selection of play activities. They are encouraged to have some control within the boundaries of the setting. As they become older, pupils should continue to be encouraged to participate in decision-making. In this way they have a degree of control over some of the aspects of school life that affect them, which helps to avoid them feeling frustrated by constantly being told what to do, as well as teaching them an essential life skill.

The strategy of discussing and setting their own targets for work and behaviour is often used with pupils, so that targets are not imposed on them without their involvement. Another strategy regularly used with older pupils is the use of school councils. These work very effectively in encouraging pupils to think about and discuss different sides of issues and then come to decisions that will be adopted by the school.

Case study K5

Involving pupils in decision-making

It is the beginning of a new school year. The class teacher and yourself need to speak to your new class about the kind of behaviour you expect to see. You have decided that you will involve the pupils in discussing a set of class rules.

- Why might this be a worthwhile exercise?
- What support would you need to give pupils?
- Have you been involved in similar activities in your own school?

Key features of effective communication and why it is important to model this when interacting with adults, children and young people

In order to contribute to positive relationships, you need to demonstrate and model effective communication skills in your dealings with others. This means that you should consider how you approach other people and how you respond to them. This is important because we are more likely to communicate information to one another if we have positive relationships. Parents and other adults who come into the school are more likely to give beneficial support if communication is strong and effective; this, in turn, benefits pupils. It is also important for pupils that we model effective communication skills, which means checking what we are saying sometimes in moments of stress or excitement, so that they can understand what our expectations in school are. If we ask pupils to behave in a particular way when communicating and then forget to do this ourselves, they find it harder to understand the boundaries of what is acceptable.

Effective communication and positive relationships do not happen by chance; you should think about the way you relate to others and the messages that this sends out. In situations where communication break down, misunderstandings lead to bad feeling. (See also K9, page 87.)

Case study

Practising effective communication

Trudy is working in a small infant school. She usually 'floats' between classes and is asked to give support where it is needed. This morning she has been asked to work with an individual pupil in Year 2 (P3) where a teaching assistant is off sick. She works in the class until playtime, then goes on duty outside and afterwards takes her break for ten minutes in the staffroom before going back into class. The teacher, who does not know that she has been on playground duty, asks her where she has been for the last ten minutes. Trudy is upset at the way she has been spoken to and tells the teacher that she has been having her coffee. However, the teacher misunderstands her and thinks that she has taken a long time coming back after playtime. Both the teacher and Trudy are unhappy and hardly speak to one another until lunchtime.

- Who is in the wrong?
- Do you think that pupils in the class will have noticed?
- How might this have been handled better by both the teacher and Trudy?

Keys to good practice

Communicating with others

✓ Make sure you are interested in the person with whom you are communicating.
✓ Use an appropriate method of communication for the other person.
✓ Speak clearly and face the person with whom you are communicating.
✓ Use positive body language and gestures.
✓ Remain calm at all times when communicating with others.
✓ Make sure you are clear about messages you are giving pupils, i.e. do not say one thing and do another yourself.
✓ Provide a variety of opportunities for pupils to communicate, e.g. class discussions, group and paired work, individual presentations.
✓ Respond appropriately.
✓ Do not interrupt or anticipate what others are going to say.
✓ Use open-ended questions to encourage communication wherever possible.

Main differences between communicating with adults and communicating with children and young people

When communicating with children, we need to be very clear and unambiguous in what we say. They need us to communicate clearly what is expected of them so that they learn to communicate well themselves. We should try not to use complicated language or long lists or instructions, which make what we are saying more difficult to grasp. Sometimes we forget the importance of making sure that children understand what we mean and might ask them 'What did I just ask you to do?' when they did not even understand the question or request.

? Thinking point
Do you always demonstrate the good practice points opposite when you are communicating with others?

As adults, we need to show children how to get along with one another and communicate effectively. We should also model the kind of behaviour we expect from them. If we are able to show them that we value and respect others, they are much more likely to learn to do the same. Children copy adult behaviour from an early age, whether this is positive or negative, as part of the learning process and because they want to seek adult approval.

Showing respect for others is crucial whether you are communicating with adults or children. You need to acknowledge what others are saying and thank them for their contributions, even if you do not agree with their opinions or ideas.

Portfolio activity K7

Demonstrating skills in communicating with pupils and adults

During an assessment visit, make sure that you give your assessor the opportunity to watch you communicating information with pupils and adults in your school, and then discuss what the differences might be when communicating with the different groups. This knowledge point can then be recorded as observed and discussed.

Valuing other adults' views and opinions

Always make sure that you show that you value the views and opinions of the adults with whom you work. This demonstrates that you are working as part of a team and that you understand the need for all individuals to be heard rather than the few who may be more assertive. All adults have views and opinions about the best ways in which to work and there should be opportunities for all ideas to be heard. This may be through forums such as meetings, but there should also be a school policy to encourage staff and other adults to present their ideas and opinions. These should then be discussed appropriately with others so that everyone feels part of the decision-making process.

Leads to a more productive working environment

Gives the right message to children

Promotes good communication

Valuing the opinions of other adults

Encourages co-operation

Shows respect for others

▲ **Figure 4.6** The importance of valuing others' opinions

The ways in which you can demonstrate that you value the opinions of others are closely linked to the methods of effective communication on page 84. If you can show that you communicate well, it is likely that you will find it easier to relate to others and therefore provide effective support for pupils.

▼ **Figure 4.7** Sharing views and opinions well can lead to a mutual improvement and expansion of knowledge

Valuing others' views and opinions

Jan has just started work in a large secondary school. Her own children have just started school and she is looking forward to working with new people and starting a new phase in her life. She is a specialist in Music, so has been allocated to work within this department, supporting teachers and contributing to school productions where needed, although she has not worked as a teaching assistant before.

You have been working in the Music department for some time and recently it has become very 'samey' with very few new staff or other changes. Your line manager has suggested having a meeting with the whole of the department to address this and also to give everyone the opportunity to meet Jan.

- Why do you think that this is important?
- How will you show that you value the views and opinions of others?
- Who will it benefit?

Communication difficulties and how these can be overcome

Communication difficulties may occur between individuals or groups of people. When working with pupils or in teams with other adults you may find that areas of difficulty arise for a variety of reasons. These may be due to an area of special needs or because individuals have different attitudes or beliefs from others in the group.

Poor communication

Often areas of conflict occur when communication has not been effective. This may be because information has not been passed on or because of a misunderstanding. The best way to resolve areas of poor communication is to discuss them to establish the cause and then find a way forward together. The important thing is not to ignore the problem or talk about it to everyone except the individual or group of people concerned.

Opposing expectations

Sometimes people do not have the same ideas about the purpose of an activity or meeting, or come with a different idea in mind. You should always clarify exactly what you are there to do and why.

Cultural differences

It may be that adults within the school team have different cultures and expectations, and therefore communicate in different ways. For example, in some cultures eye contact is not encouraged, which may mean that people do not pick up on as many non-verbal cues.

Different values and ideas

Individuals sometimes have different methods of dealing with situations. For example, whereas the school may request that pupils do things in a particular way, parental views may be very different.

External factors

You may be working with an individual who has considerable home pressures or other issues which are affecting how they communicate. As we get to know people, we can identify if they are behaving in an uncharacteristic way and ask if there is anything wrong or if we can help. When dealing with other external professionals, it is likely that they are under time and other pressures of which you are not aware.

Lack of confidence

Sometimes adults act in an aggressive way if they are not sure about what they are doing or if they lack confidence. This may come across in a personal way to others, but is more to do with how they perceive themselves and their own abilities. You need to be sensitive to this and offer them encouragement and support.

You need to show care and sensitivity to pupils and adults who have communication difficulties, as they need to take their time and not feel under pressure when they are speaking or signing. People with specific needs may not have many opportunities to speak or may be anxious or nervous and you will need to adapt the way in which you communicate to their individual needs. If they have speech disorders or conditions that make it difficult for them, allow them to take their time. Try not to fill in words for them or guess what they are going to say, as this will add to their difficulties.

You may need additional training, for example in sign language, to communicate effectively or know the most effective strategies to use. In some cases, where pupils have special educational (additional support for learning (ASL)) needs, you may need to have additional resources or equipment in order to communicate with them.

K9 Case study

Resolving communication problems

Spencer is working in a small one-form-entry primary school, which has four teaching assistants. As there are so few of them and many of the teaching staff have several responsibilities, there has been little time allocated for teaching assistants to be involved in meetings. Spencer has been in the school for the longest and has noticed that the lack of communication between teachers and other staff is starting to have a detrimental effect on the morale of the teaching assistants and other support staff in the school. The Nursery, for example, is hardly involved with the school as it is in a separate building and staff keep themselves to themselves; even breaks are taken at different times and in different rooms.

- What should Spencer do?
- Why is it important that he says something?

▲ **Figure 4.8** Take any opportunity to resolve issues as soon as possible

How to cope with disagreements with adults

It is likely that at some stage in the course of your work you will have a disagreement with other adults. This may be due to a number of reasons and should be handled carefully. Disagreements may be due to clashes of personality, but there can also be other reasons such as conflicting ideas or poor communication between members of a work team.

As adults we can sometimes misread or perceive information wrongly. We may think that someone has communicated something to us when they have not. We sometimes blame others for saying things that could be ambiguous or for having a different point of view from ourselves.

Where there are areas of conflict with other adults, you need to show sensitivity and try to resolve the situation as soon as possible. The longer a problem is allowed to go on, the more difficult it will be to put right. If you are unable to resolve a disagreement, you should refer to your school's grievance policy or procedure.

Keys to good practice

Coping with disagreements

✓ Ensure you use the correct form of address when speaking to others.
✓ Observe confidentiality.
✓ Do not make assumptions about others.
✓ Provide or obtain any vital information promptly.
✓ Be sympathetic to the needs of others.
✓ Seek advice from another adult if you cannot reach an agreement.
✓ Acknowledge the help and support of others as much as you can.

Case study

Dealing with disagreements

Duncan is working in Key Stage 3 as a language support assistant. He is based mainly in French classes but is also asked to work in some Spanish lessons as and when support is needed. Although he does not mind this flexibility and enjoys having a varied timetable, he has had some problems this week because his line manager is out of school on a trip and he has not been given the correct timetable. The following week he goes to see his line manager and has trouble disguising his annoyance.

- Do you think that Duncan should approach this meeting in the way he has?
- What would be the best way of approaching his line manager?

Why it is important to reassure adults of the confidentiality of shared information and the limits of this

Your school needs to keep a certain amount of confidential information on pupils and adults. This means that information and records that you have access to as part of your role as a teaching assistant must only be used for their intended purpose. Make sure that if you are working with information, for example updating it, you do not provide opportunities for others to gain access to it. You also need to reassure adults that any information you have the right to use is kept confidential.

> **ⓘ Key term**
>
> **Confidentiality** – only providing information to those who are authorised to have it

The kind of shared information you may have access to in school will include:

- **General records on pupils** – These include medical records, registers, names of carers, addresses and emergency contact numbers. It is very important that these kinds of records are kept up to date. Your school may also have information from other schools the pupil has attended.
- **Individual teachers' records of assessment** – These are usually kept in classrooms and should contain individual teachers' comments and assessments following their work with pupils. They also help with the planning process as they indicate the level at which each pupil is working.
- **Special educational (ASL) needs information on pupils** – This may be kept by the Special Educational Needs Co-ordinator (ASL teacher) or in the school office. It may be extensive and take the form of reports, assessments and other records from a range of professionals. These should be accessible to those who need to see them but should be stored carefully.

As a member of staff in school you have a responsibility to ensure that you observe confidentiality at all times. Under the Data Protection Act 1998, information about pupils needs to be kept in a secure place such as locked filing cabinets or password-protected computers. If you are asked to update information, you should do this while you are on school premises and not take any information off site. You should consider all information about pupils as confidential and ensure that you do not share it with others without parental permission. When discussing pupils with others, you should also take care to ensure that you only share information that they need and are entitled to know. (See also Unit 5, K4, page 101.)

Organisational policy regarding information exchange

You need to be aware of the kinds of limits on information exchange, or passing on what you know to others, that exist in schools. You should have guidelines or clear instructions in a school policy, such as the assessment, recording and reporting policy, so that you know how information exchange is to be done. If you are at all unsure about whether you should pass on information to others, it is always best to wait and to check before doing so.

There may be cases where information on pupils needs to be accessible to all staff, for example, where pupils have specific medical conditions such as asthma or epilepsy. In this case, there should be an agreed system within the school for making sure that all staff are aware of who these pupils are. Some schools will put photographs of them in staffrooms or dining areas, removing them if the school premises are used by others during the evening.

Keys to good practice

Exchanging information with others

✓ Be sure that you are clear about any information you pass on.
✓ Make sure you exchange any confidential verbal information in an environment that is not open to others.
✓ Repeat back to check what has been said to you.
✓ Ensure that details are complete and accurate.
✓ Always follow school policies for passing on information.
✓ Report any problems or breaches of confidentiality to the appropriate person.

Portfolio activity K12

Recognising your role regarding information exchange

Find out about your school's policy for exchanging information and write a reflective account to state what your role should be as a member of staff or as a volunteer working in the school.

Importance of communicating positively with children, young people and families

Children and young people always respond to positive communication with adults. They are more likely to want to be in school and to learn if they have good relationships with those who are supporting them. Occasionally the school ethos will not be in line with the beliefs or ideas held by parents and this may cause disagreement or conflict. However, this should be seen as an opportunity for adults to discuss and agree on what is best for the pupil.

It is important that schools work in partnership with pupils' families and promote the development of positive relationships between home and school. This is because pupils benefit from a shared commitment to their education and a sense that the school is part of a community that supports their education. As a result, it is likely that your school communicates with pupils and their families in a range of different ways and looks for ways of making sure that channels of communication are as positive as possible.

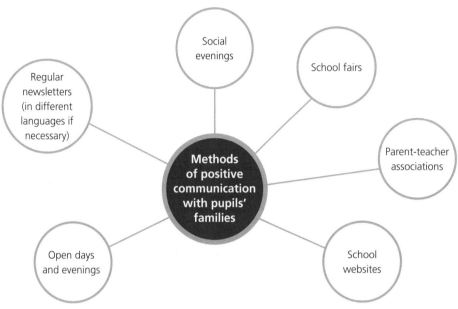

▲ **Figure 4.9** Methods of positive communication

Schools should also make sure that they do not actively discourage parents and families from entering the premises, which can appear unwelcoming, especially for families who may be less confident or do not know how to gain access. The introduction of heightened security in some schools has meant that it can be difficult to enter the premises at all. If it is not clear how to make appointments with staff or how to communicate with the school in other ways, families may be prevented from communicating important information to staff.

K13 Case study

Communicating positively with pupils' families

Steven has just started working in a primary school. The mother of one pupil in his class is often referred to by the class teacher as being 'difficult'. In addition, the teacher is often too busy to speak to the mother or tells her that she does not need to mention every concern she has about her child, who is fine. Steven knows that this parent is just seeking reassurance about her child and feels that it is unfair that she is being treated in this way.

● What could Steven do?
● Why is it important for both the mother and the pupil that this is resolved?

How children and young people's ability to communicate can affect their behaviour

Communication is one of the most important skills we have. Whether it is verbal or non-verbal, or through other media, it is the way in which we can pass on our thoughts and feelings to others. Any failure or interruption to the way in which we do this, at any age, makes it difficult for us to develop relationships with others.

Physical factors

These may be as simple as a speech impediment such as a stammer or may include more serious physical conditions or special needs that make it difficult or impossible for a pupil to communicate. If other means of communication are not found or if the pupil is unable to develop his/her skills in other ways, he/she may become frustrated because they are not able to put across their thoughts and feelings.

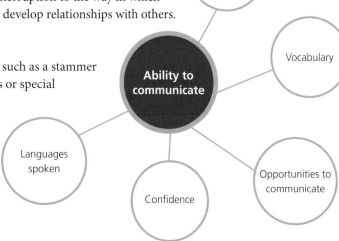

▲ **Figure 4.10** The ability to communicate

Vocabulary

Some pupils know what they want to say, but do not have the vocabulary with which to say it. For example, a very young child may know that they are upset and be able to show the emotion, but be unable to communicate why they are feeling it. For older children, being unable to express their feelings may lead to feelings of distress or frustration.

Opportunities to communicate

Pupils who have more opportunity to communicate with others are more able to develop their skills and confidence and extend their vocabulary. Pupils who are not encouraged to use language in different ways will not be as competent as those who are. Adults should be aware that if they do not make time to listen to pupils, this will have a negative effect on their desire to communicate and on their self-esteem.

Confidence

Although some people seem to have more confidence than others, it can be developed with practice. Pupils' self-esteem is linked to feelings of self-affirmation and belonging, which are very important for their social and emotional development. Often pupils who do not feel valued as they are growing up are not in a positive environment.

Languages spoken

Speaking more than one language should not mean that a pupil is unable to communicate. In the first stages of learning a new language there will always be a 'silent period', when the pupil is listening and tuning in to the different sounds they are hearing. However, bilingual pupils pick up new words quickly and, after a few weeks, their communication skills should not be hindered by speaking more than one language.

Children and young people are at the early stages of developing their skills of communication and their ability to relate to others. They are adding to their vocabulary as well as looking at the ways in which the adults around them use their communication skills. When they have difficulties in communicating, for whatever reason, they may react badly and manifest this in their behaviour. Their ability to communicate is key to the development of positive relationships and to their understanding of their own and others' behaviour.

It is also important that pupils learn to recognise their feelings because an inability to understand how and why they are feeling a particular emotion can lead them to react inappropriately. For example, if they recognise that they are angry about something, they can tell themselves that they need some time out or to speak to someone. If they know that they are feeling excited because something is happening after school, they can understand why they are feeling happy. By recognising and knowing how they react in different situations, pupils can start to manage their emotions more effectively and to talk to others about them.

One strategy that can help pupils to communicate how they are feeling is to have a bank of different coloured badges in the class, for example red for angry, green for happy, orange for excited, yellow for ok, blue for unhappy. If all adults and pupils wear a badge, others will be able to tell how they are feeling and this may encourage them to talk about it.

K14 Case study

Resolving communication difficulties that affect behaviour

Billie is 6 and has verbal and oral dyspraxia, which means that she has difficulties in the physical pronunciation of speech. She works regularly with the speech and language therapist, and also with Jane who is her individual support assistant, on exercises to develop her oral motor function. However, Billie, whose communication is limited, can become very frustrated and angry and increasingly does not want to attend therapy sessions.

- Why do you think that Billie is starting to become frustrated during sessions?
- Can you think of a way in which you could help her to be more positive about her sessions?

K1 K2 K4 K5 K6 K8 For your portfolio...

For this unit you need to show that you have good relationships with the adults and pupils with whom you work. As well as demonstrating this through the interactions you have with them, you can gather evidence for this unit through witness testimonies from adults (on headed paper from their organisation or your school), which verify how you do this. Alternatively and if it is possible, you could ask the adults you work with to speak to your assessor and you may be able to cover a considerable amount of information for your portfolio in this way.

K9 K10

If you have been involved in a situation where communication has broken down, you can tell your assessor about it during a professional discussion and ask them to record that you have told them and whether you acted appropriately. The actual incident and individuals involved do not need to be named, so you can avoid writing any sensitive information in your portfolio.

Website

www.talkingpoint.org.uk – This website gives advice and support for children and families of children with communication difficulties, and also for professionals.

5 Provide Effective Support for your Colleagues

For this unit you will have to show how you maintain effective working relationships with your colleagues that are consistent with your job role. You will need to show that you can deal with any issues that arise by using your own initiative where possible or by approaching those who have the authority to deal with them. You will also need to make sure that you understand the legal and ethical requirements concerning issues such as confidentiality of information.

When you are developing your effectiveness in relation to your role, you will need to show that you understand the expectations of your job. You should always seek feedback from others as to how you are fulfilling these expectations and work towards identifying areas for development. You will then need to show how you progress over time to strive continuously to improve the work you do in school.

For this unit, you will need to know and understand:

- School expectations and requirements about your role and responsibilities as set out in your job description

- The roles and responsibilities of colleagues with whom you work and how these relate to your own role and responsibilities

- Basic principles underlying effective communication, inter-personal and collaborative skills

- The lines and methods of communication that apply within the school setting

- The meetings and consultation structures within the school

- School expectations and procedures for fostering good working relationships, promoting team work and partnerships with colleagues

- The differences between work relationships and personal relationships and how work relationships can be maintained effectively

- Why team discussions are important and why you should contribute constructively to them

- The importance of respecting the skills and expertise of other practitioners

- Why it is important to continuously improve your own work

- How to reflect on and evaluate your own work

- The importance of taking feedback from colleagues into account when evaluating your own practice

- The formal and informal staff appraisal/performance review opportunities available to you and how you can contribute to and benefit from these

- The sorts of development opportunities available to you and how to access these

School expectations and requirements about your role and responsibilities

Whatever your role within the school, and even if you are working as a volunteer for the purposes of gaining your qualification, you need to be clear on what is expected of you. If you are an employee, it is important for you to have an up-to-date job description that is a realistic outline of your role and responsibilities. If volunteering, you should find a copy of a generic job description either through your school or local authority. This will outline the general responsibilities you might expect to have as a teaching assistant.

The role of the teaching assistant has changed considerably in recent years and you may find that various individuals in your school are known as teaching assistants but have very different responsibilities. In a primary school, a teaching assistant may be attached to a particular class for a set number of hours per week, be responsible for breakfast or after-school clubs, carry out midday supervision duties or work with individual pupils who have special educational (additional support for learning (ASL)) needs. If the teaching assistant has a subject specialism or particular area of expertise such as ICT, he/she may work only in that subject. In some cases they may do all of these things.

In secondary schools in England and Wales, it is also becoming increasingly usual for teaching assistants to support a specific subject area so that they gain expertise and experience in a subject for which they may have a particular strength. Alternatively, some secondary teaching assistants are employed to support pupils who have special educational (ASL) needs and may have expert knowledge in aspects of this. They may also carry out some administrative duties or invigilate exams.

In 2002, the DfES produced a list of 25 tasks that teaching assistants may be required to do as a result of workforce remodelling, in that teachers are no longer required to do them. The tasks are:

- collecting money
- chasing absences
- bulk photocopying
- copy typing
- producing standard letters
- producing class lists
- record-keeping and filing
- classroom display
- analysing attendance figures
- processing exam results
- collating pupil reports
- administering work experience
- administering examinations
- invigilating examinations
- administering teacher cover
- ICT troubleshooting and minor repairs
- commissioning new ICT equipment
- ordering supplies and equipment
- stocktaking
- cataloguing, preparing, issuing and maintaining equipment and materials
- minuting meetings
- co-ordinating and submitting bids
- seeking and giving personnel advice
- managing pupil data
- inputting pupil data

In addition to a job description, there may well be a person specification, which sets out the personal qualities relevant to your post. These may include:

- **Being a good communicator and enjoying working with others** – It is vital that you are able to share thoughts and ideas with others and are comfortable doing this. This means being open and honest with your colleagues at all times.
- **Using initiative** – You will sometimes need to be able to decide for yourself how to use your time if the teacher is not available to ask. There will always be jobs that need doing in a classroom, even if this means tidying up or doing some photocopying.
- **Respecting confidentiality** – You may sometimes find that you are made aware of personal details concerning a pupil or family. Remember that in such a position of responsibility it is essential to maintain confidentiality. Although pupil and school records are available to those within the school, it is never appropriate to discuss them with others outside the workplace.

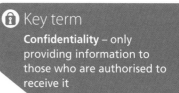

ⓘ Key term

Confidentiality – only providing information to those who are authorised to receive it

- **Being sensitive to pupils' needs** – Whether you are working with individuals or groups of pupils, it is very important to be able to judge how much support to give while still encouraging independence. Pupils need to be sure about what they have been asked to do and may need help organising their thoughts or strategies, but it is the pupil who must do the work – not you.
- **Having good listening skills** – A teaching assistant needs to be able to listen to others and have a sympathetic nature. This is an important quality for your interactions with pupils and other adults.
- **Being willing to undertake training for professional development** – In any school there will always be occasions when support staff are invited or required to attend training and these opportunities should be taken whenever possible. You may also find that your role within the school changes due to being moved between classes, departments or year groups. You need to be flexible and willing to adapt to different expectations.
- **Being firm but fair with pupils** – Pupils always quickly realise if an adult is not able to set fair boundaries of behaviour. Adults should always make sure that they make these boundaries clear when they start working with pupils.
- **Enjoying working with children or young people and having a sense of humour** – You will need to be able to see the funny side of working with pupils and a sense of humour is often a very useful asset!

K1 Portfolio activity

Understanding your job description

Find a copy of your job description for your portfolio. You will also need to refer to it or highlight specific aspects of your role for mandatory Units 1 and 3, and for some of the optional units you select.

Roles and responsibilities of colleagues and how these relate to your own role and responsibilities

In Unit 1 you looked at how your role and the role of the teacher complement one another within the learning environment. However, teachers and support staff are part of a wider picture within the school. You need to be aware of how all members of staff fit together so that you can build up a picture of how they work as a team. Obtain a school staff list, which will give the names of all of your colleagues and may also list their responsibilities within the school.

Depending on the type of school, different members of staff may have overlapping responsibilities. In a primary school the staff structure may be very different from a secondary school, although all schools have a senior management team. It is very important in all schools that all members of staff are valued and that lines of communication are always open, through formal and informal opportunities for discussion (see also K4, page 101.)

ⓘ Key term

Colleagues – people with whom you work on a regular or occasional basis, for example teachers, other professionals and support staff, voluntary helpers in the school

On a daily basis it is likely that you will have contact with:

- teachers (class- or subject-based)
- other teaching assistants or support staff such as computer technicians, midday supervisors, office staff etc.
- outside agencies who come into school; these professionals are often concerned with pupils who have special educational (ASL) needs, for example educational psychologists, or specialists from the local behaviour management unit; you may have more contact with outside agencies if you are an individual support assistant for one pupil
- other adults within the school, who may be voluntary helpers such as parents or students on work experience.

Portfolio activity K2

Identifying staff with whom you work

Obtain a copy of your school's staff list. Annotate or highlight it to show those members of staff with whom you work directly.

Basic principles underlying effective communication, and interpersonal and collaborative skills

As you will be working as part of a team, you need to have good communication, collaborative and interpersonal skills. This means that you need to be able to get on with other members of staff and support others. These could be members of the team in which you work all the time or those who you only meet occasionally. You need to know the principles underlying these skills so that you are able to apply them.

Effective communication skills

These are vital when working with others. You will need to show that you:

- listen to what others have to say. Always listen actively to others, so that you take in what they are saying to you. (See also Unit 4, K6–K8, pages 83–8)
- make time to talk to others in your team and take up all opportunities to attend meetings so that you are aware of all that is happening within your school
- ensure that you contribute to team discussions, even if you do not feel confident about putting your ideas across, without being over-confident or dominating the discussion.

▲ **Figure 5.1** Make sure you are not over-confident in discussion

Effective collaborative skills

This means that you need to be able to work effectively with others for the benefit of the whole school. The kinds of skills your team should have may include:

- being clear about objectives and goals – understanding and knowing how the school is developing
- being open about confronting and resolving any problems
- working in a positive atmosphere of mutual support and trust
- conducting regular reviews with other staff
- having sound decision-making procedures that include all members.

You may be in a school where you are aware of your team's objectives and goals, but not be clear about what you are working towards in terms of your own career development. If you find that this is a problem, speak to your line manager so that you are clear about your own development objectives.

Effective interpersonal skills

This means that you need to be able to get along with different personalities within your work team. You may find this harder to do with some people than with others, but you should be able to relate to all members of your work team. You can do this by making sure that you are always friendly and have time to speak to all members of your team. You should be sympathetic to the needs of others and encourage those who may be finding work challenging or difficult (which could be due to factors outside school that are on their mind).

◀ **Figure 5.2** Issues outside school may make it difficult to concentrate on problems in the work environment

Lines and methods of communication that apply within the school setting

The lines of communication within the school will depend on its structure but should be kept open through routine procedures so that each member of staff has access to new information. This is to ensure that everyone is aware of their responsibilities and knows what is happening within the school. Information can be passed on in many different ways.

- **Meetings** – These may be separate for governors/School Parent Council, senior managers, teaching staff, departments, and different support staff such as teaching assistants, midday supervisors and so on. Their regularity may depend on the kind of information that needs to be shared or distributed. Meetings may be at the same time each week or take place as the need arises.
- **Daily book, bulletin board or school email** – This is usually checked on a daily basis and will give all members of staff details of what is happening on that day.
- **Notice boards or newsletters** – Notice boards may be displayed inside the school or regular newsletters sent home to both staff and parents, perhaps on a particular day of the week so that they can look out for it.
- **Informal discussions** – Staff may discuss information informally during breaks or other times outside the classroom. This is fine, but may mean that important information does not reach all members of staff.
- **Parent–teacher associations (PTA)** – Schools usually have some form of PTA, which gives a great deal of support through fund-raising and other activities. Information about the PTA may be displayed on notice boards, in regular newsletters or on the school website.

If you are working with one class teacher in a primary school, you may find that receiving information is straightforward because they are your main point of contact. However if you are supporting learning throughout a secondary school, receiving information may be far more difficult. In both cases, however, you should have a line manager who is responsible for passing information on to you. In a large school there may be regular meetings especially for teaching assistants, but if your school is smaller, it is important to make sure that you have regular access to general information. Remember that any sensitive information you receive is confidential and should only be given as necessary to colleagues who have the authority to receive it and use it, in school.

You need to be fully aware of the implications of confidentiality and the importance of being mindful of this at all times. All staff should be given guidelines for the use of personal information and their responsibilities when dealing with records and security of any documentation. Confidentiality of information applies to both verbal and written information.

> **? Thinking point**
>
> **Which** of the following would you consider confidential?
>
> - information about a pupil who has special educational (ASL) needs
> - minutes of meetings
> - playground rumours about a family in the school that has been involved in drugs offences
> - documentation surrounding the school development plan, made available to you as a member of staff
> - school policies

Meetings and consultation structures within the school

It is important that schools play an active part in providing opportunities for support staff to share information about the school and pupils. If possible, these times should be made available formally as many teaching assistants work part-time or in one class with one pupil. All staff should have the chance to share ideas and experiences with others so that they do not feel isolated in their role. Opportunities should include:

- regular meetings for all support staff
- staff working together to support classes, taught subjects or individuals
- teaching assistants being invited to speak to professionals from outside agencies
- notice boards and departmental or year group meetings.

Meetings are part of a communication process that should take place within the school for passing information between all staff. If the passing of information is left to chance, it is unlikely that it will be received by all those who need to have it.

K4
K5

Portfolio activity

Identifying lines of communication in your school

Write a reflective account about the lines of communication that exist in your school. You may find it easiest to do this with a chart or diagram showing how information is passed round. Remember to include methods that are listed here. You may need to find out about meetings that take place between all staff including governors and how regularly they occur.

School expectations and procedures for fostering good working relationships

When you are working with others in a professional environment, you need to be able to offer mutual **support** and encouragement. Because of the way in which schools are organised, you will not be able to work independently and should offer support to others in different ways. It is likely that your school will expect you to work closely with others and will suggest ways in which colleagues can work together, for example a newly qualified teacher might work with an experienced teaching assistant.

 Key term

Support – the time, resources and advice that you give to colleagues and their activities and those that colleagues give to you and your activities

The ways you can offer support to colleagues include:

- **Practical support** – Helping others if they need assistance or advice with finding or using equipment and resources
- **Informative support** – Helping those who do not have the right information
- **Professional support** – You could be in a position to help others on a professional level with issues such as planning how to carry out activities with pupils. You may also be asked to write records or reports on particular pupils
- **Emotional support** – It is important to support others through day-to-day events and to retain a sense of humour.

Your staff handbook may set out the school's expectations or list how you should work with others for the benefit of pupils. You may sometimes be asked to support out-of-school activities or take part in fund-raising events such as school fairs and quiz nights.

Differences between work relationships and personal relationships and how work relationships can be maintained effectively

When working with others as part of a team, be aware of the difference between personal and professional relationships. Although people often become good friends through working together, it is important to establish good working relationships first. As well as the areas already discussed, such as the ways in which you can help others, you need to develop other strategies for contributing to the team, so ensure that you consider the following keys to good practice.

Keys to good practice

Working with others

✓ Ensure that you are considerate towards other members of your team.
✓ Carry out your duties cheerfully and to the best of your ability.
✓ Speak to the appropriate team member if you have a problem that you cannot resolve.
✓ Acknowledge the support and ideas of other team members.
✓ Do not gossip or talk about other people in your team.
✓ Always be open and honest with your colleagues.

Case study K7

Maintaining a distinction between work and personal relationships

Carol works as a teaching assistant in a primary school. She started volunteering at the school when her daughter first went into Reception (P1) the previous year and then applied for a job when it came up. Although Carol enjoys her job, she is finding it difficult to balance being a mum and a member of staff when she is talking to other mums. They are constantly asking her what it is like to work in the school and telling her that it doesn't matter that she tells them about it.

Carol also finds her role within the school hard. She still feels like a mum in the staffroom and thinks that other staff view her with suspicion. She feels that she needs to prove herself as a reliable and professional member of staff.

● Should Carol say anything about how she is feeling to other staff?
● Is there anything proactive she could do to develop her working relationships with others?
● Why do you think that this role is hard for Carol to balance?

Why team discussions are important

Meetings and opportunities for discussion do not need to be long, but are an important part of your role. They are also an opportunity for you to put your ideas across and you should do this when the chance arises. (See also K4 and K5, pages 101 and 102.)

Depending on your own experiences, you will bring a unique level of expertise to the school. You may have had specific training or experience, for example in an area of special educational (ASL) needs, and be able to offer advice to others. You should remember that each individual in the school has their own experience and expertise, which at some point may be useful to another person. If you find that you require advice or support you should always consider going to others in your team in the first instance.

K8 Case study

Contributing ideas

Zoe is a teaching assistant in a secondary school and has been working there for six months. She has been asked to attend the first teaching assistants' meeting held by the school. On the agenda is a discussion on support staff being assigned to a particular subject area, which is something other secondary schools in the area are trialling. Zoe has some ideas about the subject but in the meeting she feels daunted by the number of people there and keeps her ideas to herself.

- Why should Zoe have voiced her opinions during the discussion?
- Is there anything the school could do to encourage the participation of all those at the meeting or to gather their ideas?

Importance of respecting the skills and expertise of other practitioners

Although you will be working in a team, you may have limited contact with some team members due to the way in which you work and you will probably get on with some of them better than others. Always respect the opinions and knowledge that others bring to the team, to benefit the team effort and develop good working relationships. Bad feeling can quickly cause problems and unrest within teams.

K9 Case study

Showing respect for others' skills and expertise

You are part of a large primary school, which holds weekly or fortnightly meetings for all teaching assistants as required. This week, two of the teaching assistants who work in Year 5 (P6) are presenting some of the strategies they have been using with their classes to manage playground behaviour following a course they have attended. Some of those in the meeting are talking through the presentation and are clearly not listening. One of them even answers her mobile phone during the presentation.

- Why is it important that schools give all staff opportunities to feed back to colleagues following development opportunities?
- Give two reasons why all staff should be attentive in this situation.

Why it is important to continuously improve your own work

As part of a school, you will know that your role requires you to look at and evaluate what you are doing with pupils. Always look at all aspects of your role and consider how you might improve on it so that you can develop your practice. If you work closely with teachers, you may do this anyway to a certain extent as you will have opportunities to plan and evaluate work you do with pupils together. However, this is only one aspect of evaluating your work (see also K11 below and Figure 5.4 on page 106).

How to reflect on and evaluate your own work

In recent years, the role of the teaching assistant has become a professional one. Although you may be working as a volunteer, you need to learn how to reflect on and evaluate your work as part of your S/NVQ. This is especially important when working with pupils, as your personal effectiveness will have a considerable impact on them and their learning.

Reflecting on your work means thinking about and evaluating what you do and then working out any changes that could be made. It relates to all aspects of your work (see Figure 5.4 on page 106). You should learn to reflect on a regular basis and should have opportunities to discuss your thoughts and ideas with your colleagues or with fellow S/NVQ students. By doing this you will be able to identify areas of strength as well as exploring those that need further development. Teaching assistants often have quite diverse roles within schools and inevitably you will find that you are more confident in some situations than others. By reflecting on your practice and how you work with others, you will come to be more effective in your role and gain in confidence.

▶ **Figure 5.3** Always review the work you have completed

◀ **Figure 5.4** The importance of reflection and evaluation

Your role when supporting pupils' learning

Think about activities you have carried out with individuals or groups of pupils and evaluate how the sessions went. Even if you always work in a particular way, which seems to go well, consider different ways of approaching work you do with pupils. Here are some questions you could ask yourself at the end of a session.

- What went well?
- What did not go as well as anticipated? Why?
- Did pupils achieve the learning objectives for the session?
- What would I change if I did the activity again?

In this way your evaluation will encourage you to develop and change what you are doing if you need to, so that you can ensure that you are working effectively with pupils. As part of your S/NVQ, your assessor will also observe you working with pupils and give you feedback about the way you approach your work with them. They may be able to offer you suggestions and help you work though ideas.

◀ **Figure 5.5** Think about and evaluate the work you do with pupils

Your professional development

In most professions, individuals need to think about their role on a regular basis. As a teaching assistant, this involves looking at your job description and thinking about areas for development. Think about how you can develop in your role so that you are always giving yourself opportunities to extend your knowledge and practice. If you are working as a volunteer, take the opportunity to speak to colleagues about this, both in school and as part of your college course or training.

Working with colleagues and other adults

This important aspect of your work is about your relationships with your colleagues and others. Think about how you relate to others and the support you offer to them both individually and within different school teams, such as year groups, subject teams or key stages. If you support pupils who have special educational (ASL) needs, you may also work with other professionals outside school such as speech and language therapists or educational psychologists. Another group of adults you may work with includes parents, particularly if you work closely with one pupil. You may need to think about ways in which you can develop relationships with them so that the pupil is supported more effectively. You should think about:

how you greet other adults

- whether you offer help or support to them if you can
- if you recognise their contributions to the team
- how you respond to any issues that arise
- whether you actively listen to their concerns
- if you are positive and offer encouragement to others.

Planning, assessment and feedback

As a teaching assistant, and particularly if you are volunteering, you may or may not be involved with devising plans, but it is important that you have an awareness of the process and have opportunities to speak to the class teacher about the pupils' progress following activities you have undertaken with them. Part of your role is supporting teaching and learning and so your feedback to the teacher forms part of the cycle of planning. You should know how the teacher plans for the class and also for the groups and individuals with whom you will be working. You need to consider:

- whether you know and understand the learning objectives for each session
- whether any of the pupils have particular targets to work on and your role in this
- pupils' backgrounds or circumstances that may affect their behaviour or learning
- how you feed back to the teacher (it may be written or verbal, at a set time or spontaneous).

Managing pupil behaviour

This can be one of the most challenging aspects of your work. In order to manage behaviour effectively you need to be firm and consistent with pupils and be part of a whole school approach. It is also important to be proactive and not reactive when managing behaviour; in other words setting firm boundaries, ensuring pupils are aware of the consequences and

> **? Thinking point**
>
> **Think** about occasions on which you have had to confront pupils about their behaviour.
>
> - Do you know what strategies you can use to manage behaviour?
> - Does your school have a scale of sanctions that all adults can apply?
> - How do you reward positive behaviour? Have you checked that this is school policy?
> - What aspects of behaviour management do you find challenging?

pointing out both their responsibilities and those of others. You should be aware of the contents of your school's behaviour policy. This includes knowing what strategies you can use to manage behaviour and what sanctions to apply if pupils do not behave appropriately. You need to reflect on what aspects of behaviour management you are confident with and which areas may need development. (See also Unit 2.)

Keys to good practice

Reflecting on your work

✓ Be honest with yourself and others.
✓ Make sure you evaluate successes as well as failures.
✓ Include all areas of your work.
✓ Ask a colleague for help if required.

K11 Case study

Reflecting on professional practice

Sobiga has been working in Year 6 (P7) for four years. She enjoys her work with the pupils and gets on well with the class teacher. She has been asked to go on a training course to develop her Numeracy skills as she has never been confident with Maths.

Sobiga goes on the course reluctantly, but is very pleased with her progress and surprised that she enjoys it and is able to do the work easily. She goes back to school and says that she is thinking about going on a course to retake her Maths GCSE (equivalent to Scottish Standard Grade) as she does not have the qualification.

- How has the Maths course benefited Sobiga?
- How does this show that she is reflecting more on her practice?
- How will this help in other aspects of her role?

Importance of taking feedback from colleagues into account when evaluating your own practice

Although you may have evaluated your own practice before and have considered all areas of your work, it is important that you also seek feedback from your colleagues. This is because others may have more experience or be able to point out aspects or further opportunities that may not have been obvious to you. They may also be able to give you advice in situations where you have had difficulties in your working relationships or professional role.

Using colleagues' feedback when evaluating practice

Andy has been working in a secondary school for two years. He enjoys his job as a teaching assistant and learning mentor and is having a meeting with his line manager about his progress. He has considered his own practice and thought about different aspects of his role, although he is having difficulty in identifying areas for development.

At the meeting, Andy's inclusion manager, Julia, discusses his progress with him, in particular with regards to his learning mentor role. She tells him that his work so far in this area has been very successful and that the pupils and their families have responded well, and asks him whether he has considered further training in this area rather than in his teaching assistant role. Julia also speaks to Andy about an observation of his work that she carried earlier in the year in which she identified other areas for development.

- Why would this discussion help Andy to evaluate his work?
- How would this then take his professional development forward?

Formal and informal staff appraisal/performance review opportunities available to you

Formal opportunities for review

As part of your role in supporting teaching and learning in the school, as with most other professions, you will be required to think about how you can extend your own professional development. This means that you need to think about how you are going to progress within your own career. Formal meetings to discuss this usually take place once a year and are known as performance management or appraisal meetings.

The main consideration in staff appraisal is to improve staff performance, but an important part of the process is that it is positive and non-threatening. Every member of staff, including headteachers, should be appraised once a year by the person who has responsibility for managing them. In the case of the headteacher, the school governors (or in Scotland the Local Authority Quality Improvement Officers) are responsible. As a member of support staff, you will be appraised by your line manager or the member of staff responsible for teaching assistants. If you are working as an individual support assistant, you may be appraised by the school's Special Educational Needs Co-ordinator (SENCo, or ASL teacher).

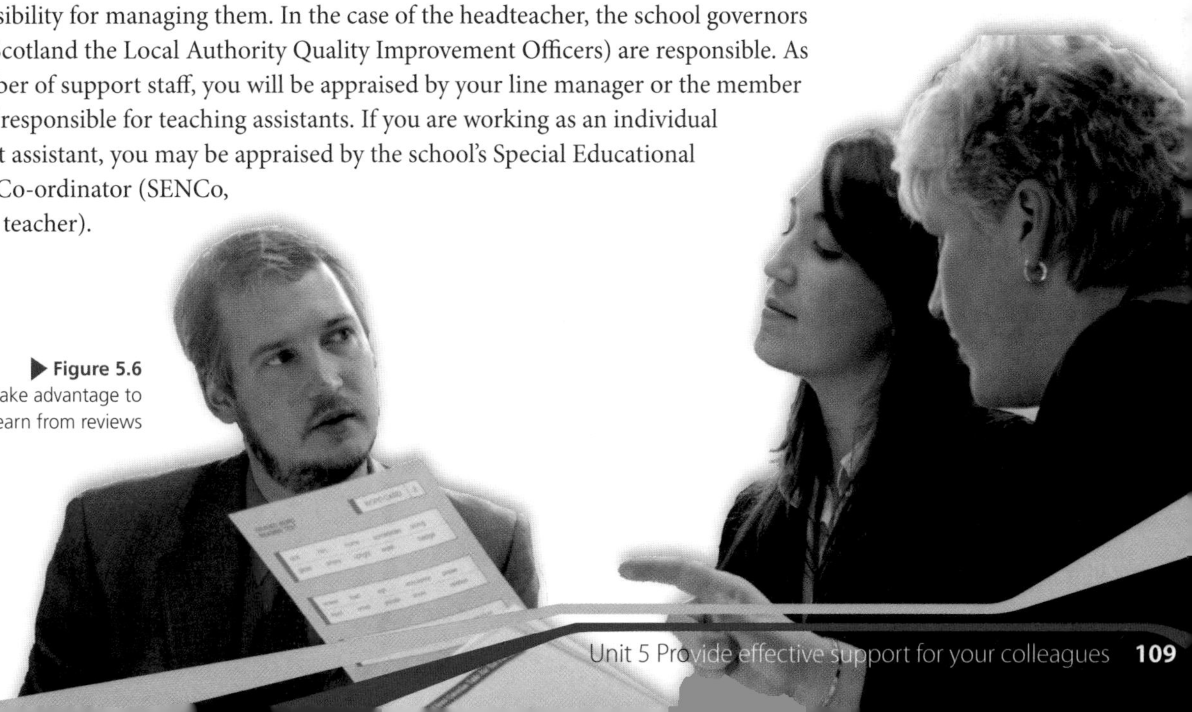

▶ **Figure 5.6**
Always take advantage to learn from reviews

You may find that the appraisal process is a good opportunity to discuss issues that may not otherwise come to light. It is also a useful time to discuss with your line manager anything that has been more or less successful than you had thought.

> **ⓘ Key term**
>
> **Personal development objectives** – your agreed priorities for learning and development including, where relevant, personal ICT skills

Before you go for your appraisal, you may be asked to fill in a general form, such as the one shown on page 111, which will help you to think about your own performance. It will also give you some idea about how your discussion might be structured.

During the interview, you will set targets or **personal development objectives** for the coming year with your line manager. It is important that you take an active part in setting these targets. Over the year you will work on these objectives and should look at them again from time to time to check your progress. At your next appraisal, you will review them with your line manager.

When thinking about areas for development, it may help to divide your knowledge and experience into sections. As an example, these might be knowledge and experience of:

- the curriculum
- behaviour management
- ICT
- relevant or new legislation
- health and safety
- working with or managing others
- record-keeping
- special educational (ASL) needs.

You then need to think about your level of confidence in each of these areas so that you can begin to see areas of strength and those which may need further development. You will need guidance in order to turn these into targets, which need to be SMART:

Specific	Ensure that your target says exactly what is required.
Measurable	Ensure that you will be able to measure whether the target has been achieved.
Achievable	Ensure that the target is not inaccessible or too difficult.
Realistic	Ensure that you will have access to the training or resources required.
Time-bound	Ensure there is a time limit in which to achieve your target (otherwise you may continually put it off to a later date).

If you are unable to achieve any of your targets for any reason, this should be recorded at the next appraisal along with the cause. You can then discuss whether to add it to the new list of targets.

Informal opportunities for review

If you are working as a volunteer or if your school does not carry out appraisals for teaching assistants, it may not be possible for you to have a formal meeting with school staff about your progress. However, you should have a chance to discuss how you are doing with school staff, if this is not carried out and recorded in a formal way. It is also important for your NVQ that you have thought about your performance and discussed areas that you would like to work on. Your assessor should be able to help you to draw up a short list of targets near the beginning of your NVQ, which you can both sign and date. You can then review this with your assessor when you are close to completing the course. There should really be a period of at least six months between setting and reviewing targets to allow you time to progress. (See also For your portfolio... at end of this unit.)

General Self-appraisal

It would be useful if you could bring this information with you to your initial meeting, to help you to identify your needs as part of the appraisal process.

1 Do you feel that your job description is still appropriate? Do you feel that there are any changes that need to be made?

_____

2 What targets were set at the last appraisal/when you started your job? Have you achieved your targets?

_____

3 What are the reasons for not having achieved your targets?

_____

4 What aspect of your job has not been as successful as you had anticipated?

_____

5 What part of your job satisfies you the most?

_____

6 Are there areas of your work that you would like to improve?

_____

7 What training have your received? Has it been successful?

_____

8 What are your current training needs?

_____

9 What are your needs for career development?

_____

Sorts of development opportunities available to you and how to access these

Although you may not realise it, you are constantly taking on new information while working in a school. You will also have opportunities to go on staff training or courses and should also be invited to INSET days as and when they occur.

However, you will also have other opportunities for developing your professional competence through working with other people whose expertise and experience you will be able to call on for advice and through having access to a range of other resources.

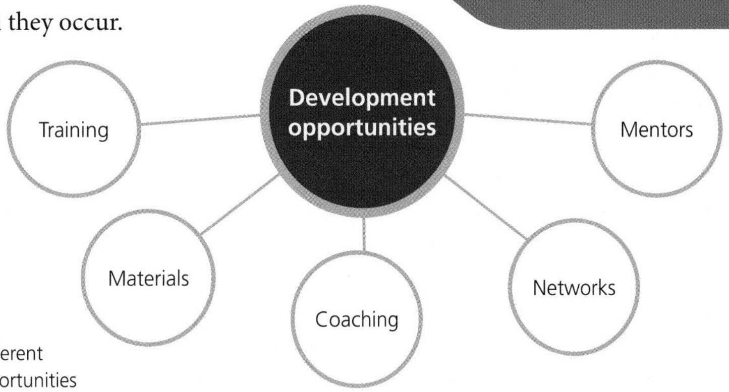

> ⓘ Key term
>
> **Development opportunities** – the people, resources and other opportunities available to you to help you develop your skills

Development opportunities

Training · Materials · Coaching · Networks · Mentors

▶ **Figure 5.8** Different development opportunities

Mentors

These may be school or college based but will be individuals who support you in your professional development. You should have a contact who is able to guide you through aspects of your career and advise you about the opportunities available to you and how to best access these.

Networks

These may be across the school or between schools and will be opportunities for teaching assistants to share experiences and ideas. Many schools now have cluster networks within their locality to provide this kind of support. Your college group is also an opportunity for you to network.

Materials

New materials for educational use are constantly being tried and tested and it is likely that your staffroom will have a selection of educational magazines or other publications that may advertise some of these. You will also have the opportunity to share new resources such as computer programs, books or web-based materials. Try to find time to look at any additional resources that become available and share these with others if possible.

Coaching

Coaching is a relatively new concept, which is often used in business. If your school is part of the coaching programme, you will be allocated a coach who will work with you at regular intervals. During these sessions you will be invited to discuss aspects of your role that you find challenging and will be supported in finding a resolution over time.

K14 # Portfolio activity

Identifying and accessing development opportunities

Find out about the kinds of **development opportunities** that are available to you. Write up or describe to your assessor what is available and how you can access it.

5.2, P2
5.2, P3
5.2, P4
5.2, P5
K13

For your portfolio...

In order to gather evidence for this unit, you need to reflect on and discuss your role and think about your achievements, strengths and weaknesses. You should then find a way of setting professional development targets and, after a period of at least six months, reviewing them with a teacher or line manager in your school. If you are employed by the school, you may already do this as part of the appraisal cycle and you will be able to use your review forms in your portfolio. If you are a volunteer, you need to set targets at the beginning of your course, or a month or two into it, with your assessor so that you still have time to review them before the end date.

6 Support Literacy and Numeracy Activities

This unit is for those who support literacy and/or numeracy activities in schools. You may be working in a mainstream or special school and be supporting Literacy and/or Numeracy as part of the daily lesson or in activities that are designed to promote literacy and numeracy development. You should work closely with teachers to ensure that you are clear about the extent of your role and are able to work towards learning objectives in whole class, individual pupil and group situations. You will need to use a variety of strategies to enable pupils to develop literacy and numeracy skills, including the use of specific support programmes and targeted activities. You will also need to be able to provide feedback to teachers about how well the activities went and how the pupil or pupils responded to them.

What you need to know and understand

For this unit, you need to know and understand:

- The school policies for Mathematics and English, Welsh or language as appropriate to the setting

- The literacy and numeracy skills expected of the pupils with whom you work

- How pupils develop reading, writing, speaking/talking and listening skills, and the factors that promote and hinder effective learning

- The interactive use of speaking/talking, listening, reading and writing to promote literacy development in pupils

- How pupils develop mathematical skills and the factors that promote and hinder effective learning

- The nature of any special educational needs or additional support needs of pupils with whom you work and the implications of these for helping them to develop:

    a) language and literacy skills

    b) mathematical knowledge, understanding and skills

- How to encourage and support bilingual pupils to participate in learning activities to develop literacy and numeracy skills

- The strategies and resources used at your school for developing pupils':

    - a   reading skills

    - b   writing skills

    - c   speaking/talking and listening skills

    - d   mathematical knowledge, understanding and skills

- How to use praise and assistance to maintain the pupils' interest in and enthusiasm for understanding and using the full range of literacy and numeracy skills

- The sorts of problems that might occur when supporting literacy and numeracy activities with individuals and groups

- The importance of working within the boundaries of your role and competence and when you should refer to others

School policies for Mathematics and English, Welsh or language as appropriate to the setting

If you are supporting pupils' literacy or numeracy development, you need to be aware of your school's English/Literacy and Mathematics/Numeracy policies. These outline your school's approach to the teaching of each subject and should follow local and national guidelines. The guidelines are different depending on whether your school is in England, Northern Ireland, Scotland or Wales. In each country there is a separate curriculum, which follows a recommended structure for the teaching of Literacy and

Numeracy/Mathematics in mainstream and special schools throughout the time that pupils are in school, including during the early years of schooling.

It is likely that your school policy identifies how literacy is taught throughout the school and how standards are monitored and assessed. Make sure that you are also up to date with the latest national developments in your home country, which are now available online (see at the end of this unit).

Portfolio activity K1

Identifying your responsibilities with regard to Mathematics and English/Welsh policies

You need to show that you know your school's policies for Mathematics and English or Welsh. You can do this by showing the policies to your assessor and talking through your responsibilities with regard to them. Alternatively, write a reflective account to demonstrate your school's aims and objectives.

Literacy and numeracy skills expected of the pupils with whom you work

You need to show that you have an awareness and understanding of the literacy and numeracy skills expected of pupils. As well as knowing about individual teachers' long-, medium- and short-term plans and how they fit together (see Unit 1, page 8), you should have an idea how these fit into the Early Years Foundation Stage or National Curriculum and the Literacy and Numeracy frameworks or other curriculum requirements relevant to your home country. As these change from time to time, make sure that you keep up to date through reading educational publications and checking websites (see the end of this unit).

As you get to know individual pupils and the curriculum for the year group in which you work, the expected skill levels will become more apparent. For example, when working on numeracy activities with young pupils, you often need to use practical examples and spend time checking their verbal comprehension of new concepts before embarking on recording work with them. When working on reading activities, you need to give pupils opportunities to use the different cues in the text and discuss the ideas being presented. As you become more experienced, you will get to know whether pupils are working at the levels expected for their age and year group.

Portfolio activity K2

Identifying the literacy and numeracy skills expected of pupils

Speak to your assessor about the pupils with whom you work, identifying the curriculum you are working from and the literacy and numeracy skills pupils are expected to have.

How pupils develop reading, writing, and speaking/talking and listening skills

Pupils' reading and writing, speaking and listening skills develop at different paces. Some pupils develop their skills more slowly and this could be because they have fewer opportunities to practise or because they have special educational (Additional Support for Learning (ASL)) needs, which give them difficulties with particular aspects of literacy (see page 118). Teachers and teaching assistants need to be aware of those pupils who are working above or below the class average.

Reading

At the time of writing, the focus is on teaching reading through phonics, using programmes such as 'Letters and Sounds'. Pupils need to be taught to read with an emphasis on word recognition and language comprehension, in line with the 'simple view of reading' proposed by the DCSF.

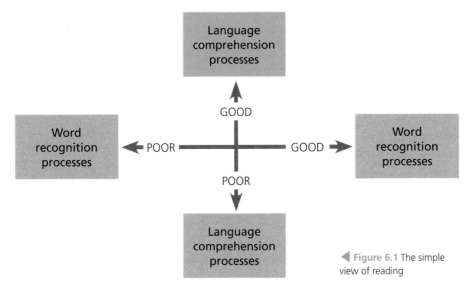

◀ Figure 6.1 The simple view of reading

The simple view of reading is based on recent research, which has shown that the ability to read depends on both word recognition and language comprehension processes. Pupils develop reading skills by recognising and understanding the words on the page. They then develop comprehension skills and begin to understand a range of different forms of written and spoken language. Pupils need both sets of skills before they can read fluently, as the skills do not work in isolation. (For more information, see http://www.standards.dfes.gov.uk/primaryframeworks/foundation/early/simple/.)

The support pupils receive through literacy activities in school will promote the development of these skills.

Writing

You need to support pupils' writing, not only in Literacy lessons, but across all areas of the curriculum as they learn to use different forms of writing for a variety of purposes.

The way pupils learn to write differs from the way they learn to read because they need to remember more information. In reading, they have cues on the page in front of them to work on, but in writing they need to formulate and structure ideas for themselves. They also need to have the fine motor skills necessary to hold a pen or pencil and form letter shapes. The skills they need for writing can be divided into word-, sentence- and text-level skills. Pupils build on their skills at each level, reinforcing what they know and learning new vocabulary as their reading and writing skills interact.

Keys to good practice

Supporting reading and writing in the classroom

✓ Confirm the pupils you will be working with and agree organisation.

✓ Clarify your understanding of pupils' learning needs with the teacher.

✓ Find out the learning objectives of the session.

✓ Agree any strategies to be used.

✓ Obtain any resources needed.

✓ Encourage and praise pupils as much as possible.

✓ Monitor pupil progress and report back to the teacher.

Speaking/talking and listening

During the Early Years Foundation Stage, the Early Learning Goals for Communication, Language and Literacy are at the heart of pupils' learning experiences. They need to experience interactions with others in a variety of situations:

- attentive listening and responses
- using language to imagine and recreate roles and experiences
- interacting with others both in play situations and to accomplish tasks.

The National Curriculum for Speaking and Listening builds on this by setting out the skills to be developed over Key Stages 1, 2 and 3. During Key Stage 1, as pupils develop their use of language, they learn to respond appropriately to different situations and to listen carefully to others. At the end of Key Stage 2, pupils should be able to adapt what they say to the purpose and to their audience. At Key Stage 3, pupils will be able to evaluate their own speaking and listening skills and participate in drama and group discussions. There is now a website for the teaching of speaking and listening in secondary schools, which is linked to the Secondary National Strategy and can be found at www.standards.dfes.gov.uk/speakingandlistening. It includes specific guidance for teaching assistants.

▼ Figure 6.2 The school's English policy should outline the shared objectives for developing pupils' speaking and listening skills

MAPLEWOOD
PRIMARY SCHOOL

ENGLISH POLICY

Objectives for the teaching of Speaking and Listening:

- to develop knowledge and understanding of the spoken word
- to develop the ability to listen to others
- to encourage pupils to express themselves effectively in a variety of situations, enabling them to match response and style to audience and purpose
- to develop a growing vocabulary and an enjoyment of words and their meanings
- to be able to give and receive instructions
- to be able to use speaking and listening skills when participating in a range of drama activities

Factors promoting and hindering effective learning in Literacy

These may vary between settings and individual pupils. The factors may include:

- **Ability of the pupil** – Pupils vary in their ability to carry out a task. Schools may decide to 'stream' pupils from an early age so that they are taught with those who are of similar ability.
- **Prior knowledge of the subject and understanding of the task** – When working on literacy activities, pupils' learning is affected by their prior knowledge and whether they understand what they are required to do.
- **Support such as praise and encouragement** – You need to make sure you support pupils effectively, using strategies such as praise, modelling the correct use of vocabulary, supporting their use of resources and explaining any ideas they do not understand.
- **Resources available** – Inadequate or insufficient resources, for example not enough textbooks, will make it more difficult for pupils to carry out the task.
- **Learning environment** – This should be conducive to learning and all pupils should have access to the equipment and resources they need.

Interactive use of speaking/talking, listening, reading and writing to promote literacy development in pupils

When pupils are developing their language skills, they are learning to communicate with others in a variety of ways. The language skills interact with each other to promote self-expression and imagination. Through the Literacy curriculum, pupils explore the ways in which language works so that they can use this knowledge in a variety of situations. The National Curriculum and primary and secondary frameworks give structure to the way pupils are taught in schools and suggested details for how this should be organised.

In a typical Literacy lesson, pupils take part in a whole class activity, which may involve some discussion and a shared reading or writing activity. They may also work with a talk partner to discuss ideas, before moving into groups or individual work to focus on specific areas. At the end of the session, they go back to a whole class or large group discussion to talk about what they have found out or worked on.

How pupils develop mathematical skills and the factors that promote and hinder effective learning

From the very earliest stages of learning, pupils should be encouraged to think of Maths as part of everyday life. There can be too much emphasis on formal recording of 'sums', which can hinder pupils' progress in thinking mathematically if introduced too early. Also be aware that Maths may be taught very differently from when you were at school. Now, great emphasis is placed on teaching the different mental strategies for arriving at an answer and developing investigation skills, particularly in the early primary phase. The curriculum is designed to give pupils a solid grounding in all aspects of Maths, on which they can base their understanding. A key aspect of developing skills in Maths is that pupils understand the purpose of each skill and how to apply it to real-life situations. Maths skills are therefore developed in the earliest stages through practical work, which gives pupils a grounding in aspects of Maths such as shape, pattern, counting, sorting and so on. As pupils progress, they build on these skills.

You need to have an awareness of the skills that pupils in your class are working towards in order to support them fully and help them to access the curriculum.

For example, the Primary National Framework in England gives a list of Key Objectives for each year group from Reception to Year 6. The skills in Reception include the ability to:

- find one more or one less than a number from one to ten
- use language such as 'circle' or 'bigger' to describe the shape and size of solids and flat shapes
- talk about, recognise and recreate simple patterns.

By Year 9, pupils are learning skills to help them:
- have a sense of the size of a number and where it fits into the number system
- recall mathematical facts confidently
- use simple formulae and substitute numbers in them
- calculate simple perimeters, areas and volumes, recognising the degree of accuracy that can be achieved
- measure and estimate measurements, choosing suitable units and reading numbers correctly from a range of meters, dials and scales.

The factors that promote and hinder effective learning will vary between settings and individual pupils, and may include:

- **Ability of the pupil** – If the pupil enjoys Maths and can work on tasks independently, this is a strong starting point. Pupils used to having support may come to rely on the reassurance of adult input.
- **Prior knowledge of the subject and understanding of the task** – If pupils have worked on similar tasks in the past and have prior knowledge, they may be more or less confident, depending on their perception of how they have managed before.
- **Support such as praise and encouragement** – Depending on their ability, pupils may need adult support to enable them to carry out the task required. It may make a huge difference to some pupils to have additional support and for an adult to notice their efforts.
- **Resources available** – Pupils need to have sufficient resources and understand how to use them to carry out the task.
- **Learning environment** – The learning environment, including noise levels, temperature and furniture, should be conducive to effective learning.

K5 Case study

Dealing with factors that hinder effective learning

Jeremy is in Year 7 (S1) and in your group for Numeracy. He has some good ideas, but finds recording his work difficult. You have been asked to support his group as they work on some activities to develop their understanding of area and volume. However, you do not have enough resources for the pupils to carry out the activity without constantly borrowing from each other. You also find that Jeremy needs a high level of support, which makes it difficult for you to give enough attention to the other pupils.

- How are the circumstances affecting your ability to continue with the lesson?
- Why is it important that you resolve the situation?

Language and literacy skills

If a pupil you are supporting has special educational or additional support (ASL) needs, make sure that you understand what the specific needs are and have discussed them with the teacher or SENCo (Special Educational Needs Co-ordinator)(ASL teacher). Always agree the strategies to be used with pupils who need extra help or who have specific educational targets or an Individual Education Plan (IEP). If the pupil has problems with reading or writing skills, these may be addressed in the form of more individual help to prompt the individual to think about points that have been discussed in class. This may take the form of a specific writing support programme or small targets that are to be built up. The school may have the resources to provide small group work for some pupils, so that they have more focused help.

Pupils who speak English or Welsh as an additional language will have different learning needs from others in the class or group, particularly if they have recently started to learn the target language. They may understand more than they are able to speak. So staff must be careful to make tasks sufficiently challenging and group such pupils by ability rather than knowledge of the target language. It is important to remember that these pupils do not have learning difficulties, and may be very able, but still have different learning needs from other pupils. (See K7, page 121 and Unit 11 for strategies for supporting them.)

In order to distinguish between these different types of learning support, it is important that staff consider the difference between bilingual pupils and those who have learning difficulties. Although some areas, such as the development of vocabulary and language skills, will overlap, some may be specific to EAL pupils:

- development of self-esteem through social and cultural reinforcement
- giving pupils more time to listen and process information
- providing dual language texts to enable pupils to develop verbal and written language together
- using pictures to support comprehension.

Mathematical knowledge, understanding and skills

Pupils who have special educational (ASL) needs may be working at a very different level from others in the class. The special needs that you experience in mainstream schools may cover a wide range of difficulties and it is not possible to include them all here. A pupil may, for example, need specific help with Maths vocabulary or have a visual impairment that makes it difficult to use some Maths equipment. Your class teacher will need to seek advice from the school's SENCo (ASL teacher) and other agencies outside the school for the best strategies to use with particular pupils. (See also Unit 12.) You may also support pupils through the use of specific programmes such as Springboard Maths. The DCSF has produced a particularly useful series of publications for supporting pupils with specific needs during the daily Maths lesson, which can be found in 'Publications' on www. standards.dfes.gov.uk/primary/ (see the end of this unit for more detail).

Pupils who speak English or Welsh as an additional language may also need specific support during Numeracy lessons in order to check their understanding and develop their learning. The introduction to the Framework for Teaching Mathematics gives guidelines for working with these pupils and places emphasis on participation with other pupils, particularly in oral work such as counting aloud, number songs and so on, and the use of practical activities. You should also seek guidance about the particular needs of these pupils from your local EMAS (Ethnic Minority Achievement Strategy) service if possible.

Identifying pupils' needs and the implications on their learning

When your assessor comes to observe you working with pupils, make sure that you are able to tell them about the pupils' needs and any specific Literacy and Numeracy targets they have. You may wish to show them IEPs and discuss the implications of pupils' needs on their learning.

How to encourage and support bilingual pupils to participate in learning activities to develop literacy and numeracy skills

As in all situations, effective use of praise is very important when working with bilingual pupils. You need to provide encouragement and support to them because they will be insecure in the target language (see also Unit 11). Through the use of a positive learning environment and opportunities for them to develop relationships with others, you will encourage and support their learning in all subjects.

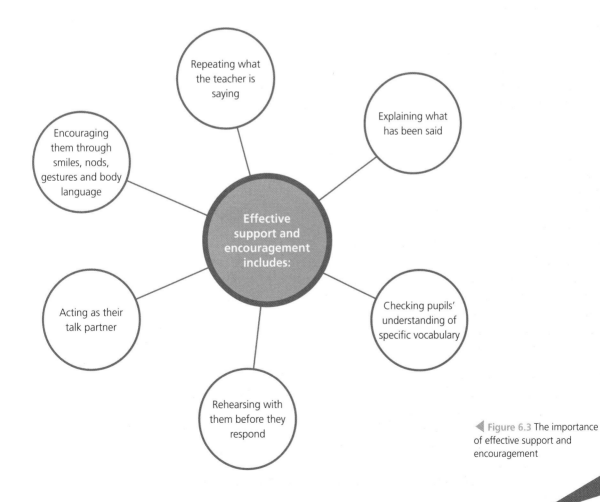

▲ Figure 6.3 The importance of effective support and encouragement

When giving pupils feedback in different learning situations and repeating back words or phrases to them, you may need to 'remodel' language or extend their responses. For example, if they use language incorrectly, such as 'I go to the shops last weekend', you could respond with 'You went to the shops last weekend? What did you buy?' rather than specifically pointing out an error. Remember that understanding language and specific vocabulary is also very important during numeracy activities.

Strategies and resources for developing reading skills

Teachers, parents and teaching assistants should all be working together to encourage pupils to enjoy and benefit from reading. The main focus of development will be through the Literacy lesson, although reading will be promoted through all areas and curriculum subjects.

You should know the different kinds of reading that take place in school so that you can support reading in a variety of situations.

- **Shared reading** – This takes place in the class situation and everyone looks at a text together. The texts should include various types, such as plays, fiction, non-fiction and poetry, and be on a range of different subjects and themes.
- **Guided/group reading** – This takes place in small taught groups within a class while other pupils are working independently.
- **Individual reading** – This usually involves pupils quietly reading books from the classroom or library, or those used during guided reading, which pupils can read without adult support. You should hear individual pupils of all ages read as much as possible as it is an important way of developing their reading skills.
- **Paired reading** – Two pupils read together with one supporting the other. They may be the same age or sometimes younger and older pupils from the same school may work together at a set time each week.

▼ Figure 6.4 Working one-to-one with a child can improve literacy skills

When supporting pupils' reading, you need to use a range of strategies. Make sure you check with the teacher whether any pupils have specific targets. However, it is important to involve all pupils if you are working with a group. Be aware if you have pupils who are reluctant to talk about what they are reading. Make sure you give them plenty of praise and encouragement to build up their confidence and reassure them when putting their ideas forward. Careful questioning will also help you find out about pupils' understanding of texts, as they may be able to 'decode', but not be able to tell you what they are reading about. Dictionaries or vocabulary lists may also help if pupils are unsure of the meaning of specific words.

Strategies and resources for developing writing skills

As pupils develop writing skills, they need support both in English/Literacy lessons and in other subject areas. With older pupils, this may take the form of planning, drafting and re-drafting work; with younger pupils, it may be supporting them as they form basic words. You therefore need to help them with the technical aspects of writing, including spelling, grammar and handwriting, and with their skills in creating and developing their own compositions. If pupils find writing acitivies challenging, the strategies in the diagram below may help them.

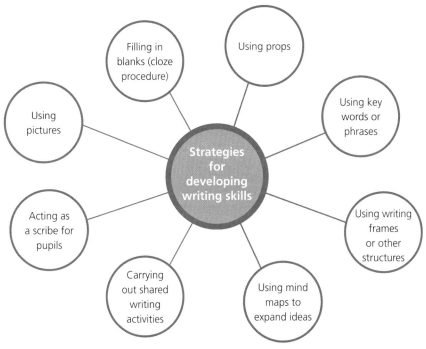

◀ **Figure 6.5** Strategies and resources for developing writing skills

Your teacher or the school's Literacy co-ordinator will also be able to give you a range of ideas for supporting specific pupils who are having difficulties with writing.

Strategies and resources for developing speaking/talking and listening skills

Pupils who are not confident when speaking need to be aware that you value what they have to say. You can show them that you are interested by:

- giving them eye-contact when they are talking to you
- smiling or encouraging them to continue while they are talking
- repeating back what they have told you, for example, 'So you think that the character is worried about what might happen?'
- asking them open-ended questions to encourage them to answer in more detail.

You can also support pupils by allowing them time to think about and formulate ideas before they give their answers.

Some pupils find it very difficult to sit quietly and listen to what others are saying. At a very young age, pupils often need to verbalise their thoughts immediately and find it hard to wait. They may find activities such as 'circle time', where they need to spend a long time listening to others, quite difficult, or easier in a smaller group. Older pupils, however, may enjoy debates and discussions about set topics, and should be encouraged to adapt their language and ideas accordingly.

Pupils who lack confidence in speaking and listening situations in class, for whatever reason, should be given opportunities to develop these skills in smaller groups, which they may find less threatening. We can develop speaking and listening skills in many different situations, not necessarily as planned events.

Literacy resources

You should be able to identify the location of literacy resources within individual classes and in the wider school. These may support basic writing with younger pupils (e.g. lists of words, line guides or sound cards) or may be books such as dictionaries and dual language texts. The school is also likely to have a range of technical resources such as computer programs and software to support literacy activities.

Strategies and resources for developing mathematical knowledge, understanding and skills

When working with pupils on Maths tasks, you will use different strategies to support the development of their skills. It is likely that you will adapt how you do this depending on the needs of the pupil, so you need to know about individual pupils' targets for Maths. You might use some of the following strategies.

- **Helping pupils to interpret and follow instructions** – Some pupils find it hard to recall instructions or follow a series of points given by the teacher. You may need to help them follow what is required.
- **Reminding pupils of teaching points made by the teacher** – Some pupils may find a task challenging because of their individual learning needs or ability to focus on it. You may need to remind them about specific teaching points to enable them to continue.
- **Questioning and prompting pupils** – It is likely that you will use this strategy regularly with all pupils, as they often need to be refocused or have specific questioning to redirect their thinking.
- **Helping pupils to select and use appropriate mathematical resources** – You may need to prompt or encourage pupils to think about resources available to them when working on Maths activities. If pupils have sensory support needs, you may need to speak to specialist teachers to find out what additional resources are available. (See also 'Numeracy resources' below.)
- **Explaining and reinforcing the correct use of mathematical vocabulary** – Always reinforce vocabulary used by the teacher, extend pupil vocabulary and check pupils' understanding of the terms used. For example, young pupils or those with English as an additional language may need to have the term 'table' explained to them in a mathematical context.
- **Introducing follow-on tasks to reinforce and extend learning** – The teacher may have given additional tasks for pupils to work on if they have finished the initial activity. More able pupils may be asked to develop concepts and find their own objectives, but it is likely that you will still need to check these with them.

Numeracy resources

Always make sure that you know how to use any resources that you need and where they are kept. All pupils should be given the opportunity to look at and explore resources before starting to use them, and some pupils may need help if they are unfamiliar with particular resources.

Resources for Maths may range from measuring apparatus for length and weight to number equipment, such as cards or counters, and games to develop different Maths skills. There will also be a range of technologies to support Maths, such as calculators, numeracy software and 'pixies'. (For more on ICT resources, see Unit 8, page 133.)

Portfolio activity K8

Using strategies and resources to develop pupils' skills

Your assessor should observe you working with pupils on both literacy and numeracy activities so that they can see you using a variety of strategies to support pupils' learning in each area. You will also need to identify where you would find literacy and numeracy resources in the school to help you to do this.

How to use praise and assistance to maintain pupils' interest and enthusiasm

You need to give praise and feedback to pupils as you support learning, not just in Literacy and Numeracy but in all subject areas. Everyone, not just pupils, works better when their efforts are acknowledged and they feel that they have been noticed by others. Provide as much feedback as is practicable to pupils when they are working, for example through discussing what they are doing. Make sure that any feedback you give them is presented in a positive way, so that it does not prevent them from continuing with their work. Also make sure that you are working to enable the pupil to do their work rather than doing it for them; you can encourage this through effective questioning techniques to check their understanding.

Your assessor should see you doing this, which will be enough evidence for this knowledge point.

Sorts of problems that might occur when supporting literacy and numeracy activities with individuals and groups

While supporting pupils, you may find that you face problems to do with the resources you are using, the environment or the pupils' ability to learn. If you find that the difficulties prevent you from continuing with the activity for any reason, speak to the teacher if possible. If the teacher is busy or elsewhere, you may have to decide what to do yourself. If there is a problem with resources (for example, you do not have enough books or equipment) or they are inappropriate for the group you are with, you may need to find them another literacy or numeracy activity to do, and speak to the teacher afterwards. If there are problems with the learning environment (e.g. there are too many distractions), it would be appropriate for you to move to a quieter area or abandon the task; it is not possible to work if pupils are unable to concentrate on what is being said. If you are supporting a group in which one pupil finds the work too difficult or too easy, you can give that pupil alternative activities or modify what they have to do. Where pupils are causing the concern (e.g. due to behaviour problems), you should not attempt to continue unless their behaviour improves. If it does not, they should be sent back to the teacher.

Importance of working within your own sphere of competence and when you should refer to others

As a teaching assistant you are working under the direction of a teacher, whether you are on or outside school premises. If you are working at NVQ Level 2, you will be very much guided by what teachers have asked you to do, although you should still have opportunities to use your own initiative. This means that you should know the boundaries of your responsibilities and be aware of when to refer to the class teacher or senior managers within the school.

Broadly speaking, you need to refer to others in situations that you cannot resolve or which:

- disrupt the learning of pupils working with you
- are indicators that the pupil does not understand the teaching points, despite being approached in different ways
- show that the pupil has a very good understanding and is working at a higher level than others in his/her group
- are issues of which others need to be aware (e.g. child protection concerns or issues that have happened at home)
- put others in danger.

For your portfolio...

**K2
K4
K6
K8
K9
K10**

In order to gather evidence for the knowledge base of this unit, you need to show that you have a clear understanding of the needs of the pupils you are supporting. Your assessor should have the opportunity to observe you in a Literacy or Numeracy session. As part of this process, you should also go through the pupils' needs, lesson plans, resources and any IEPs with your assessor. Read through the knowledge points carefully to make sure that you cover as many of them as possible.

Further reading

DfES 0514/2001: Guidance to support pupils with hearing impairments in mathematics (www.standards.dfes.gov.uk/primary/)

DfES 0511/2001: Guidance to support pupils with autistic spectrum disorders in mathematics (www.standards.dfes.gov.uk/primary/)

DfES 0512/2001: Guidance to support pupils with dyslexia and dyscalculia in mathematics (www.standards.dfes.gov.uk/primary/)

DfES 0510/2001: Guidance to support pupils with visual impairments in mathematics (www.standards.dfes.gov.uk/primary/)

Websites

http://curriculum.qca.org.uk – for the secondary curriculum

www.deni.gov.uk – for curriculum guidance for Northern Ireland

www.ltscotland.org.uk/5to14/htmlunrevisedguidelines – for Scottish guidelines

www.standards.dfes.gov.uk/eyfs – for the Early Years Foundation Stage

www.standards.dfes.gov.uk/primaryframeworks - Government Frameworks for Primary Education

www.standards.dfes.gov.uk/secondaryframeworks - Government Frameworks for Secondary Education

8 Use Information and Communication Technology to Support Pupils' Learning

This unit is for teaching assistants who work with ICT to promote pupils' learning. You may use ICT in different ways as part of your day-to-day practice in the classroom across a range of subjects. However, teaching assistants are sometimes responsible for technical or subject specialist support in ICT. You must show how you plan to utilise ICT in a way that is stimulating for pupils while ensuring that it is the most appropriate method for their needs and abilities. Children are surrounded by different technologies in the world outside school and are often very competent in the use of different ICT equipment. It is important that in school ICT is used to encourage pupils to use their enthusiasm for technologies in order to support their learning.

If you work with pupils who have special educational (additional support for learning (ASL)) needs, you may use specialist ICT equipment to enable them to have full access to the curriculum and you may need particular training in order to do this.

You also need to have an awareness of health and safety and the relevant legislation and copyright procedures that are applicable in the case of information technology.

It is important to remember that ICT does not just mean computers – it covers a broad range of learning technologies found in schools, from digital cameras and programmable roamers to interactive whiteboards.

What you need to know and understand

For this unit, you will need to know and understand:

- The school's ICT policy
- The potential learning benefits of using ICT in different ways to support learning
- How good quality ICT provision promotes pupils' physical, creative, social and emotional and communication development alongside their thinking and learning
- The relevant school curriculum and age-related expectations of pupils in the subject/curriculum area and age range of the pupils with whom you work
- The contribution that ICT can make to meeting the planned teaching and learning objectives
- Ways of selecting good quality ICT resources that encourage positive learning for pupils by applying selection criteria, e.g. allows the pupil to be in control, has more than one solution, is not violent or stereotyped, stimulates pupils' interests
- The range of ICT materials from different sources
- How to identify the benefits of ICT materials and sources of information and advice
- The school's policy and procedures for obtaining, adapting and using ICT programmes and materials
- The school's ethical code and/or equality of opportunities policies to ensure the suitability of ICT programmes and materials obtained
- How to adapt use of ICT for pupils of different ages, gender, needs and abilities
- Tools and techniques for adapting ICT programmes and materials
- The need to comply with copyright and licensing agreements for different ICT materials
- How to use ICT to advance pupils' learning, including those with special educational needs or additional support needs, bilingual pupils and gifted and talented pupils
- The importance of having high expectations of all pupils and how this is demonstrated through your practice
- Strategies for gathering information on pupil learning and progress through ICT, and how to plan for and use these in teaching and learning activities
- The importance of health, safety, security and access
- The specific requirements to ensure the learning environment is accessible and safe for pupils using ICT resources
- How to use screening devices to prevent access to unsuitable material via the Internet
- Safeguarding issues for pupils who access the Internet
- How pupils use ICT as a tool to support learning in many curriculum areas and in doing this what they learn about ICT as a subject in its own right
- How to select and use appropriate teaching and learning methods to develop pupils' ICT skills and enhance subject teaching and learning

- The types of support pupils may need to use ICT effectively and how to provide this support
- The importance of pupils having time to explore and become familiar with ICT activities and equipment
- How ICT can be used to assist implementation of equality of opportunity, inclusion and widening participation policy and practice
- How to monitor and promote pupil participation and progress in learning through ICT
- The sorts of problems that might occur when supporting pupils' learning using ICT and how to deal with these
- How to evaluate the effectiveness and suitability of ICT resources and materials for promoting pupils' learning
- Useful online and offline resources that support appropriate use of ICT
- As ICT is a rapidly developing and changing area, how you will need to keep up to date in order to ensure you provide the best support and opportunities for pupils' learning through the use of ICT

The school's ICT policy

The school should have an ICT policy, which will give you guidelines for using and working with ICT in the classroom. There may be set routines and guidance for the use of equipment that all individuals should follow, for example pupils or adults signing a checklist to say when they have borrowed equipment such as digital cameras. The school policy should give the aims and objectives of the school with regard to pupils' experiences and opportunities in ICT.

There will also be school requirements for safety, and for the storage and security of ICT equipment. There may be a borough or school policy on use of the Internet and the availability of websites that are suitable for schools. (For more on health and safety, see page 137.)

This unit is also intended to include and encompass new technologies as they become available and are used in schools.

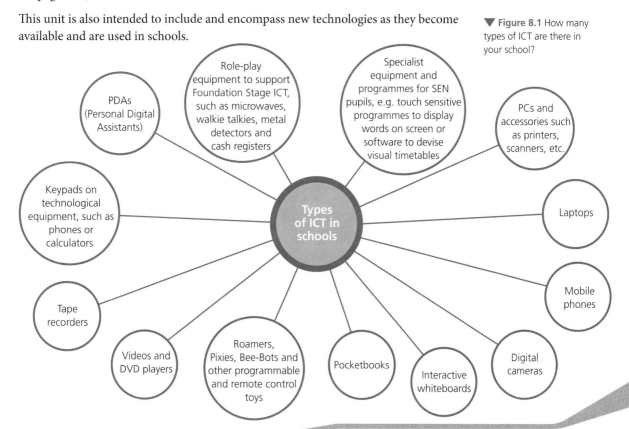

▼ Figure 8.1 How many types of ICT are there in your school?

Portfolio activity

Identifying school policy to support pupil learning through ICT

What does your school policy say about how you should support pupil learning? You could write a reflective account, fill in a blank policy document form (there is one in the related *Interactive Tutor Resource File* for this course) or highlight the policy itself.

Potential learning benefits of using ICT in different ways to support learning alongside pupil development

ICT can be used in many ways to benefit pupil learning as it is cross-curricular, as well as being an individual subject area. By its very nature, it is ideal for problem-solving and finding things out, and can support sustained thinking and group work. Research by the Department for Education into the use of ICT has shown that it '… has been found to be positively associated with improvement in subject-based learning in several areas'. If planned effectively, ICT can support whole class, group and individual activities.

Most pupils enjoy learning through ICT and, as it is an area that is constantly changing, they will benefit from new and innovative technologies as they come into school. Below are some examples of how ICT can be used in a number of different ways to support learning and pupil development.

▼ Figure 8.2 The potential learning benefits of using ICT in different ways to support learning alongside pupil development

Whole class sessions

The use of interactive whiteboards (IWB) in recent years has transformed whole class teaching. Pupils and adults are able to use this technology and many of the programmes available encourage participation. The use of IWB technology also enables teachers to display files downloaded from the Internet, as well as CD-ROMs, and builds interactivity to encourage active learning.

Group work

ICT is effective during group work as it can be used to enhance teaching and encourage pupils to develop their technological skills. For example, programmable toys such as a pixie, bee-bot or roamer can be used in small groups to develop pupils' understanding of programming, directional vocabulary and spatial development in Maths.

Individual work

Individual pupils can be given opportunities to experiment with different technologies, for example using digital cameras during project work, or specific resources can be used with pupils who have special educational (ASL) needs.

▲ **Figure 8.3** Allow children to use different technologies

Portfolio activity

K2
K3

Promoting pupils' development through ICT

Giving examples of ICT work you have carried out with pupils, show how you have promoted their physical, creative, social and emotional development alongside thinking and learning activities.

The relevant school curriculum and age-related expectations of pupils in the subject/curriculum area and age range of the pupils with whom you work

Since you may be supporting ICT through other subjects you will need to be aware of how what you are doing with pupils fits in to the school curriculum. The best way of doing this is through speaking with teachers and checking plans so that you can see how your work with pupils fits in. For example, if you are working in a secondary school you should know about the curriculum at Key stages 3 and 4 and what pupils are expected to attain in different subject areas.

If you are supporting activities in ICT you should be aware of the curriculum guidance and the attainment targets which pupils are expected to be working towards. If you are unclear about these you will need to check with either your class teacher or teacher of ICT, or the ICT co-ordinator. You should also make sure you have read the school's ICT policy. If you work with pupils of a particular age group for any length of time you will get to know their expected abilities.

Contribution that ICT can make to meeting the planned teaching and learning objectives

ICT is a cross-curricular subject, which means that it can be used in most other curriculum areas. For example, you may be working with a pupil in Literacy asked to write up their work on a computer or you may be supporting a group of pupils using digital cameras to record geography in the local area. When planning, both you and the teacher should be thinking about ways in which ICT can enhance pupil learning and help pupils to meet the planned learning intentions. If there are pupils in the class with special educational (ASL) needs, there may be specific ways in which ICT can enable them to access the curriculum more fully. As new equipment becomes available, you may be able to think of increasingly imaginative ways in which ICT may be used to support learning.

K5 Case study

Identifying the contribution of ICT to teaching and learning objectives

Martha is working in a small village primary school, which has mixed age classes. She and the Year 3/4 (P4/5) teacher have planned a Literacy session in which the learning objective is for pupils to identify and discuss stories that have a moral. One of the groups in the class is asked to investigate and feed back to the others about stories they have found through searching on the Internet.

- How might the use of the Internet enhance the teaching and learning in this lesson?
- Give an example of a lesson you have supported in which ICT has contributed to pupils meeting the planned teaching and learning objectives.

Ways of selecting good quality ICT resources that encourage positive learning for pupils by applying selection criteria

In recent years, schools have been allocated money through local authorities specifically to spend on multimedia resources to support teaching and learning. This has led to a wide range of new resources becoming available. As with all areas of learning, you should always be on the lookout for good quality new materials. If you are specifically asked to look for new ideas, you may need to consult with others, particularly if you have limited experience of the kinds of resources that are available (see also K8 below). You may also find that your school staffroom has a range of magazines and educational publications that advertise new resources and equipment as they come on to the market.

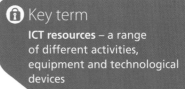

Key term

ICT resources – a range of different activities, equipment and technological devices

ICT resources are often expensive and you will need to bear in mind how much any new equipment will actually contribute to positive learning. For example, programmes and resources should meet criteria such as the following:

- allows pupils to be in control and encourages independent thought rather than 'leading' them to a specific conclusion

- encourages pupils' interests, for example in Maths or Music
- allows pupils to be creative and use their own ideas
- are not violent or aggressive
- avoids stereotyping.

The range of ICT materials from different sources

The range of ICT materials that is available is increasing all the time. You may find that even in the time you are completing your NVQ, different equipment and materials become accessible.

You could use existing suppliers known to the school if you need to find specific software or equipment for use. There are also a number of websites which give advice for tried and tested resources that are educationally worthwhile and encourage pupils to use their own ideas (see end of this unit).

How to identify the benefits of ICT materials and sources of information and advice

If you are not sure about the benefits of using particular software or equipment because it is not apparent from the learning objectives or from speaking to the teacher, you may need to consult your school's ICT co-ordinator or local authority ICT consultant. You can also check recommended products through your local authority website. BECTA and TEEM offer useful information on procurement and evaluation of software (see the end of the unit for contact details).

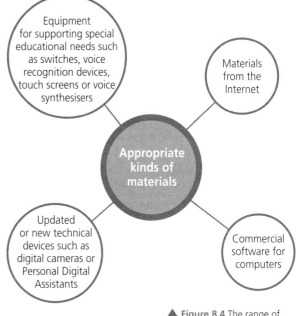

▲ **Figure 8.4** The range of ICT resources

The following points (from Lewisham LEA) are useful when considering software and resources.

Design
- Do pupils find it easy to work out how to use it?
- Is it fairly self-explanatory?
- Is it easy to navigate? Can pupils use it independently?
- Is it straightforward to enter data or instructions?
- Does it give feedback and if so what kind?
- Can you customise it to suit the needs of the pupils you are working with?

Content

- Are there useful support materials with the package?
- Is the language and information suitable for the age range and special needs of the pupils you are working with?
- Is the content non-sexist? Are both girls and boys in active, positive roles? Is the subject interesting and motivating to both sexes?
- Does it encourage cultural diversity?
- Is it relevant to your scheme of work?
- What links are offered to other websites?

Teaching and learning

- How long will it retain pupils' attention, interest and motivation?
- Does it support a range of teaching and learning styles and models of classroom management?
- Does it encourage open or closed responses from pupils?
- Will it support the learning of less able pupils?
- Can it extend the learning of highly able pupils?
- Will it support and enhance teaching? In what way?
- Does it support the teaching of Literacy and Numeracy?

School's policy and procedures for obtaining, adapting and using ICT programmes and materials and how to ensure the suitability of those obtained

If you are involved in obtaining ICT programmes and materials, you need to read your school's ICT policy and find out what materials are available to you for use in school. You should not bring in your own software to be used on site or install any programmes without the knowledge of the ICT co-ordinator. This is because your school needs to have the appropriate licence or permission to use programmes, which also need to be checked for suitability. You may also unwittingly import viruses on to school systems. Resources and materials used in school should be accessible to all pupils and be appropriate for educational use. In addition, any electronic equipment that you bring into school to use should be safety checked.

How to adapt use of ICT for pupils of different ages, gender, needs and abilities, and tools and techniques for doing this

You may need to adapt how ICT is used in the class in which you are working so that it is more accessible to different groups of pupils. Ensure that you plan such adaptations into the session as much as possible so that you are prepared for different eventualities.

Age

If you have a mixed age range, you may need to group children so that older pupils support younger ones.

Gender

You may be using programmes or equipment that appeals more to boys or girls, or pupils of one sex may be more likely to dominate. You need to monitor this or have a rota system so that all pupils have access to programmes or equipment.

Needs

You may need to work in smaller groups with pupils depending on their needs so that they have adequate support. Adapting materials may mean preparing templates for pupils to work through, for example. Pupils may sometimes need to work alone so that they can develop a specific skill or consolidate what they have done.

Abilities

The most challenging part of supporting ICT is that pupils have a wide range of abilities. For example, for your first session with a group, make sure that your plans are not over ambitious as this will make the task much harder to manage.

Case study K11 K12

Adapting the use of ICT

You are working in Reception and have been allocated a timetabled slot in the ICT suite each week. The class teacher has asked you to take half the class each time so that you each have smaller groups to work with. This is the first session and you have planned to use a sorting programme with pupils so that you can assess their confidence at using computers. However, during the session you have to spend a lot of time working with two pupils who have very poor mouse skills and find it difficult to manage the task.

- How might you have adapted the task in this instance?
- How could you work with the teacher to support each other?

Need to comply with copyright and licensing agreements for different ICT materials

It is important that you are aware of the copyright and licensing agreements held by the school in relation to different ICT programmes and materials. Licensing agreements vary, which can cause confusion, so the safest option is to check on individual programmes.

Copyright

If the school has CD-ROMs and other software, these must only be used by the school and not by other parties, and multiple copies of programmes should not be made.

Software licensing

You need to be aware of the licences held by the school with regard to software. There are different kinds of licence depending on the intended use of the software; for example, single use or across a network. (For more information go to the Becta or British Educational Suppliers' Association websites at the end of the unit and search for licensing.)

How to use ICT to advance pupils' learning, including those with special educational needs or additional support needs, bilingual pupils and gifted and talented pupils

If you are working with pupils who have specific or individual support needs, you need to find out about ICT resources appropriate for their use. You should have access to specialist support teachers in the areas concerned and also need to be aware of the kinds of websites you should check on a regular basis to ensure that you have up-to-date information. (See also the individual units on special educational (ASL) needs and supporting bilingual and gifted and talented pupils.)

The importance of having high expectations of all pupils and how this is demonstrated through your practice

High expectations of learning and behaviour should be part of a whole school approach and give pupils a sense of pride in their achievements. It is vital for pupils to feel part of a whole school and whole class, and to understand the importance of the contribution of each individual. In this way, children will develop a positive attitude to learning. In ICT, you should encourage pupils through being positive about the subject and through your own enthusiasm. It may also be helpful to buddy pupils who are less confident with those who are.

Strategies for gathering information on pupil learning and progress through ICT, and how to plan for and use these in teaching and learning activities

Your school may keep pupil records on computer systems, which are accessible to staff and may also give you additional information on pupil progress. You may be required to update pupil records on computer systems as you work with pupils. Although you may prefer to use paper-based systems and transfer the records to computer later, this will take more time. You may need to plan time into sessions so that you can assess pupil learning as you go, although this can be challenging if you are supporting groups on your own. You will need to have clear assessment criteria so that you can observe pupil progress. This can be more difficult if pupils are working in pairs or groups. To aid assessment it may help to ask pupils to self-assess if they have experience of doing this. It is important to remember that only the planned focus should be assessed, whether that is ICT or another curriculum area. You need to be clear on the assessment criteria and should discuss these with the teacher who has asked you to carry out the assessment.

K16 Case study

Gathering information on pupil progress through ICT

You have been working with Year 4 (P5) on using the Internet to gather information. You have to assess their skills at presenting the information they have gathered and saving it to a document so that they can add to it later. They are working in pairs.

- Explain two different ways that you might go about assessing the pupils' skills.

Importance of health, safety, security and access

When developing ICT skills in pupils, you should be aware of the risks associated with using equipment and how these can be minimised. Equipment should be safe as long as it is used properly and checked regularly. However pupils will need to be regularly reminded of the correct procedures. Pupils should always be taught to switch on, log on to and shut down computers correctly; computers can be damaged and work lost if they are turned off incorrectly. Work that pupils save on school networks or intranet will usually be password protected and in a named folder for their own class.

Specific requirements to ensure the learning environment is accessible and safe for pupils using ICT resources

Your school policy should give guidelines outlining the specific requirements you should follow when supporting ICT. It is important that you are aware of what kinds of risks pupils may face and what to do if you discover any hazards or faults. Many schools have a book in which faults are recorded and these are then checked and corrected by technicians when they come in.

Wireless technology has enabled increasing use of portable equipment such as laptops in schools and so security is even more important. Many schools will now have special storage devices or digitally locked cupboards to ensure that equipment is stored securely.

Keys to good practice

Maintaining health and safety when using ICT

✓ Check the equipment regularly and report any faults immediately.
✓ Ensure you know how to operate equipment before the lesson.
✓ Use only the correct accessories with each item of equipment.
✓ Ensure that pupils are sitting correctly on height-adjustable chairs if applicable.
✓ Ensure that computer screens are at the correct height (eye level).
✓ Limit the amount of time pupils spend seated at computers.
✓ Never overload sockets.
✓ Ensure that the equipment is being used safely and intervene when it is not.
✓ Store equipment safely and securely when not in use.

There are also dangers involved in the misuse of the Internet, chatrooms, email and mobile phones. Pupils should be aware of what the dangers are and what they should do if they have any concerns. Cyber-bullying affects increasing numbers of children. For information and support on the safe use of the Internet, see the contact details at the end of the unit.

How to use screening devices to prevent access to unsuitable material via the Internet and safeguarding issues

Your school will have screening devices and filters to prevent pupils from accessing unsuitable material via the Internet. These are usually put in place automatically by all schools. You should also be on the look out when pupils are using the Internet in case they inadvertently come across inappropriate websites. In most schools, pupils are not permitted access to the Internet unless there is an adult present to monitor what they are doing. Pupils may also use their own personal devices, such as memory sticks, so the school also needs to have a policy on their use. If you have any cause for concern, you should report it immediately to your school's ICT co-ordinator so that it can be resolved.

K20 K21 Portfolio activity

Investigating screening devices in use in school

Find out what screening devices your school has in place to prevent pupils finding unsuitable material when using the Internet. You may need to look in your school's ICT policy or speak to the co-ordinator or technician.

How pupils use ICT as a tool to support learning in many curriculum areas and in doing this what they learn about ICT as a subject in its own right

ICT is a valuable tool for supporting learning as it extends teaching and learning in many ways. It enables teachers and pupils to use visual and auditory media to extend learning and encourages pupils to become actively involved. It encourages access to a wide range of information and communication opportunities and enables pupils to store and retrieve, draft and redraft, test and analyse. Through using ICT in different curriculum areas, pupils can apply what they know in a range of situations. This means that they can see what different technologies and software can do alongside their other learning.

How to select and use appropriate teaching and learning methods to develop pupils' ICT skills and what support pupils may need

You need to consider a number of different teaching and learning methods when supporting ICT. ICT activities may be more appealing to a particular type of learner. Some pupils will be particularly able when using particular kinds of equipment and you will want to encourage them, while also supporting those who are less confident. Depending on the task you are working on and the abilities of the pupils, you may need to give them different levels of support.

▲ Figure 8.5 Pupils can use ICT equipment for their own activities, such as presentations

Importance of pupils having time to explore and become familiar with ICT activities and equipment

In ICT, as in other subject areas, it is important that pupils have a chance to become familiar with activities and equipment when they are first asked to use them. They will need some time for this so that they can concentrate on what they have been asked to do rather than *how* they are going to do it. By giving them time to explore and become familiar with ICT activities and equipment, you will be saving time in the long run as pupils will be less likely to be distracted by using something new.

Case study

Recognising the importance of familiarisation

You have been asked to work with a group of Year 3 (P4) pupils using light sensors. The pupils have not used them before, but you do not have time to allow them to explore their use before starting on the teaching and learning activity. As a result the pupils are too excited about using the new equipment and unable to give their full attention to the activity.

- Why should you build exploration time in when planning pupil activities?
- Can you relate this example to your own experience with ICT equipment?

How ICT can be used to assist implementation of equality of opportunity, inclusion and widening participation policy and practice

The use of ICT will enable you to support all pupils and give more pupils fuller access to the curriculum. You may find that the use of ICT enhances the learning experience of pupils with limited access to the curriculum. The work they carry out will also enhance the work of other pupils. They can work alongside others in pairs or groups to support one another or teach one another how to use particular software or equipment.

▼ Figure 8.6 A wide range of ICT resources can be used

Implementing equality of opportunity through ICT

Think about the following pupils:

- Jed, who has very poor fine motor skills and difficulty with handwriting
- Anya, who has difficulty staying on task in the classroom
- Phillip, who has dyslexia
- Somera, who speaks English as an additional language.

How could you use ICT to support them, while also encouraging pupils to work alongside others?

The QCA website also has some guidance on inclusion in ICT (see the end of the unit).

How to monitor and promote pupil participation and progress in learning through ICT

If you are supporting groups of pupils or whole classes during ICT sessions, it is likely that they will be enthusiastic and keen to participate. Most children are interested in using different technologies and will be keen to join in. However, this can also mean that young children become overexcited, particularly if you are working in a different part of the school from their normal classroom.

You may be supporting pupils who are less familiar with different programmes or ICT equipment. In this situation, it will be difficult to get around a large group or the whole class even if you are working alongside the class teacher. It may be useful to pair up a more confident or able pupil with a less confident or able pupil, so that they need your assistance less often. In order to monitor pupil learning, ensure that you move around the group, as individuals may appear to be fully absorbed in the task but reliant on the input of others. It may be useful to have a list of pupils' names so that you can make a note of who has met the learning objectives and add your own comments.

If your school has resources such as PDAs (Personal Digital Assistants), you may be able to work with the teacher to track pupil learning during the lesson. With this technology you will be able to look at how pupils are progressing as they work.

The sorts of problems that might occur when supporting pupils' learning through ICT and how to deal with these

Unfortunately, when working with ICT, problems often arise and you need to have a list of strategies available to deal with these. Problems are most commonly to do with:

- technical issues – you may have problems loading or using programmes or equipment may be faulty
- discrepancies between pupils' abilities within a group or class, which will become too demanding
- not having enough equipment for the number of pupils
- not having had sufficient training or experience yourself to use the equipment.

In order to minimise problems, always be clear before the lesson what you will be doing during it and ensure that the equipment you need is available and not booked by others. Make sure you have worked on any new programmes and checked the ICT suite or equipment beforehand to make sure that you will be able to operate it when pupils are present.

K27 # Case study

Dealing with problems when using ICT

James has been asked to take half of a Reception class to the IT suite for 20 minutes to use some Maths programmes with them. He has paired pupils up but two of the computers are not working. He also nearly forgets to give out headphones, which will avoid pupils making too much noise. He eventually starts pupils off on the task, but finds he has little time left and at the end of the session feels dissatisfied with what they have achieved.

- How could James have improved his session with the pupils?
- What could he have done to enable him to monitor pupil progress further?

K27 # Portfolio activity

Reflecting on the problems of using ICT

Write a reflective account of some of the problems you have had to deal with when supporting pupils for ICT and how you have dealt with these.

How to evaluate the effectiveness and suitability of ICT resources and materials for promoting pupils' learning

As with other subjects, it is useful to take time following an ICT lesson to evaluate how it went and think about the resources or materials you have used, especially if these have not been trialled before. (See also the checklist of criteria for ICT resources, from Lewisham LEA on pages 133–4.)

Evaluating the effectiveness of ICT resources

Use the questions below to help you evaluate the effectiveness of ICT resources you have used to promote pupil learning.

- Did the ICT resources help pupils to achieve the learning objectives?
- In what ways was the task successful/unsuccessful?
- How was ICT used to support learning in other areas of the curriculum?
- Were you confident about using the resources or do you need additional training in how to use them?
- Were/was there sufficient resources/software available for all pupils to use?
- What might you do differently if you were to use the resources again?
- Would you recommend use of the resources to others?
- You might also ask pupils to evaluate the resources and activities to help with this.

Useful online and offline resources that support appropriate use of ICT

You should work with your school's ICT co-ordinator and with the class teacher to develop lists of online and offline resources that you can promote for use in school, although some are listed at the end of this unit. You may also be able to liaise with your local authority ICT consultant if you need more information or help.

How to keep up to date with developments in ICT

If you regularly support pupils in ICT, you will need to make sure that you are up to date and trained in any new equipment or software that you are asked to use. It may also be useful to speak to your ICT co-ordinator on a regular basis so that you can discuss any new use of technology in teaching.

Keeping up to date with ICT developments

Write a reflective account to show how you keep up to date with ICT now to ensure that you offer the best support to pupils and how you will continue to do so in the future.

For your portfolio...

This unit has a long list of knowledge points to cover. To avoid using too many case studies and reflective accounts, you could ask your assessor to come into school to observe you working with pupils using ICT equipment. In this way you can cover as much as possible through direct observation. Make sure you show how you have planned to meet the needs of all pupils and are aware of health and safety issues.

Websites

www.bbc.co.uk/teachers/ – this site has a number of ideas and links for teaching curriculum subjects across all four key stages

www.becta.org.uk – British Educational Communications and Technology Agency

www.besanet.org.uk – British Educational Suppliers' Association (BESA)

www.bullying.co.uk – online help and advice service for combating all forms of bullying

www.bullyonline.org/schoolbully/mobile.htm – provides information on bullying by mobile phone, specifically aimed at children

www.curriculumonline.gov.uk – this website offers a large number of resources and teaching materials listed by subject and key stage

www.inclusive.co.uk – this site gives a guide to some of the ICT equipment available for pupils who have special educational (ASL) needs

www.kidscape.org.uk – general bullying resource with specific information on cyber-bullying

www.stoptextbully.com – NCH website on text bullying

www.teem.org.uk/ – educational software evaluation

References

QCA, *A Scheme of Work for Key Stages 1 and 2 in ICT* (ISBN 1-85838-333-1)

9 Observe and Report on Pupil Performance

This unit is about how you can support teachers through carrying out observations on pupils. You will need to be aware of methods of observation and how the process may affect the pupils you are observing. You will also need to know the purpose of any observations you undertake so that you can pass on the required information to the teacher. There are different methods of observation and ways of organising pupils, so this unit gives a breakdown of situations in which you may find yourself when carrying out observations. You should also make sure that when you are observing pupils your presence is not a distraction to them and that you are acting in a supporting role to both pupils and teachers. Finally, you will need to be able to record your observations so that you are able to report back information to the teacher.

What you need to know and understand

For this unit, you will need to know and understand:

- The basic principles of how children and young people develop
- The range of behaviours which might be expected of the age and stage of development of pupils with whom you work
- How to and why record features of the context and off-task behaviours when making observations of pupils' performance on specific tasks and activities
- Potential sources of distractions and disruptions during observations of pupils and how to minimise these
- How to tailor instructions and requests to pupils to match their age and stage of development
- The basic concepts of reliability, validity and subjectivity of observations
- The various roles that observers might play in enabling pupils to demonstrate their full potential
- Possible cultural, social and gender based influences on pupils' responses to being observed
- The protocols to be observed when observing pupils
- How to summarise and present information from observations of pupil performance
- *The importance of confidentiality, data protection and sharing information according to the procedures of your setting* (See Unit 2, K4, page 28)

Basic principles of how children and young people develop

As already seen in Unit 1, page 11, the intellectual development of children and young people is influenced by a range of different factors. They will be developing not only their cognitive skills, but also their skills across all areas of learning. You may be asked to observe pupils' performance in any one of these. (See also Unit 2, K1, page 27.)

The types of learning you may be asked to observe will include the following:

- social and emotional skills – how pupils relate and respond to others
- physical skills – how pupils use gross and fine motor skills
- intellectual and cognitive skills – how pupils interpret and apply concepts and knowledge
- language and communication skills – how pupils communicate with others and understand language structures and vocabulary.

Social and emotional skills

You may be asked to observe pupils who are working or socialising with their peers in order to look at how they relate to others. You may also be asked to ensure that the pupil is unaware that you are watching, as this could have an influence on how they behave.

Children and young people develop their social skills by watching the behaviour of others and through influences in their own social environments. Adults have a strong part to play in supporting the development of social and emotional skills as they can guide children and young people as to the kinds of behaviour that are acceptable.

Developing social and emotional skills is more difficult for some children and young people. This may be for a variety of reasons such as immaturity or a more urgent need for attention due to their individual background. In this kind of situation, you need to observe the pupil's interaction with others, whether they are proactive in seeking out others with whom to socialise and whether they behave appropriately when they are with others. Those pupils who spend breaks on their own or are not confident when socialising with others, may need support in school to help them to develop these skills.

Physical skills

As children and young people grow and explore the world around them, their physical skills become practised and develop. They learn to have control over their bodies and can demonstrate competence in many physical skills such as running, jumping, riding a bicycle and so on.

You may be asked to observe pupils in situations where they are demonstrating their physical skills because they may not be developing in an age-appropriate way or because the teacher needs to have a record of younger pupils' physical development. A typical scenario is that you may be asked to record progress during PE lessons. For example, if the lesson is in games and the objective is to learn about throwing and catching, you might record which pupils are finding the skills more challenging. Sometimes a particular pupil may display difficulties with gross motor skills, which

▼ **Figure 9.1** Young children need to be encouraged to hone their physical skills

needs to be recorded as evidence so that the school can seek additional support for them. You may also be required to observe pupils who have difficulties with fine motor skills, such as using scissors or a pencil. These skills may not be well developed when pupils first come into school or they may have an area of special educational (additional support for learning (ASL)) need and adults need to be aware of those who need extra support.

There are also occasions in the classroom or other areas in school when a teaching assistant may be asked to record how pupils with disabilities are organising themselves within the learning environment. These pupils need careful monitoring at all times and if you see a particular problem you should report it to the teacher straightaway.

Intellectual and cognitive skills

There have been many theories about how children learn and develop and the kinds of influences on their learning. You need to be aware of what is expected of the pupils with whom you work so that you can assess what kind of support they need. (For more on this see Unit 2, page 32.) As part of your role, you will often be asked to work with groups and individuals to support teaching and learning so that pupils can complete tasks. You may also be asked to sit back from a group and observe how they interact with each other or manage their learning independently. Teachers should give clear instructions as to why you are observing the individual or group, whether your role is purely to observe or also to join in the task, and to guide you on exactly what you need to record.

You may need to look at how a pupil or group is approaching the task, for example, if the pupil is methodical when undertaking a Maths activity such as identifying the number of ways to make ten. You could also be looking at whether the pupil has understood a new concept or one that should be familiar. It is also useful to observe whether the pupil approaches the task with confidence or waits for assistance from other pupils or adults.

Language and communication skills

Language and communication skills are closely linked to pupils' learning. If they have difficulty with processing language or communicating, their ability to rationalise and think through what they are doing may be affected. Those who experience difficulties when communicating with others may need to be observed both in the classroom and in other environments, such as the playground or dining hall.

You may be asked to observe and monitor the behaviour and interaction with others of pupils with communication difficulties, such as autism. Agencies that support social and communication difficulties may be available to offer help and advice to support work with these pupils. The school may also have been given advice and targets from a speech and language therapist about how to maximise the pupil's speech development, so that the school, parents and therapist can work together.

Make sure you have a clear idea of what you are expected to observe and whether you should intervene. Also always be aware of individual pupil's targets, particularly if supporting those with special educational (ASL) needs, so that you know what areas the pupil is working on. If you have not seen the targets of the pupil you are supporting, you should ask to speak to the Special Educational Needs Co-ordinator (ASL teacher).

Range of behaviours which might be expected of the age and stage of development of pupils with whom you work

As can be seen from the table below, children display a range of behaviours at different stages in their development. The behaviours in the table are typical for the ages shown, but individuals vary and when working with a particular age group or pupils at a particular stage of development, you will quickly learn the kinds of behaviours that are 'normal' for the group. You will also get to know different personalities and be able to tell if individual pupils are acting differently from their normal behaviour.

Stages of social and emotional development

Age	Stage of development
4–6 years	Child generally feels much more confident in itself and starts to be proud of its own achievements. Close friendships are increasingly important.
6–8 years	Pupil starts to develop a sense of fairness and is more able to share items and equipment. Pupil has greater self-awareness, can be self-critical and starts to compare itself with peers. Friendship groups can be problematic if children fall out with one another. Pupil also makes some gender friendships in this age group.
8–12 years	Pupils are already aware of how they fit into groups, the co-operation necessary and what the acceptable levels of behaviour are. They are aware of their own achievements and capable of self-criticism. Friendships are already important to them. Throughout, they are growing in maturity and able to take on greater responsibilities. They respond well to small group activities. They have a strong need to feel accepted and worthwhile. Leaders should provide reassurances and support.
12–15 years	This age group is keen to plan activities together and enjoy teamwork. They may enjoy taking part in activities that are away from home. This is a time of emotional swings and the biggest period of challenges to a pupil's self-concept. Staff need to take time to talk about values with this age group.
Years 11 and 12 (S5–S6)	Give teenagers opportunities to interact in mixed groups. They are learning to co-operate with others at an adult level. They need increasingly greater responsibilities to allow for independent thinking and decision-making. Consistent treatment by staff is important. Be willing to listen to and accept each one as an individual.

Pupils who display abnormal behaviours for their age usually show the following types.

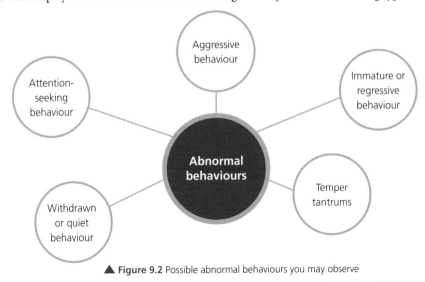

▲ **Figure 9.2** Possible abnormal behaviours you may observe

When observing pupils, you should record if they are not on task for reasons of behaviour. Depending on the circumstances, you may need to intervene. However, if you are observing a type of behaviour and how often it occurs, you may have been asked not to intervene and should only step in only if the pupil is putting themselves or others in danger. It is important to clarify the boundaries of behaviour and how to deal with any problems in advance with the teacher because if the behaviour continues, you need to have agreed strategies for how to proceed. It is important for adults to be firm and for pupils to know what is expected of them. Your school should also have a behaviour policy, which you can refer to if you are unsure of the kinds of sanctions you should apply.

K2 Portfolio activity

Recognising different behaviour patterns

Write a reflective account outlining the behaviour patterns of the age range with which you work. If you are supporting learning in different age groups, do this for each group.

How to and why record features of the context and off-task behaviours when making observations of pupils' performance on specific tasks and activities

You may be asked to observe pupils carrying out:

- normal learning activities
- formal test tasks to be administered in a controlled way
- specific tasks with verbal instructions such as 'copy this in your best handwriting' or 'find out the weight of these objects'.

It is likely that you will need to note down the context of the work or activity pupils are undertaking as part of the record of your observations, so that those who look at your records later are aware of any issues that may have affected how pupils performed. Depending on the age of pupils, circumstances will affect them differently, for example the ability of a pupil to concentrate may well be affected if he/she needs to leave school early for a hospital appointment.

> **Key terms**
>
> **Observations** – systematically watching pupils engaged on tasks and activities designed to elicit specific behaviours; observations may be carried out on individuals working on their own or as part of a group, or on groups of pupils working together
>
> **Performance** – the skills and behaviours to be observed

Potential sources of distractions and disruptions during observation of pupils and how to minimise these

It is important to make sure that you record only information that is relevant to the observation you have been asked to carry out (see page 155 on how to record information). This is the case unless you notice something that you feel needs to be reported to the class teacher, which could include one of the following:

- pupil is distracted or showing disruptive behaviour which is preventing them or others in the group from completing the task

- pupil is showing uncharacteristic behaviour, for example being unusually quiet during the session
- pupil is playing up to being observed, so the observation may not be a realistic interpretation of his/her abilities
- there are environmental factors and interruptions, which could be caused by physical factors such as noise levels, that prevent the task being carried out successfully.

If a pupil is disruptive or does not participate in the activity owing to disturbance by others, this should be recorded as part of the observation because it will have an effect on whether pupils are fulfilling the required learning objectives of the lesson.

You may be aware of potential causes of disruption and should always speak to the teacher who has asked you to carry out the observaton if you anticipate any problems. It is also important to maintain the normal rules and routines of the school or classroom before undertaking any observations so that pupils are not working in an artificial situation. If you set out the activity in a different environment, the pupils may find this too much of a distraction to focus on the activity.

Other potential sources of disruption include:

- pupil's own behaviour
- task being too difficult or too easy for pupils
- physical factors such as noise or light levels
- interruptions by other pupils in the class
- insufficient space, materials or equipment to carry out the task
- faulty equipment.

Case study K3 K4

Difficulties when observing pupils

You are observing pupils in Reception (P1) using speaking and listening skills for their Foundation Stage profiles (similar to reports on pupil progress in Scotland). Three pupils are using the home corner as a hospital. One of them is uncharacteristically quiet because her pet dog has just died. Another has noticed you are watching the group and keeps coming to see what you are doing.

- Would you record the context of this observation?
- Is it worth continuing?
- What would you do in this situation?

How to tailor instructions and requests to pupils to match their age and stage of development

Depending on the task you have been asked to observe, you need to be sure that the pupils understand what they have to do. You should have some experience with the age range of the pupils so that you have an idea about the way in which instructions should be given.

Very young pupils or those with special educational (ASL) needs need instructions and requests to be straightforward and not long-winded, otherwise they find them difficult to remember. This is even more important if you are observing them, as you may not have the opportunity to repeat what pupils have to do. Make sure that the vocabulary you use is appropriate to their understanding.

Older pupils are able to read or write down more complex instructions if they need to, but they will also find tasks less challenging to remember if they understand what they have been asked to do.

If you are a participant observer (see K9, page 153), you will be working alongside pupils as you observe them and will have more of an opportunity to give them instructions and direct what they have to do.

Basic concepts of reliability, validity and subjectivity of observations

While you are completing records of observations, check that the information you have is valid and makes sense. As you carry out observations, you may find that you are recording a large number of different things, some of which may not be relevant. Make sure that you read through information before filling it in and that it has been filled in correctly. Check that any dates required are correct and ensure that any discrepancies are dealt with straightaway, as you may not remember to come back to them later.

Reliability

In order to be sure your observations are reliable, record only what you see and not what others have told you or what you think you know a pupil can do. Check through what you have written following an observation to make sure that it is based on facts.

Validity

Keep the reason for the observation in mind and think about whether all you have recorded is valid information. For example, if you are observing a pupil's social skills, it is not valid to add information about how they cope on their own with a mathematical problem.

Subjectivity

When you are observing, only record what you see and not your own opinions. Pupil observations are to give the teacher an idea about the pupil's progress or how they manage in particular situations. Do not be tempted to give any further information than is needed.

> **? Thinking point**
> You are observing Nico in Year 4 (P5) and have been asked to complete a free description of his gross motor skills during part of an apparatus lesson. Your description includes the fact that he spends some of the time talking to his friend and you record what they say to one another. You also record that he becomes very upset when he is unable to manage one of the tasks he has been asked to do. Are either of these pieces of information a valid part of the observation?

Keeping observations valid and reliable

Johann is working in a mainstream school with a special educational (ASL) needs unit. Adam, with global learning delay, has just started at the school in Year 3 (P4) and Johann has been asked to observe him across all four areas of development. He has been given some of Adam's records from his previous school, but is not sure whether to read them as he wants to make his own judgements about Adam and what he can do.

- What should Johann do in this situation?
- Do you think he is right in being wary of reading the records first?
- Will his observations be valid and reliable?

Various roles that observers might play in enabling pupils to demonstrate their full potential

Before you start to observe pupils, you need to plan what you are going to do. Your teacher will tell you whether you are a participant or non-participant observer so that you know whether or not you are supporting the task.

Participant observers can ask pupils to do a particular task rather than wait for them to do it without being asked. This may help if you need to fill in a checklist because you can make observations straightaway. You can also talk to pupils as they are working and question them on their approach to the task. However, a disadvantage is that pupils may feel under pressure to respond in a particular way or say what they think you want to hear.

Non-participant observers can record their observations more freely because they are not interrupted by having to speak to pupils. It is likely that the pupils will be more relaxed as they will not be so aware of the observation, although it may be difficult to find a place which enables you to see and hear clearly without being in the way.

Keys to good practice

Planning an observation

✓ Make sure you have permission if required.
✓ Plan the type of observation and have any required paperwork.
✓ Decide exactly what you are going to observe.
✓ Ensure that you know if and when you should intervene.

Possible cultural, social and gender-based influences on pupils' responses to being observed

You may need to encourage pupils who find it difficult to demonstrate the extent of their knowledge or skills when being observed. It can sometimes be helpful, therefore, to have some prior knowledge of the pupils before undertaking the observation. Some pupils will be able to work on a task without being distracted by an observer, while others may play up to the adult to seek attention.

You may also need to put the pupil or pupils at ease so that they are more likely to work constructively with one another. You may need to encourage some individuals to participate so that you gain a clearer idea of their understanding.

Groups of pupils need to be chosen carefully so that they do not include individuals who disturb or influence the reactions of one another. These outcomes may be due to a number of reasons.

Cultural factors

In schools with a high percentage of mixed cultures and where a high number of pupils speak English as an additional language, there may be problems of language and understanding. Bilingual teaching assistants are employed by schools in areas where this is the case (see also Unit 11, K1, page 176). Currently, there are also developments to raise the achievements of pupils from ethnic minorities and traveller families, as many of them are underachieving. Your school may have a strategy for helping these pupils to achieve their full potential and your local authority may offer training so all staff can help to raise attainment.

Social factors

Some pupils feel unable to work with those who are more able or confident and consequently will be less likely to put their ideas forward when being observed. Pupils with a high level of self-esteem are more likely to be involved and to gain more from what they are doing.

Gender-based factors

These pupils are not comfortable, or find it difficult working, with those of the opposite sex. Depending on their age, this may involve a group of pupils who are more confident or who have preconceived assumptions, such as boys are better at Science or girls are better at Art. This may make them less likely to volunteer information when working in a group. This factor may lead older pupils to show off or draw attention to themselves in a mixed group.

Pupils who are being observed individually may be working on their own or as part of a group. Those who are working on their own may not react to the observation in the same way as if they had been working in a group, mainly because they will not be interacting with others to complete the task. When you are observing a pupil working on their own, you may need to ask them questions about what they are doing so that you have more understanding of their approach to the task. Questioning strategies need to be consistent with the objectives of the task, as well as the pupil's age and understanding.

Case study K8

Acting on pupils' responses to being observed

You have been asked to observe a mixed group of Year 7 (S1) pupils, who are working on a problem-solving activity. The task requires them to manage themselves and to decide on how they are going to proceed. As the pupils have not been together as a group for very long (it is the autumn term), some of them do not know each other very well. As they start the activity, you notice that the pupils are having difficulty in deciding what to do as there are some strong personalities in the group. Two of the boys have taken over and are keen to direct what is happening, while one of the girls is calling out and making it as difficult as possible for them to proceed. The group are aware that you are observing them.

- What factors do you think are influencing the way the pupils are behaving?
- What would you do?

Protocols to be followed when observing pupils

When you are asked to observe pupils, make sure that you understand what you are expected to do and whether you should intervene in the activity at all. Although you will have been given guidance by the school and class teacher on exactly what is required when carrying out pupil observation, there are other factors you need to consider. It is important that you always keep the lesson objectives and required observation in mind, so that you can redirect the pupils to what they are doing if they start to go off task. You must also be aware of how you can maximise the pupils' interest and focus on the task, through questioning and directing their work. Make sure that you continue to check on the purpose of your observation as you work to ensure that you are only recording reliable, valid and subjective information (see K6, page 152). Your school will have informed parents and carers about the need to observe pupils, but remember to think about confidentiality.

Keys to good practice

Observing pupils

✓ Make sure that you are clear on what you are observing.
✓ Follow the required format.
✓ Record clearly.
✓ Keep information reliable, valid and subjective.
✓ Remember confidentiality.
✓ Follow school guidelines.

How to summarise and present information from observations of pupil performance

The teacher with whom you are working should give you information about the **format** of the observation and method of recording. Observations may be presented in a number of ways depending on their purpose. Some different types of recording are listed below.

> ### Key term
> **Format** – the way in which results of observations are recorded and presented

Free description

A free description enables you to write everything down during the period of the observation (usually 5–10 minutes). This means that the observation may be quite short because it is very focused on the pupil. Free descriptions need to include what the pupil says to others, how they express themselves non-verbally (e.g. body language or facial expression) and the way in which the activity is carried out. They are used when a lot of detail is required about how the pupil is carrying out an activity and are usually written in the present tense.

Structured description

This type of description may require the observer to record what the pupil is doing against specific headings or in response to pre-determined questions. Structured descriptions are to be used to guide the observer on what needs to be recorded, for example, a series of steps towards achieving a task.

Checklist

These are used to check and record whether pupils can carry out a particular activity quickly and in a straightforward way. They usually require the observer to make a judgement on whether a pupil is able to achieve a task; the focus is not on how they do it but on whether or not they can. Checklists may take different forms and schools can devise their own easily, depending on what is being observed.

Event sample

This method is used to record how often a pupil displays a particular type of behaviour or activity. Event samples need to be carried out without the observer participating in the activity to retain objectivity.

Informal observations

You may be asked to 'just keep an eye' on a pupil or watch them during break time, especially if there have been any specific concerns, and then feed back to teachers. In this case you can make your own notes, but should be careful about confidentiality if you are writing things down and remember not to leave notebooks lying around, particularly if you have recorded pupils' names.

K10

Portfolio activity

Recording observations

Show your assessor or include in your portfolio an example of an observation you have carried out on a pupil. Remember to remove the pupil's name if it is on the observation.

K2
K3
K4
K5
K7
K9
K10

For your portfolio...

The best way of gathering information for this unit is for your assessor to observe you observing pupils and for you to have a professional discussion afterwards taking into account the knowledge points above. You will need to know the pupils and be prepared to talk about any background information, as well as discuss what happened and your method of recording.

10 Support Children's Play and Learning

This unit is designed for those who support children's play and learning in the early years, so it is about supporting very young children in school. You will need to know and understand how children learn and some of the stages of learning and development. You should also have a working knowledge of the Early Years Foundation Stage Curriculum in your home country (Level A in Scotland) and how it affects your work with children. Teaching assistants may be asked to support pupils in school nurseries as well as Reception (P1) classes, and if you have not worked with this age range before, you may need to attend specific training. You can also gain information through speaking to others in school who have worked with this age range.

What you need to know and understand

For this unit, you will need to know and understand:

- How to support children's communication, intellectual development and learning in your setting (see Unit 2, page 37)

- How to support children's play and communication development in bilingual and multilingual settings and where children learn through an additional language (see Unit 2, page 37)

- A basic outline of the expected pattern of children's physical, communication and intellectual, social, emotional and behavioural development for the age group with which you are working (see Unit 2, page 31)

- How the activities and experiences for children and babies and children under three years relates to formal curriculum frameworks and frameworks for babies and young children in your home country

- The importance of play in children's learning and development

- Types of music, movement, songs and games to encourage communication that are appropriate for the children with whom you work

- How to use ICT to support play and learning

- Appropriate language to use to encourage children's communication and learning to include: benefits of open-ended questions, the use of language to extend learning, such as use of mathematical language or encouraging children to question

- The scope and benefits of play where children use their imagination to make one thing stand for another and to play out different roles

- How drama and imaginative play can be used to encourage children's learning, including the types of materials, equipment and props that support this area of play

- Recognising that children will play out roles they see at home and in the world around them and the need for sensitivity in dealing with stereotypes

- Why it is necessary for children's imaginative play to flow freely and with minimal adult intervention, while recognising that sometimes sensitive intervention may be necessary to move the play along

- The importance of encouraging creativity and the scope of activities involved

- How you would display children's work to its best effect

- How to support children's confidence and self-esteem when they make and create things, making sure that the emphasis is on the process of creating something rather than the end product

- Suitable activities for the development of children's fine and gross motor skills

- How physical play can help children to assess risk in a safe and controlled environment

- The benefits to children of physical play and exercise and the need for sensitivity in dealing with those who find it more difficult to participate

- The kind of objects that engage children's interest at different ages and with different needs and abilities

- The benefits to children's learning of grouping together objects with similar characteristics and learning to sort and classify

- The benefits to children's learning of knowing about their own background and community

- How to provide a stimulating environment and not stifle children's curiosity, problem-solving and exploration

- The importance and scope of practical daily activities such as cooking and gardening to enhance children's learning

- How you set up activities to help children learn and the most effective types of activities, toys, equipment and experiences

- How to lay out furniture and equipment to make the best use of space and help children gain access to play and learning activities

- The use of everyday routines to support play and learning

Influence of curriculum frameworks for babies and young children

In each UK country, the formal curriculum begins at around age 5, and there are separate guidelines covering the care and education of children under 5 years old. If you have not worked with children under 5 before, you may need to have additional training or guidance from your school. You should also speak to your class teacher about how planning takes place in Early Years classes. The curriculum for children under 5 in all UK countries is based on the concept of learning through **play**, rather than through more formal education, because play has been shown to be an important vehicle for children's early learning.

Key term

Play – an activity children are motivated to do from within themselves. It is freely chosen and children play in their own chosen way

In English and Welsh schools, the Foundation Stage Curriculum runs from the ages of 3 to 5 years and is therefore used in Reception classes and in nurseries. At the time of writing, the new Early Years Foundation Stage Curriculum is due to replace the existing Foundation Stage Curriculum in September 2008. This will set out one standard framework for learning, development and care for all children from birth to the end of the Reception year (for more information see www.standards.dfes.gov.uk/eyfs). It brings together the Birth to Three Matters framework, the Foundation Stage, and aspects of the National Standards for Under 8s Day Care and Childminding. If your school has a nursery, you may also be asked to work with these children, although in a school setting you will not be asked to work with babies.

In Scotland, the curriculum is focused around the document, *A Curriculum for Excellence – Building the Curriculum 3–18*. The curriculum for 3–5 year olds and the early primary phase (P1) are presented as one level. This means that, although in Scotland there is a distinction between the phases, children only start to have more formal teaching when they are ready. There is also a strong emphasis on active learning and on increasing pupils' depth of knowledge.

In Northern Ireland, pupils in Years 1 and 2 (equivalent to Reception and Year 1 in England) are in the Foundation Stage. Key Stage 1 in Northern Ireland comprises of Years 3 and 4, and Key Stage 2 of Years 5, 6 and 7. Although the year groups are divided up differently from those in other countries, the Foundation Stage remains distinct from the Primary Curriculum and again only introduces children to formal learning when they are ready.

The early years frameworks aim to prepare young children for formal learning in a structured way, which allows effective monitoring of a young child's progress. The way in which learning is usually managed in the early years is that adults work alongside children on focused activities that involve specific concepts, such as using numbers or carrying out writing or language activities. Children also work independently within the class on activities that they choose themselves and which allow them to develop their skills.

K4 Portfolio activity

Understanding the curriculum frameworks

For this knowledge point you need to look at examples of how the curriculum for very young children is reflected in settings. You should give examples of the kinds of activities that children are carrying out and relate them to specific areas of the Early Years Foundation Stage curriculum or other frameworks relevant to your home country. If your school has a nursery, you may be able to ask staff about how they plan and carry out activities. You should also relate activities planned in Reception classes to the curriculum.

Importance of play in children's learning and development

Play is a vital element of children's learning. In the early years of school they are learning more about the world around them and discovering a range of new experiences. They must be given opportunities to explore different environments and use their imaginations. We need to give all children equal opportunities to take part in a range of play situations to promote their learning.

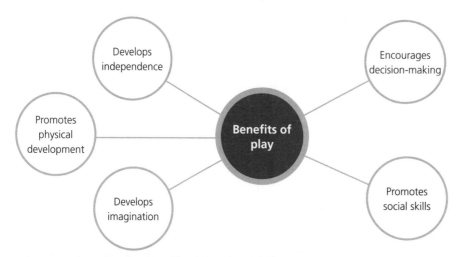

◀ **Figure 10.1** The main benefits of play

Observing children's play

Observe children carrying out play activities in the learning environment over one day. Make a note of the kinds of activities taking place and what skills and opportunities they are encouraging.

Music, movement, songs and games to encourage communication

All children should be given the opportunity to explore their world through the use of music, movement, songs and games. Music and games can help to develop all areas of children's learning and in particular encourage communication. This is because children learn to respond to rhythm, repetition and both competitive and non-competitive games in different ways.

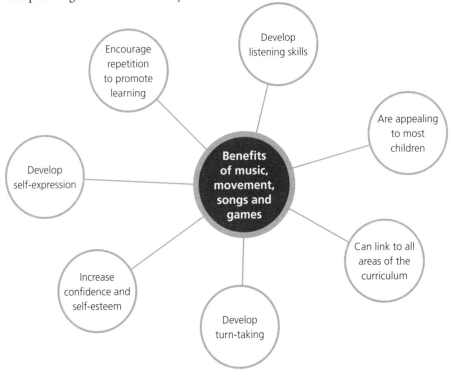

▲ **Figure 10.2** The main benefits of music in encouraging communication

It is likely that you will be using games, nursery rhymes, traditional songs, and music and songs from different cultures to develop pupils' skills in music and communication. When thinking about aspects of movement linked to music, you should encourage the use of different aspects such as rhythm, actions to songs, musical instruments and dancing.

The use of music, games and other activities is beneficial to children's communication skills as they encourage them to take turns and share with others.

Examples of music and games activities you might use with young children are:

- traditional board games such as lotto and matching games, dice games, puzzles
- singing and counting games such as 'Ten green bottles', 'Five little ducks', various nursery rhymes
- physical or action games such as 'Follow my leader', 'Farmer's in his den', 'Ring o' roses' or variations on 'Hunt the thimble'.

K6 Case study

Using music, rhymes and games

Trudi is working in a Reception class and is planning a topic with the teacher around houses and homes. What kinds of musical activities, rhymes or games might she suggest to the teacher to support this topic?

How to use ICT to support play and learning

It is important to remember that using ICT does not simply mean using computers. New technologies suitable for use in schools are being developed all the time and it is likely that you will be asked to support their use in Early Years classes. Make sure that you have had some training if technologies are new to you and that you can speak to others about what is available to pupils in school. Your ICT co-ordinator may be able to help you and give you ideas. If pupils are asked to work with ICT or have opportunities to use it, they should be instructed on its safe use before they do so. They should also be encouraged to help one another.

ICT can be used in different situations and across all areas of the curriculum. It can promote skills of creativity, collaboration and investigation, and can be used both in structured and play activities.

Examples of ICT equipment pupils might use may include:

- tapes and CD recorders
- interactive whiteboards and projectors
- computers and printers
- digital cameras
- programmable toys such as a Pixie, Bee-Bot or Roamer
- electronic keyboards
- mobile phones.

Technologies can also be used in other areas, for example the use of a Dustbuster-type mini-vacuum cleaner to clear up sand off the floor. Equipment designed for use by pupils with special educational (Additional Support for Learning (ASL)) needs may also be used for the benefit of others. Young children's attention and imaginations will be easily captured by technology and they are often competent in using it at an early age.

Appropriate language to use to encourage children's communication and learning

During the Early Years Foundation Stage, the Early Learning Goals for Communication, Language and Literacy are at the heart of children's learning experiences. The Scottish and Northern Irish curricula give equal importance to communication, language and literacy at the early stages of schooling. Children need to experience interactions with others in a variety of situations:

- attentive listening and responses
- using language to imagine and recreate roles and experiences
- interacting with others both in play situations and to accomplish tasks.

The school's English policy should outline the shared objectives for developing children's speaking and listening skills (for example, see the policy on page 117).

The Early Years Foundation Stage (EYFS) also sets out models of effective practice for Communication, Language and Literacy – Language for Communication for each age group from birth to 5 years old. The EYFS website (see the end of this unit) gives the following examples of the kind of language, including open-ended questions, you should use with pupils aged 40–60 months (3–5 years) in order to extend their learning.

- Encourage conversation with others and demonstrate appropriate conventions: turn-taking, waiting until someone else has finished, listening to others and using expressions such as 'please', 'thank you' and 'can I…?'. At the same time, respond sensitively to social conventions used at home.
- Show pupils how to use language for negotiating, by saying 'May I…?', 'Would it be all right…?', 'I think that…' and 'Will you…?' in our interactions with them.
- Model language appropriate for different audiences, for example, a visitor.
- Encourage pupils to predict possible endings to stories and events.
- Encourage pupils to experiment with words and sounds, for example, in nonsense rhymes.
- Encourage pupils to sort, group and sequence events in their play, using words such as: first, last, next, before, after, all, most, some, each, every.
- Encourage language play, for example, through stories such as 'Goldilocks and the Three Bears' and action songs that require intonation.
- Value pupils' contributions and use them to inform and shape the direction of discussions.

Scope and benefits of imaginative play

Children should have different opportunities to use their imaginations through the use of **role-play** and 'small world' activities. They can do this either on their own or with their peers, finding different ways to develop their language and communication skills as well as their confidence. Role-play and **drama** activities allow children to imagine that they are other people and to act out different situations.

Key term

Imaginative play/drama/ role-play – pretending, role-play (i.e. acting the role of another person either alone or in groups), acting out scenarios, drama activities with or without adult support

How drama and imaginative play can be used to encourage children's learning

Most Early Years classrooms have an area such as a home corner set up to enable pupils to develop their imaginative play. This area should be changed regularly to represent a range of role-play opportunities. You should also ensure that there are multicultural opportunities for pupils and opportunities for using different equipment and resources. It is also important to recognise that role-play and drama activities do not need to be 'set up' by adults. Children will also make up their own activities using small world equipment such as Duplo or Lego and Playmobil toys, or use imaginary play in an outdoor environment.

Portfolio activity

Supporting imaginative play

Fill in a table such as the one below to show how the suggested home corner scenarios could encourage pupils' learning and what materials and props you might use to promote this.

Scenario	Learning opportunities	Materials and props
Vet		
Opticians		
Estate agents		
Three bears' house		
Café		

Recognising that children will play out roles they see around them

At this stage in children's learning they will be taking in a large amount of information and making sense of the world around them. They will also naturally play out what they see in their own home environments. You may find that you need to intervene if it is clear that they are not sensitive to others or have ideas that are inappropriate.

Case study

Dealing with stereotyping

Mikey is in the home corner, which is currently set up as a house. He is playing with two girls who are busy in the kitchen area and have told him that they are getting his dinner for him. One of them asks him to lay the table, but Mikey says that they have to do it because they are girls.

● Would you intervene and say anything here?
● Why?

Why it is necessary for children's imaginative play to flow freely and with minimal adult intervention

While it is important for children to have opportunities to play freely, you may sometimes find that it is necessary to interrupt or intervene. This will usually be if pupils become too loud or if there is a safety issue you need to resolve. However, the activities should be child-led and allowed to flow as much as possible. This is because pupils need to feel that they have control over their play and that adults are not limiting their opportunities to direct their own experiences.

Keys to good practice

Promoting role-play opportunities

✓ Encourage the involvement of all pupils.

✓ Provide a safe and secure environment and limit numbers if necessary.

✓ Use both indoor and outdoor environments for role-play.

✓ Encourage pupils to make their own signs and labels, for example price lists and notices in shops.

✓ Use a variety of resources and equipment to sustain pupils' interest.

✓ Consider the needs of all pupils.

✓ Use multicultural resources and discourage stereotyping or inappropriate language.

Importance of encouraging creativity and the scope of activities involved

Creative play is important because it encourages children to explore a range of activities and materials, allowing them to develop their own ideas. It enables them to create their own work using their imaginations and to develop skills in all areas of their learning. This is highly beneficial to their learning as it encourages initiative and gives pupils greater confidence. It also enables them to experience a feeling of achievement and success through their own ideas.

Adults can encourage pupils in specific ways, for example, by ensuring that there is always a choice of activities, including practical activities such as painting or modelling. Remember that creativity encompasses activities such as dance, music and movement, which also rely on children's imaginations.

> **(i) Key term**
>
> **Creativity/creative play** – this is where children develop and communicate their own ideas using art, design, making things, music, dance and movement. Children can express their **creativity** in every area of play and learning

▼ **Figure 10.3** Pupil displays help produce a positive atmosphere

Displaying children's work to its best effect

It is important to use displays creatively to make a stimulating and welcoming learning environment for pupils. When displaying their work, you need to make sure that you display the work of all pupils and not just the most appealing. All pupils should be able to see their work on display as it encourages them to take pride in their work and promotes their self-esteem. You can add labels and children's names to displays, but make sure that these are easy to read and spelled correctly. When creating displays, you should also consider the height of any print and the positioning of pupils' work so that they are able to see it.

There are many different ways of displaying pupils' work. In any Early Years environment you should use a variety of these in different areas of the classroom.

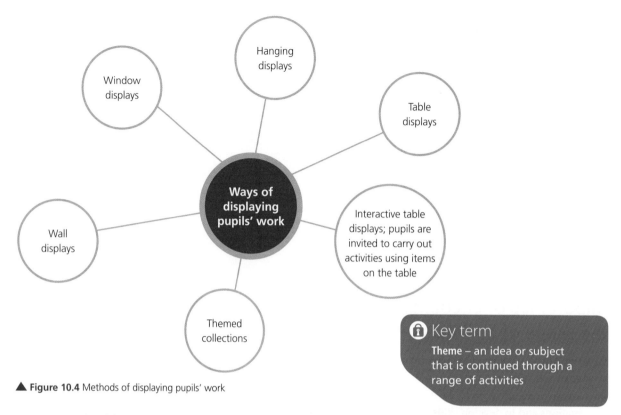

▲ **Figure 10.4** Methods of displaying pupils' work

Your setting should be able to provide a range of materials to enable staff to create effective displays. You can make displays more stimulating by choosing colours carefully, by creating three-dimensional effects using covered boxes and by using fabrics and other materials. Make sure you use a paper cutter to ensure that you follow any straight lines!

If you are inexperienced at displaying work, you may need to seek help from more experienced teaching assistants as there are many ways of doing this.

🔒 Key term

Theme – an idea or subject that is continued through a range of activities

❓ Thinking point

If you can, make regular opportunities to look at displays in other areas of your school to help you to gather ideas and see what kinds of materials are available.

Keys to good practice

Displaying pupils' work

✓ Think carefully about what you are going to do before you start.
✓ Prepare the background or choose backing paper and borders.
✓ Decide where to put any captions or information.
✓ Position pupils' work using pins first so that it can be moved as you work and stapled at the end.
✓ Use cross-cultural displays to promote positive images.
✓ Check displays are safe.
✓ Involve pupils and ask for their ideas if possible.
✓ Ensure all pupils' work is named.
✓ Do not be annoyed if pupils use interactive displays!

How to support children's confidence and self-esteem when they make and create things

You can support children's confidence and self-esteem in a variety of ways as they make and create things in different curriculum areas.

Suitable activities for the development of children's fine and gross motor skills

Children need to be given the opportunity to explore a range of activities in order to develop their physical skills. They need to develop muscle control so that they can build up both their fine and gross motor skills.

Gross motor skills

It is important to remember that although gross motor skills can be developed through running, hopping, skipping and so on, opportunities to enhance these skills should also include a wide range of activities such as climbing, riding bicycles, dance and games. Pupils need to have control over their bodies in different situations and to practise skills such as balance and co-ordination.

Fine motor skills

Young children may find these skills more difficult to acquire and need opportunities to develop skills in dressing and undressing (including buttons, zips and shoelaces), cutting, threading, holding and using a pencil, using a knife and fork, using a keyboard and mouse. Activities in sand and water can also develop fine motor skills, for example playing in wet sand will strengthen pupils' hands.

K16

Portfolio activity

Recognising opportunities to develop pupils' physical skills

Look at your class plans for the week and see how many opportunities there are for pupils to develop both their gross and fine motor skills.

How physical play can help children to assess risk in a safe and controlled environment

Children should be encouraged to play in different environments and with a range of equipment. They should always be supervised during **physical play**, as they are still developing their abilities to take responsibility for their safety and to understand how to assess risk. As they extend their experiences, they will be more able to anticipate the kinds of risks that may occur and actions that they can take to avoid them. They should be aware of any rules for the use of larger equipment and understand why these are necessary for everyone's safety.

> **ⓘ Key term**
>
> **Physical play** – play focusing on movement of the body.

Benefits to children of physical play and exercise

It is important to recognise that physical play and exercise are beneficial to all children as they are learning to develop their control over their bodies. They also need to learn how to recognise danger in their environment and act accordingly.

You may find that you have to manage pupils who find physical play challenging. This may be because they are over enthusiastic and/or unable to anticipate dangers to themselves or others. You may also find that you are supervising pupils who are overanxious about participating in physical activities. In both cases, such pupils may need to have individual supervision or be encouraged to stay with another pupil so that they are able to take part safely.

Keys to good practice

Supporting physical play activities

✓ Ensure pupils are supervised.
✓ Give pupils clear boundaries.
✓ Speak to pupils about the importance of safety and being aware of others.
✓ Give individual support where necessary.

Case study

Managing physical play safely

You are supervising a group of pupils in the outside area. There is a range of activities, including tricycles and scooters, sand, and large construction toys. The rules for the outside area state that the ride-on toys should stay in a particular area away from any activities under the shelter. You have had to speak to Molly and Orla because they are riding very close to the construction toys, which is making pupils playing in that area anxious. One of them, David, says that he wants to go inside as he is scared they will run him over.

- Why is it important that Molly and Orla understand the rules for the outside area?
- What would you say to pupils to resolve this problem?
- Should you encourage David to stay outside?

Kind of objects that engage children's interest at different ages and with different needs and abilities

For the purpose of this unit, you need to know about the kinds of **objects of interest** that engage pupils in Early Years classes. Your classroom should contain a range of materials and objects that encourage pupils' interest and enable them to use their senses. The kinds of objects that are appropriate may be educational resources, but can also be things you or the teacher have collected and brought to school. They should be displayed on interest tables or interactive displays so that all pupils have access to them.

> **🔒 Key term**
>
> **Objects of interest** – this includes any objects that interest children and can extend their learning, such as fossils or stones, living things like insects, and food items

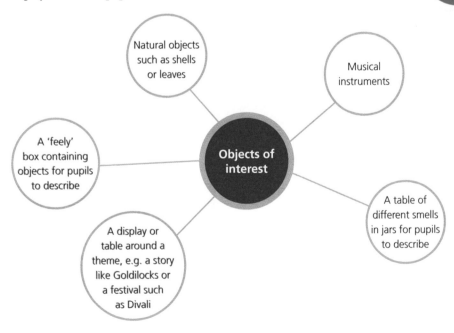

▲ Figure 10.5 Possible objects of interest

The objects should be suitable for the age range you are supporting and be available to all pupils whatever their needs. If you do not want pupils to touch particular objects, it is not appropriate to put them out on general display – children naturally want to explore whatever is available.

Benefits of learning to sort and classify

Children benefit from having the opportunity to group objects together because this helps them to practise their language and mathematical skills. Encourage them to think about and discuss the criteria by which they are sorting different objects. For example, if pupils are working with shapes, they should be able to tell you about the properties of the shapes, such as the size and the number of sides. They may be able to think of additional ways of classifying which you had not anticipated but which may be just as valid.

Keys to good practice
Using and sorting objects

✓ Check that items being used are safe.
✓ Make sure that objects cannot be damaged easily.
✓ Encourage pupils to explore objects using their senses.

K20 Case study
Supporting sorting activities

You are working with Cheryl and Nadeem in Year 1 (P2) to group together a series of objects they have been given. The items include readily available classroom equipment – Unifix counters, a variety of construction toys, small plastic bears of different sizes and a set of farm animals. The pupils are in a lower ability group for both Literacy and Numeracy and you have been asked to carry out the activity with particular attention to their language skills and ability to describe the objects.

● Name three different ways the pupils might sort the objects.
● What will be the benefits of this activity to their learning?

Benefits to children's learning of knowing about their own background and community

Young children in the early years of school are starting to understand that they have separate identities and personalities from one another and that they come from different backgrounds and cultures. Through learning about their community and where they fit in, children develop confidence in themselves and knowledge about their own local environment.

> **ⓘ Key term**
>
> **Community resources** – resources found in the local community, such as parks, allotments, libraries, people and organisations

Supporting a knowledge of community

Think about the kinds of opportunities pupils have in your school for developing their knowledge of their own community. Create a list or brainstorm the kinds of activities and **community resources** you might use to help them to do this.

How to provide a stimulating environment and not stifle children's curiosity, problem-solving and exploration

Classroom environments should:

- be welcoming, with bright and meaningful displays, and involve all in the class
- be accessible to all pupils, with areas clearly labelled for pupils to read
- contain different cultural representations of a multicultural society and make all pupils feel involved
- be changed or added to regularly, to create a 'living' environment, reflecting pupils' learning experiences
- represent different areas of the curriculum: role-play area, mathematical displays, hands-on investigative displays, creative area, etc.
- be maintained effectively, ensuring things are put away after use and pupils are involved in keeping it tidy.

You can provide a stimulating environment by thinking about different ways of attracting and sustaining pupil interest, for example through the use of interactive displays. It is important that you allow pupils time and opportunity to explore different activities without trying to 'take over' what they are doing and give so much adult intervention so that they are unable to direct themselves.

Importance and scope of practical daily activities such as cooking and gardening to enhance children's learning

Young children should have opportunities within the learning environment to take part in activities they can relate to their day-to-day experiences outside school. It is important that school is not seen as something separate from and unrelated to their daily lives and the kinds of activities you carry out with pupils should reflect this. Both cooking and gardening are examples of everyday activities that can be very beneficial learning experiences.

Creative development	• Planning and setting out where to grow different plants • Designing a garden • Creating different types of garden, e.g. sensory, flower or herb garden
Knowledge and understanding of the world	• Visit to shop or garden centre to buy plants and seeds • Predicting what will happen when seeds are planted • Growing plants for use in cooking and eating • Learning about seasons and which plants grow in different temperatures • Taking photos to record growth
Physical development	• Developing motor skills through digging, weeding, clearing, planting out.
Communication, language and literacy	• Naming plants and tools • Discussing the planting process • Making labels for seed trays • Learning new vocabulary
Problem-solving, reasoning and numeracy	• Sorting seeds • Working out cost of seeds and plants • Measuring water and growth of plants
Personal, social and emotional development	• Working in a group • Thinking about safety • Taking turns

How to set up activities to help children learn

When you are preparing activities, make sure that you have considered whether they are appropriate for the pupils with whom you are working. The most effective types of activities and equipment will be those that meet the needs of the pupils and provide them with a wide variety of experiences. An important aspect of this is thorough preparation.

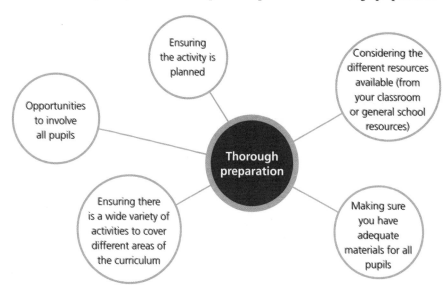

◀ Figure 10.6 Strategies for thorough preparation

How to lay out furniture and equipment to make the best use of space and help children gain access to play and learning activities

Part of your role in supporting play activities is to set up learning environments to enable all pupils to participate. As a member of staff in school, you must be aware of the rights of all pupils to have **equality of access** to the curriculum. Make sure that the layout in the classroom and outside area does not prevent any pupils from taking part in activities alongside their peers. In particular, you should think about the following points.

> **Key term**
>
> **Equality of access** – ensuring that discriminatory barriers to access are removed and allow for pupils' individual needs

Children who have a physical impairment

A physical impairment may hinder access to the curriculum for some pupils. When planning activities, ensure that any pupils who have impairments are not discriminated against, for example ensure all pupils can hear or see what is happening, and are able to participate.

Encouraging all pupils to allow their peers to have access

You may need to speak to younger pupils about allowing others to use resources or equipment. In an Early Years environment and, in particular, if pupils have a choice of activity, there may be pupils who like to dominate some areas of the classroom, for example involving sand or water play activities, or use of the computer. It is important to have some kind of system, allowing all pupils to have opportunities with different activities.

Involving and celebrating all cultures

Make sure that you include representations from other cultures through your plans and activities. This may be through stories, religious festivals, displays and talking to pupils from all cultures about their experiences.

Ensuring 'boy' and 'girl' activities do not become an issue

It can be the case that a group of boys or girls dominate certain activities in Early Years classrooms and you may need to encourage the involvement of particular pupils to ensure that everyone takes part and has the same opportunities.

In most Early Years classrooms there are different areas, which are set aside for particular activities.

Areas in Early Years classrooms
Role-play areas
Sand and water play
Quiet or book corners
An area for construction toys
An outdoor area
An area to listen to story tapes or CDs
A computer table or area
A painting table

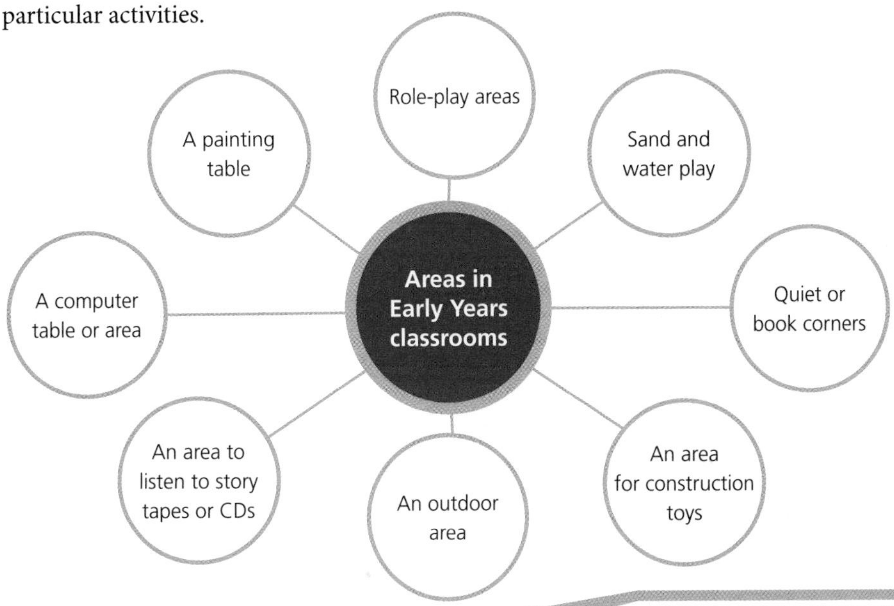

Figure 10.7 Areas in Early Years classrooms

Use of everyday routines to support play and learning

Your learning environment should be set up so that it supports play and learning through a range of activities, both indoor and outdoor, and including whole class, individual and group activities. Ways of approaching this will vary between settings, for example the timetable may mean that your class is only able to use the outside area at particular times of day. However, there should be opportunities for all pupils to experience the whole range of activities and equipment available. This means that planning and preparation should take account of any constraints such as timetables while ensuring that no groups of pupils are excluded from any activity. In many Early Years settings there will be opportunities for 'free play' activities, but you should ensure that particular pupils do not dominate these.

K13
K14
K19
K22
K24
K25
K26

For your portfolio...

This activity could also cover other knowledge points, depending on the activity, for example an ICT activity would include K7.

Plan and carry out a play activity which focuses on a particular curriculum area (e.g. creative development). Your plan should include:

- the resources you will use
- the skills pupils will be developing
- the kinds of opportunities pupils will have to develop their skills
- the extent of any adult intervention
- a risk assessment showing any health and safety issues to consider
- how you will set up the area to make the best use of space
- where the activity will fit into your daily routine.

If possible, after you have carried out the activity, create a classroom display to demonstrate how you can show the pupils' work to its best effect and take a photo of it for your portfolio.

Websites

www.acurriculumforexcellencescotland.gov.uk – curriculum for Scotland

www.nicurriculum.org – curriculum for Northern Ireland

www.opsi.gov.uk/ACTS/acts1998/19980029 – Data Protection Act

www.standards.dfes.gov.uk – curriculum for England and Wales

www.teachernet.gov.uk/teachingandlearning/EYFS – The Early Years Foundation

11 Contribute to Supporting Bilingual/Multilingual Pupils

This unit is for staff who support bilingual and multilingual pupils in the target language (English or Welsh) and looks at the way in which pupils develop their language skills. Pupils from bilingual and multilingual backgrounds need more support in the classroom when developing these skills. Teaching assistants will need to be aware of the way in which all children process language and the importance for bilingual and multilingual pupils of retaining their identity through valuing and promoting their home language. In this unit, you will identify strategies for promoting pupils' development in speaking/talking, listening, reading and writing in the target language, which may be English or Welsh. You will need to build on the pupils' experience when developing their skills in the target language and encourage them to develop as independent learners.

For this unit, you will need to know and understand:

- The school's policy and procedures for supporting bilingual/multilingual pupils

- The school's policies and practices for inclusion, equality of opportunity, multiculturalism and anti-racism

- The stages of language acquisition and the factors that promote or hinder language development

- Strategies suitable for supporting pupils in developing their language skills in the target language (see also K11, page 187)

- The interactive use of speaking/talking, listening, reading and writing to promote language development in pupils

- How to use praise and constructive feedback to promote pupils' learning

- The role of self-esteem in developing communication and self-expression and how to promote the self-esteem of pupils through the support you provide

- The curriculum plans and learning programmes developed by the teachers with whom you work when supporting bilingual/multilingual pupils

- How to obtain information about a pupil's language and educational background and skills, individual learning targets and language support needs

- How to provide appropriate support for bilingual/multilingual pupils according to their age, emotional needs, abilities and learning needs

- Strategies suitable for supporting pupils in developing their language skills through different learning activities and experiences across the curriculum

- How to feed back information on pupils' participation and progress in learning activities to teachers and contribute to planning for future learning

School's policy and procedures for supporting bilingual/multilingual pupils

According to government statistics, over 200 languages are spoken in the homes of pupils who attend British schools. If you have been asked to support bilingual and multilingual pupils, you need to think about how you can promote the development of the target language while valuing each pupil's home language and culture. This is particularly important if there is only one bilingual or multilingual pupil learning the target language in the class or group. The school should have its own

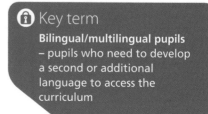

Key term

Bilingual/multilingual pupils – pupils who need to develop a second or additional language to access the curriculum

policies and practices for how pupils with English or Welsh as an additional language are supported and you need to know what your school has in place if you are supporting them. The different types of strategies may include:

- school policies to promote positive images and role models
- school policies and practices on inclusion, equal opportunities and multiculturalism
- identification of bilingual and multilingual pupils, for example, photos in that staffroom so that all staff are aware who the pupils are
- providing opportunities for pupils to develop their language skills
- having established school and class routines
- finding opportunities to talk with parents of bilingual pupils and encourage links with the school
- celebrating linguistic and cultural diversity.

Many schools also now have a governor and/or designated teacher with overall responsibility for EAL (English as an additional language) pupils, whose role is to advise other staff on the kinds of strategies that are most effective.

Portfolio activity K1 K2

Identifying policies that support bilingual and multilingual pupils

Find out what policies your school has which may be relevant to pupils from bilingual or multilingual backgrounds. How are bilingual pupils and their families supported within your school community?

School's policies and practices for inclusion, equality of opportunity, multiculturalism and anti-racism

You should also be aware of how your school's inclusion and/or equal opportunities policies relate to the needs of bilingual and multilingual pupils. Along with the policies for multiculturalism and anti-racism, they will give you guidelines for working with bilingual and multilingual pupils. For example, most schools celebrate a range of cultural festivals throughout the year and actively encourage community involvement to raise awareness of the different languages spoken in the school. Multicultural and anti-racism policies will outline the different ways in which the school recognises and celebrates different languages and cultures. Depending on the location and intake of your school, you may have a very high or very low number of these pupils and the policies will take account of this.

Stages of language acquisition and the factors that promote or hinder language development

In order to build up a picture of how we learn language, it is important to consider the two stages that linguists consider all children pass through. These are known as the pre-linguistic and the linguistic stages.

The pre-linguistic stage is during the first 12 months, when babies begin to learn basic communication skills. During this time they start to attract the attention of adults and repeat back to them the different sounds they hear. This is true of any language and, although babies are born with the potential to make the same sounds all over the world, by the age of 12 months they can only repeat back the sounds that they have heard around them.

The linguistic stage is when babies start to use the words that they are hearing and to learn how to make sentences. Children develop this stage gradually over the next few years so that by around 5 years of age they are fluent in their home language. Children who are learning more than one language may learn to speak slightly more slowly as they absorb different language systems. This should not, however, affect their overall language development. As children develop language, they need to have it reinforced through continuous stimulation so that as they become older their vocabulary expands from around 1,000 words at the age of 4 to around 20,000 at 16 years old.

Stages of language development in children

Age	Stage of development
0–6 months	Babies try to communicate through crying, starting to smile and babbling. They start to establish eye contact with adults.
6–18 months	Babies start to speak their first words. They start to use gestures to indicate what they mean. At this stage, they are able to recognise and respond to pictures of familiar objects.
18 months–3 years	Children start to develop their vocabulary rapidly and make up their own sentences. At this stage, children enjoy simple and repetitive rhymes and stories.
3–8 years	Children start to use more and more vocabulary and the structure of their language becomes more complex. As they develop their language skills, they are able to use language in a variety of situations.
8 + years	Children continue to develop the complexity of their language skills and their confidence in the use of language should begin to flourish. The attainment targets in the English National Curriculum set out the specific language skills expected of pupils at the different Key Stages.

Adults need to support pupils through all of the stages of development shown in the table above in order to encourage and promote their language development. At each stage, the role of the adult may be different. For example, a baby needs positive recognition of its attempts to communicate through eye contact and speech. A 5- or 6-year-old may need adults to help them extend their vocabulary through the use of open-ended questions or 'what if?' strategies. An older child may need to have specific vocabulary explained or guidance around the different nuances of how language may be interpreted.

Where children's language progresses more slowly through these stages, there may be other factors involved, such as:

- learning more than one language
- a communication difficulty such as autism
- a speech difficulty such as a stutter
- lack of stimulation from others
- a hearing impairment.

Research has shown that children need to 'tune in' when learning languages. It can be difficult for one person to speak two or more languages with a child, before the child's language development is properly established. In other words, children need to make an association between a language and the person with whom they speak it: a child who is learning to speak Arabic and English will be better equipped to distinguish between languages if they can link each language to different individuals.

Opportunities for developing language

Children and young people from all backgrounds, whether they are learning one or more languages, need to be given opportunities to develop their language skills in a variety of different ways. If pupils come to school only speaking their home language and needing to develop their English or Welsh, they need to have more support in order to do this. However, you should also remember that when learning a new language, it is normal to have a 'silent phase' when the learner is 'tuning in' to new sounds and vocabulary. It is important not to push pupils to speak before they are ready.

Keys to good practice

Developing language opportunities

✓ Creating a secure and happy environment where pupils and their families feel valued and part of the class and school
✓ Raising cultural awareness in school for all pupils
✓ Reinforcement of language learning using resources such as dual language texts
✓ Reinforcement of language learning by giving pupils immediate verbal and non-verbal feedback and praise
✓ Giving pupils time to think about questions before they respond
✓ Creating more opportunities for speaking and listening, such as paired conversations with others

Strategies suitable for supporting pupils in developing their speaking/talking, listening, reading and writing skills in the target language

Speaking/talking and listening skills

These skills need to be developed in EAL pupils and you may find that you are working with individuals or small groups to facilitate this. In very young children the approach may be different than for older pupils, but the strategies should be the same and should apply across the curriculum.

▲ **Figure 11.1** Working closely with children on lingual skills to help build their confidence

Opportunities to talk

Children and young people need to be given as much opportunity as possible to talk and discuss ideas with others. At a very young age this would include opportunities such as role play, whereas older children may enjoy discussions.

Physical cues and gestures

These might include gestures such as thumbs up, thumbs down, which enable pupils to make sense of the situation more quickly.

Songs and rhymes

Younger children develop concepts of pattern and rhyme in language through learning nursery rhymes and songs. These are also an enjoyable way of developing pupils' language skills as well as being part of a group. You may also be able to introduce rhymes and songs in other languages for all pupils to learn and so develop their cultural awareness.

Games

Opportunities for games are useful as they help pupils to socialise with others as well as practise their language skills.

Practical examples

These can help pupils when they are being given instructions, for example showing a model when a group is going to work together.

Discussing with a partner first

This may help EAL pupils gain confidence when they have to tell their ideas to the class. They should work with a variety of partners who will provide good language models.

Appropriate vocabulary

Staff need to think about the language they use with bilingual and multilingual pupils to ensure that it is appropriate to the individual's age and level of understanding. If a teacher talks to the group and uses language that is difficult to understand, you may need to clarify what has been said for the bilingual and multilingual pupils.

Purposeful listening

If pupils have entered school with very limited experience of the target language, you may be asked to work with them on specific areas of language. For example, the teacher may be focusing on positional words to ensure that pupils understand words such as 'behind', 'above', 'below', 'next to' and so on. You could work with pictures or other resources to help the bilingual or multilingual pupil develop their understanding of these words.

Explain the purpose of the activity

Pupils should be aware of why they are undertaking a particular activity and what they are going to learn from it.

Reading and writing skills

Pupils who are learning to speak English or Welsh as an additional language will need to have opportunities to read and listen to books in the target language. This is so that they can associate their developing verbal and written skills with the printed page. Bilingual pupils will also benefit from working with the rest of the class or group during Literacy sessions. They should be able to share texts with the class or group, although the teacher may need to use additional strategies so that they maximise learning opportunities. These strategies should be clear to you so that you can support pupils through reinforcing the skills that are being taught. Such strategies may include:

- using repetitive texts
- revising the previous week's work to build confidence
- using pictures to point out individual words
- making sure they pace the lesson to give bilingual pupils time to read the text
- grouping EAL pupils according to their actual ability rather than their understanding or knowledge of English or Welsh
- pairing EAL pupils with a partner or an adult to work on shared writing activities
- displaying and referring to a selection of vocabulary that is relevant to the topic
- giving praise and encouragement wherever possible
- using computer programs to help with reading.

Pupils who are also learning to speak English or Welsh may need adult support to decipher the meaning of some words when they are learning to read. They may need more support during shared or guided reading sessions, but should benefit from these as they will be able to model good practice from other pupils. As with their peers, they need to experience a wide variety of texts, both fiction and non-fiction, in order to maximise their vocabulary. Even if a pupil is able to read and understand more than expected, staff should continue to extend their vocabulary by discussing the text further.

Case study

Supporting pupils in developing their speaking/talking skills

You are working in a large inner-city secondary school in which 40 per cent of pupils speak English as an additional language. You work closely with the teacher who has responsibility for Ethnic Minority Achievement Strategy (EMAS) in the school and take groups out of classes every day to develop their English language skills through targeted activities. Today you have a new pupil in one of your groups. You did not have any notice that she was coming and she is very self-conscious about speaking in front of others.

- What might you do to support her, both initially and in the long term?
- Give examples of the kinds of strategies you could use if she remains reluctant to speak.

How to use praise and constructive feedback to promote pupils' learning

As with all situations, effective use of praise is very important when working with bilingual pupils as they may be insecure in the target language. Through the use of a positive learning environment and opportunities for them to develop relationships with others, you will encourage and support their learning.

Examples of this might be:

- repeating what the teacher is saying
- explaining what has been said
- rehearsing with pupils before they respond
- acting as a talk partner with pupils
- encouraging pupils with smiles, nods, gestures and body language.

When giving pupils feedback in learning situations, you may also need to 'remodel' language when repeating words or phrases back to them, or to extend their responses. For example, if a pupil uses an incorrect tense such as 'I go to the shops at the weekend', you could respond 'You went to the shops at the weekend? What did you buy?' rather than specifically pointing out the error.

Role of self-esteem in developing communication and self-expression and how to promote the self-esteem of pupils

It is very important for all bilingual pupils that staff in school are aware of their home language and culture. This is because a bilingual pupil's perception of how others see them will affect their self-esteem and their confidence when using language. It is especially important for pupils' names to be pronounced correctly and for everyone to be aware of this. If their parents do not speak English, this may be the pupil's first experience of having to communicate with others in a language other than their own. It is important for the pupil to be able to communicate in school and, although bilingual pupils usually pick up language reasonably quickly, this can be a difficult time for them. If you notice that any pupils are finding it hard to make friends, it is important to discuss this with teachers. You may also be able to help pupils to socialise with others through clubs and extra-curricular activities.

▶ **Figure 11.2** Encourage children to socialise

Case study K7

Supporting the development of self-esteem

Amal is a new pupil in your year group and she does not speak any English. Although she has made friends and is involved in class activities, you have noticed that at breaks and lunchtimes she is often on her own.

● What kind of support does Amal need and why?
● List three strategies you could use to help her to develop her self-esteem.

Curriculum plans and learning programmes

Bilingual pupils should be integrated into whole class or year group teaching and learning programmes alongside their peers as much as possible. You need to support them to develop their social as well as their academic skills, and through involvement with others and access to the school curriculum they will have the ideal base from which to develop these skills. The curriculum plans developed by the teacher will give opportunities for bilingual pupils to practise speaking and listening skills in the target language, and additional strategies or opportunities should be outlined in the plans to which you should have access.

Portfolio activity K8

Identifying how plans support bilingual and multilingual pupils

Using a daily or weekly plan, show how work is differentiated for bilingual pupils. Highlight examples of the kinds of activities or specific vocabulary that you focus on with these pupils. Alternatively, show a copy of the plan to your assessor when he/she comes to observe you in school.

How to obtain information about a pupil's language and educational background and skills, individual learning targets and language support needs

When a pupil from a different background, culture or language from others in the class or year group enters school, it may be a difficult experience for them, particularly if they have not been in an educational environment before. They may find it hard due to lack of confidence or self-esteem, and staff need to be aware of their needs. The different backgrounds and skills of individual pupils as they come into school will all influence their learning and the development of the target language. It can be very difficult to assess the needs of bilingual pupils and staff need to find out whatever they can about each pupil when they first enter school in order to support them fully.

Usually the school will have systems in place when pupils first enter school so that they are aware of those who speak English or Welsh as a second language. Parents will have been asked to fill in forms before the pupils enter school and home visits can sometimes be a valuable way of gathering information. Sometimes bilingual assistants will be employed, especially where there are a large number of pupils who speak one particular language. Specific assessments or observations may also be carried out on pupils.

Educational backgrounds

When pupils first enter a new school at any stage, there should be records from their previous school, which will give some indication of their progress in the target language to date. If your school is the first contact the pupil has had with the target language, the school will need to devise educational targets for them to work on so that they can begin to develop their new language skills.

It is important to gain as much information as possible from the pupil's previous school if they have transferred. The previous school is required to send records of assessment and attainment, but these may take some time to come through and teachers may need to contact the school, particularly if there is an area of concern.

When pupils come from very different educational backgrounds from others in the class or year group, they may take more time to settle into school, for example, if they have come from an area where there are many bilingual pupils to one where there are very few, or from an area where learning styles are different.

Other agencies such as speech therapists may also have been involved with the pupil's development and records from these professionals will be useful in finding out about pupil background.

Home backgrounds

These will be varied and have the greatest influence on pupils. Those such as refugees whose home backgrounds have been traumatic may have had wide and varied educational experiences. The school needs to obtain as much information as possible about the pupil's background and if possible seek the help of an interpreter to discuss this directly with the parents or carers.

A pupil's past experiences may affect their behaviour. It may also be difficult to obtain information from home and this can cause problems with issues such as sickness notes or information forms being completed and returned to school.

Pupils who come from backgrounds with a different culture or religion from the majority of others in the school may feel isolated and it is important for them that the school values cultural diversity. Staff also need to be aware of religious issues that can affect pupils' learning, such as fasting during Ramadan. Issues of health and physical development may have been discussed with other professionals and these checks should also be included in the pupil's records.

Language backgrounds

Pupils who come into school with English or Welsh as a second language or those who are multilingual may find settling in difficult due to the development of their language skills in the target language or to a combination of factors. If staff know that a pupil has never been exposed to the target language before, this knowledge can help them to devise their educational plan. However, pupils who come into school at 4 years old need a different level of support from those who come into school at 10 or 14 years old. Teachers need to ensure that each pupil has a plan that takes individual learning needs into account, including specific targets where appropriate.

Case study

K9

Gathering information on language and emotional support needs

You have been asked to work with Robina, a Pakistani pupil who has just come into school in Year 3 (P4). This is her second English-language school and she does speak some English.

- How would you go about gathering information on her language support needs?
- What emotional support might Robina need?

How to provide appropriate support for bilingual/ multilingual pupils according to their age, emotional needs, abilities and learning needs

Pupils may feel differently about the experience of learning an additional language for a variety of reasons. You need to know how these factors might affect how you support their learning.

Age

A pupil's age may make a difference to how they learn language. Older pupils may find it more challenging due to the demands of the curriculum and the fact that they need to learn to speak, read and write in English in order to access it. They may also be self-conscious and, as a result, less likely to attempt to speak. A younger pupil may be less anxious about acquiring language and more relaxed about attempting to speak. Research has shown that the younger the child, the easier it is for them to learn additional languages. For individuals to initiate language, they need to feel relaxed and confident that their contributions will be valued.

Emotional needs

Bilingual pupils may have to make significant adjustments to life in a new country. They will often have found it a real 'culture shock' and have great anxiety, not only about communicating with others, but also in adapting to their new environment. However, it may also be an advantage to them to be in a structured and secure environment if they have experienced trauma or an unsettled period.

A pupil's emotional needs can result in the following effects:

- pupil becomes withdrawn
- pupil is frustrated by being unable to communicate and displays behaviour problems
- pupil is anxious and reluctant to participate in class activities.

All of these effects make it difficult to participate in classroom activities so make sure that you develop as many strategies as possible for pupils who need emotional support.

▼ Figure 11.3 The importance of responding to pupils' needs

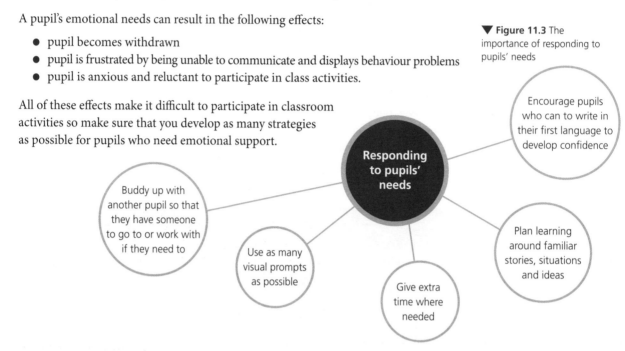

Abilities and learning needs

Remember that the fact that pupils speak additional languages is not a reflection of their general ability. Speaking two or more languages is a gift and should be celebrated, but pupils may be of higher or lower general ability in the same way that all learners are. However, it may take longer to determine if these pupils have any additional needs and this is another reason why it is important to monitor their development of the target language.

K10 Case study

Supporting different abilities and learning needs

You are working with a group of primary pupils of different ages who all speak Tamil. Although they have the language in common, their needs and abilities are all different. Dayalan speaks very little English and has just come to this country. Gangesh has lived in this country all his life, but has always spoken Tamil at home, needs extra support with his English and is of average ability. Nithila is bilingual and able in her work, but is very anxious and reluctant to speak English, although she is able to.

- Would you approach the support you give these pupils differently even if you had to group them together?
- How could you balance the different needs of the pupils while supporting them effectively?

Supporting pupils through different learning activities and experiences

When supporting bilingual and multilingual pupils, you need to use a variety of strategies to support them as they develop their language skills. Think about:

- whole school strategies for supporting these pupils (see K1, page 176)
- strategies for developing speaking and listening, reading and writing skills (see K4, page 176)
- class or group strategies that particularly support bilingual or multilingual pupils in different situations or subject areas (K6, page 182 and K8, page 183)
- individual targets where appropriate (K9, page 184).

Although you may be working across the curriculum in many cases, language will be the vehicle through which pupils are learning and many of the strategies you should use will be similar to those used to develop literacy skills. If pupils have access to a broad and balanced curriulum, they develop their language skills all the time during learning activities. After consultation with teachers, you may find that you need to adapt and modify the learning resources pupils are using in order to help them to access the curriculum more fully. You may also need to explain and reinforce the vocabulary used in class, for example during a topic or particular subject area. Often the types of resources and vocabulary that benefit bilingual pupils are also useful for other pupils in the class or group.

▼ **Figure 11.4** It is useful to have examples of what you are discussing so that pupils can quickly and easily relate them to their experience

How to feed back information on pupils' participation and progress

When working with bilingual and multilingual pupils, you need to provide frequent feedback to others on their progress. You will need to report to other professionals such as form tutors, individual teachers, the Special Educational Needs Co-ordinator (Additional Support for Learning Teacher) and possibly EAL teachers who visit the school. You should have opportunities to contribute to meetings and/or paperwork such as Individual Education Plans concerning pupils with whom you are working. It is important that there is a 'joined-up' approach from all those who are working with bilingual pupils so that their progress can be measured.

K4
K5
K6
K7
K8
K9
K10
K11
K12

For your portfolio...

Your assessor should have the opportunity to observe you working with the bilingual or multilingual pupils you support. Be prepared to talk to your assessor about the pupils' backgrounds and language needs as well as showing a range of strategies for supporting their learning. Check with your assessor that you have covered all the learning points above.

Websites

The following websites are regularly updated with articles and information to support the inclusion of speakers of additional languages.

www.becta.org.uk/inclusion/inclusion_lang/community – Becta community languages website

www.britishcouncil.org

www.dfes.gov.uk – the standards site has information under EAL learners

www.freeenglish.com – has resources for those wishing to learn English

www.mantrapublishing.com – this company produces a range of books in different languages

www.naldic.org.uk – the National Association for Language Development in the Curriculum aims to raise attainment of EAL learners; the website contains a number of links and resources

www.qca.org.uk – qualifications and curriculum authority

www.teachernet.gov.uk – type in 'EAL' under 'search'

12 Support a Child with Disabilities or Special Educational Needs

This unit is for those who work in mainstream or special schools with pupils who have special educational (additional support for learning (ASL)) needs or disabilities. This role requires you to have skills in a number of areas. You may have a high level of responsibility for working with these pupils and need to work in partnership with the pupil and with others who support them, both at home and to provide education. You will need to be able to relate well to a variety of different people, including parents, carers and other professionals.

For your S/NVQ, you will need to show how the needs of the pupil or pupils impact on the support you provide both to them and their families and how you adapt what you do to manage them. You will have to identify the resources available to you and it would be sensible to access any training as it becomes available.

However, the situations that cause pupils to have 'difficulty in learning' will differ because individuals have special educational (ASL) needs during different periods in their schooling. Some pupils may have learning needs and require support for short periods during their school careers but may eventually cease to need help. A pupil with a disability may also require varying degrees of support from the school and local services at different times. Other pupils may be traumatised by bereavement or the separation of parents and need to have close support for a time to enable them to continue to access the curriculum.

What you need to know and understand

For this unit, you will need to know and understand:

- Laws and codes of practice affecting provision for disabled children and young people and those with special educational needs within your home country

- Specialist local and national support and information that is available for disabilities and special educational needs

- Partnerships with parents and families are at the heart of provision as they know most about their child and how partnerships can be encouraged

- The importance of not labelling children and young people and having realistic expectations

- How integration/inclusion works in your setting and local area and the reasons for its benefits or otherwise

- Details about particular disabilities or special educational needs affecting the children or young people in your care

- How to use Alternative and Augmentative Communication and assist children or young people through use of all their available senses

- Planning for each child or young person's individual requirements in partnership with other colleagues

- What barriers may exist preventing children or young people's participation and how to remove these barriers

- How to make sure what you do is suitable for all the children or young people you work with, according to their age, needs and abilities

- What specialist aids and equipment are available for the children or young people you work with and how to use these safely

- The possible impact of having a child or young person with a disability or special educational need within a family

Laws and codes of practice

You need to have some idea about the kinds of laws that affect the provision your school makes for pupils who have disabilities and **special educational (ASL) needs**. There have been many changes to the relevant legislation in the UK over recent years. A very brief outline is listed below.

Education Act (Handicapped Children) 1970

Until this time, children with special educational (ASL) needs were looked after by the health service. This act transferred the responsibility for their education to the local authority and as a result many special schools were built.

 Key term

Special educational (ASL) needs are defined in Code of Practice 2001 as the child having:

- 'a significantly greater difficulty in learning than the majority of children the same age'

- 'a disability which prevents or hinders them from making use of educational facilities of a kind generally provided for children of the same age'

The Warnock Report 1978

This was a Report rather than an Act of legislation, but it had an impact on subsequent Acts of parliament as it was a study of the needs of SEN (special educational (ASL) needs) children. It introduced a number of suggestions as to how children with these needs should be supported – through access to the curriculum, changes to the curriculum and changes to the environment. It influenced the Special Educational Needs (SEN) Code of Practice 2001 through its focus on inclusion.

Education Act 1981

This was based on the findings of the Warnock Report and gave additional legal responsibilities to local authorities as well as power to parents.

Education Reform Act 1988

This introduced the National Curriculum into all schools in England and Wales. Although this meant that all schools had to teach the same basic curriculum, it allowed schools to change or modify what was taught for pupils' special educational (ASL) needs if the basic curriculum was not appropriate for them.

Children Act 1989

The welfare of the child must be considered at all times and their rights and wishes should be taken into consideration. The Scottish equivalent is the Children (Scotland) Act 1995.

Education Act 1993

This required that a Code of Practice be introduced for guidance on the identification and provision of special educational (ASL) needs. The role of the SENCo (Special Educational Needs Co-ordinator)(ASL teacher) was introduced in schools and parents were able to challenge local authorities about providing for SEN (ASL) pupils.

Disability Discrimination Act 1995

This made it illegal for services such as shops and employers to discriminate against disabled people.

Carers and Disabled Children Act 2001

This was the first Act that recognised the needs of carers as well as those of children.

SENDA and Special Educational Needs (SEN) Code of Practice 2001

The Special Educational Needs and Disability Act (SENDA) strengthens the rights of parents and SEN (ASL) children to a mainstream education.

Every Child Matters 2005

This was put into place to ensure that all organisations and agencies involved with children between the ages of birth and 19 years should work together to ensure that children have the support needed to be healthy, stay safe, enjoy and achieve, make a positive contribution and achieve economic well-being. The acronym SHEEP can help you remember this:

Stay safe   **Healthy**   **Enjoy and achieve**   **Economic well-being**   **Positive contribution**

Specialist local and national support and information that is available for disabilities and special educational needs

You need to have access to additional support for the pupils you are working alongside, as do their parents and carers. This support may come through services within your school, local authority or NHS trust, or you may find it through your own research into particular conditions or impairments. You may need to have training if you have not worked with SEN (ASL) pupils before or to ask your SENCo (ASL teacher) where local support might be available.

Some teaching assistants work with pupils on the autistic spectrum. It is likely that your local authority will have information and support will be available to schools. It will also be able to refer you to any local or national support groups.

Partnerships with parents and families and how they can support others

Many parents who have children with disabilities or special educational (ASL) needs have become experts on the particular need or condition. They may have researched in detail what support is available and have access to special groups or other sources of help. With their experience of the difficulties as carers, they will also be in a good position to offer sympathy and support to other families in similar circumstances. Partnerships with parents and families are crucial to the process of working with SEN (ASL) pupils. Schools will also need to ensure that they are as supportive as possible through clear communication and discussion with parents.

K2 K3 Portfolio activity

Accessing additional support and working with families

- Show how you have sought additional support for a pupil with specific needs, indicating what support was available locally and nationally.
- Explain how parents and carers of pupils with special educational (ASL) needs have been involved in supporting and helping other pupils and their families in the community.
- Explain how you have worked in partnership with the parents of pupils you support.

(See also the websites at the end of this unit.)

Importance of not labelling children and young people and having realistic expectations

Medical and social models of disability, from *Disability Discrimination in Education Course Book: Training for Inclusion and Disability Equality*.

Medical model	Social model
Pupil is faulty	Pupil is valued
Diagnosis	Strengths and needs defined by self and others
Labelling	Identify barriers/develop solutions
Impairment is focus of attention	Outcome-based programme designed
Segregation or alternative services	Training for parents and professionals
Ordinary needs put on hold	Relationships nurtured
Re-entry if 'normal' or permanent exclusion	Diversity is welcomed and pupil is included
Society remains unchanged	Society evolves

When you are working with pupils who have special educational (ASL) needs, you will find that many professionals and parents speak about the danger of 'labelling' pupils. This is because it is important that we look at the needs of the individual first, rather than focusing on the pupil's disability or impairment. In the past, the **medical model of disability** has been used more frequently than a **social model** and this kind of language has promoted the attitude that people with disabilities are individuals who in some way need to be corrected or brought into line with everybody else. This has sometimes led to unhelpful labelling of individuals in terms of their disabilities rather than their potential.

You should also be realistic about the expectations you have of pupils and consider their learning needs. For some, although not all, the curriculum will need to be modified and pupils may need support. However, it should not be assumed that SEN (ASL) pupils will always need support and you need to encourage them to be as independent as possible.

> **🛈 Key term**
>
> **Social and medical models of disability** – the medical model reflects the traditional view of disability, that it is something to be 'cured', treating the individual as a sick patient. The social model considers that it is society that needs to change and that disabled people have rights and choices

How integration/inclusion works in your setting and local area and the reasons for its benefits or otherwise

Inclusion/**integration** is a process by which schools, local education authorities and others develop their cultures, policies and practices to include all pupils. It does not refer only to pupils with special educational (ASL) needs, but aims to give all pupils the benefits of equal opportunities in school. However, inclusion has become more closely associated with special educational (ASL) needs as the term has been used widely since the introduction of the SEN Code of Practice 2001. The theory is that with the right training, strategies and support nearly all SEN (ASL) pupils can be included successfully in mainstream education.

> **🛈 Key term**
>
> **Integration** – inclusion of pupils with disabilities, special educational (ASL) or additional support needs in a mainstream setting

The benefits of inclusion should be clear – that all pupils are entitled to be educated together and are able to access the same education without any form of discrimination or barriers to participation.

You need to speak to your assessor about your school's inclusion or equal opportunities policies (see also Unit 14, page 203) and identify the ways in which pupils who have special educational (ASL) needs and disabilities are integrated into school. Alternatively you could carry out the portfolio activity below. You should be able to identify the measures taken in your school to promote inclusion and the kinds of attitudes staff and parents have towards pupils with special educational (ASL) needs.

In some cases, it may be the view of parents or the school that provision for SEN (ASL) pupils would be better met in a specialist school or unit. This can be difficult if the school's view does not match the view of the parents, particularly because if the pupil has a Statement of Special Educational Needs (Co-ordinated Support Plan), parents have the final say in where the child is educated. The SEN Code of Practice, page 190, gives some guidance and advice to schools where it is felt that the pupil's needs would be better met in a different school.

Keys to good practice

Promoting inclusion in your school

✓ Have high expectations of pupils.
✓ Celebrate and value diversity rather than fear it.
✓ Be aware that all pupils have more in common than is different.
✓ Encourage the participation of all pupils in the curriculum and social life of the school.
✓ Work to include pupils in the main activities of the class wherever possible.
✓ Develop 'can do' attitudes in pupils through appropriate degrees of challenge and support.

K5 Portfolio activity

Identifying how inclusion works in your school

● What can you say about inclusion in your school?
● How effective is it in your experience?
● Do you think that its advantages outweigh any disadvantages you can identify?

Details about particular disabilities or special educational needs affecting the children or young people in your care

For this knowledge point, you need to identify the specific details of the disabilities and special educational (ASL) needs of pupils with whom you work and discuss how you have managed them with the support available to you. You need to show how you have worked with others in the school and local authority to provide a high-quality service to these pupils. For example, you should have information from the school's teachers and SENCo/ASL teacher about each pupil's needs. You may also work with professionals such as occupational or physiotherapists, who may advise you on the kind of provision that should be provided by the school and give suggestions as to how you can best support the pupils.

How to use Alternative and Augmentative Communication and assist children or young people through use of all their available senses

As part of your role in supporting teaching and learning in the classroom, you need to be aware that pupils who have communication difficulties may need specialist resources or equipment. You may also need to have training in the use of communication technologies such as voice recognition software.

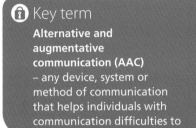

ⓘ Key term

Alternative and augmentative communication (AAC) – any device, system or method of communication that helps individuals with communication difficulties to communicate more easily

Case study K7

Assisting pupils to communicate

You are working with Jenny, a hearing-impaired pupil in Year 1 (P2). She has just been given a new digital hearing aid and you have been asked to help her with it as you have supported a hearing-impaired child in the past. However, this hearing aid is different from the one you are familiar with, Jenny's mother has not shown you what to do and the sensory support teacher is only in school on Thursdays.

- What would you do, both in the short and long term?
- What alternative communication devices have you used in your work with pupils and how have they made use of the pupils' available senses?

Planning for each child or young person's individual requirements in partnership with other colleagues

Lesson plans should always include differentiated activities for pupils who have special educational (ASL) needs. If you plan alongside the teacher you may be able to make suggestions at this stage for the pupils you support. You may also have had input from other professionals as to the kinds of strategies or equipment you could use. Any additional training you have had around the needs of the individual may also give you ideas about the kinds of activities and resources that will be beneficial.

You may still need to adapt work, however, if the pupil is finding it challenging. Monitor pupil participation and intervene if necessary so that they are able to achieve the learning intention.

Portfolio activity

Planning for individual needs

Using a plan you have devised alongside the teacher, show how you have planned for the needs of different pupils in your class, including those who have special educational (ASL) needs. If you have had to adapt the plan to make it more accessible for pupils as you work, annotate the plan to show this.

What barriers may exist preventing children or young people's participation and how to remove these barriers

All pupils, whatever their needs and abilities, have an equal right to education and learning. Equal opportunities should include not only access to provision but also to facilities within and outside the school setting. Schools and other organisations that offer educational provision must by law ensure that all pupils have access to a broad and balanced curriculum.

▲ Figure 12.1 Barriers to inclusion

Provision in schools may be affected by any of the above **barriers to participation** if the school does not take active steps to make sure that they do not occur. It is important that schools:

- have high expectations of pupils and develop their attitudes of self-belief through appropriate challenges
- celebrate and value diversity, rather than fear it
- are aware that all pupils have more in common than is different
- encourage the participation of all pupils in the curriculum and social life of the school
- work to include all pupils in the main activities of the class wherever possible.

🔒 Key term

Barriers to participation – anything that prevents the pupil participating fully in activities and experiences offered by the setting or service

Barriers that prevent participation

You have just started to work with Kayleigh, who uses a wheelchair, in Year 5 (P6). One of the parents in the class comes to see you and says that Kayleigh won't be able to go on a week-long residential trip due to take place early in Year 6 (P7) as there are no facilities for 'children like that'. You are concerned both by the attitude of the parent and by the possibility that Kayleigh may not be able to go on the trip.

- What would you do?
- How can schools go about removing social barriers such as these if they exist?

How to make sure what you do is suitable for all the children/young people you work with, according to their age, needs and abilities

You need to know how the pupils you are supporting differ from their peers in their expected pattern of development. If you routinely work with pupils of a particular age range, it will be easier for you to identify whether they are fitting the normal pattern of development for their age. (See Unit 2 for stages of physical and cognitive development, page 31.) You will also get to know what they are capable of doing, or if tiredness or medication is affecting whether or not they can continue.

If you are supporting pupils with special educational (ASL) needs, both you and the teacher need to make sure that planned activities are appropriate for the pupils' specific needs. If tasks are too difficult or unsuitable, they may become frustrated or anxious, which will make them reluctant to attempt further activities. If you are unsure of the kinds of activities that are suitable, always find out exactly what pupils are capable of and about their specific needs by asking parents, professionals who work with them or others who have supported them in the past.

Figure 12.2 Finding the right activity will increase learning and enjoyment

Case study

Identifying appropriate approaches

You work in a junior school, which is separate from the infant school on the same site. This year you will be working in Year 3 (P4) and supporting Tom, who has a severe visual impairment and has come up from the infants. You and the class teacher have been given plenty of paperwork detailing Tom's needs, which you have read, but you do not feel that you 'know' him yet.

● How would you find out more about Tom's needs and the kinds of approaches that might be helpful?

What specialist aids and equipment are available for the children/young people you work with and how to use these safely

If you work with specialist equipment, you need to show it to your assessor and explain how it is used. For example, you may work with a pupil who needs to use mobility equipment such as a walking frame in order to fully access the curriculum. In this instance you should talk through its use and your role in setting it up and using it

▲ **Figure 12.3** Access must be equal for all

safely for the pupil. If you are unable to show the equipment to your assessor, you need to have a professional discussion or write about what is involved. The increased use of technology in schools means that pupils will often use aids that will require you to have specific training.

Possible impact of having a child or young person with a disability or special educational need within a family

If you are working with pupils who have special educational (ASL) needs and disabilities, you need to have an awareness of how their needs affect those closest to them. If a pupil has had a disability or special educational (ASL) need throughout their time in school, the family will have had time to become used to the fact that they may need additional support. However the everyday pressures of caring for their child, for example coping with the reactions of others, could mean that they may become tired or find their child's needs difficult to manage on a day-to-day basis. Parents and carers have varied responses because each child and situation is different, and need to be treated accordingly.

Parents may feel angry or isolated when their child's needs are first identified or may not want their child to go for assessments because they do not want them to be 'labelled'. They may need to have access to appropriate specialist support groups and organisations, which are available to families of children who have special educational (ASL) needs or disabilities. (See the end of this unit for examples.)

Case study K12

Recognising the impact of special needs on the family

You are working in a special school. Before pupils start at the school, it is normal practice for home visits to take place so that staff can meet the pupils and parents in their own homes. Today you are visiting the home of Ben, who has severe learning needs. Your school is expecting him to start the following week and you are being accompanied by your colleague, who is a teacher in the school. When you arrive at the house, you are greeted by the child's grandmother, who says that his mother is unable to meet you, and that she regularly cares for Ben as his mother gets very tired. Ben also has two younger brothers who are very lively.

- What sort of impact might Ben's needs be having on his family?
- How might the school be able to assist the family in getting help and support?

For your portfolio...

The most useful way of gathering knowledge-base evidence for this unit is to have a professional discussion with your assessor. Decide beforehand what you would like to cover so that you are ready to answer, but be prepared to talk about the particular needs of the pupil or pupils you support and your role in relation to this. An example of a plan for discussion might be:

K6
K8
K10
- look through and talk about the pupil's Individual Education Plan and discuss their needs

K3
K5
K12
- describe the relationship between the school and the child's parents, and specific support that is needed

K2
K7
K11
- explain how you plan to support the pupil's individual needs and explain the use of any specialist terminology or equipment

Further reading

There are a number of magazines and periodicals available for school staff who support SEN (ASL) pupils, such as *Special Children* and *Special! Magazine*. You should also keep up to date by reading the *Times Educational Supplement* and checking websites such as those listed below.

Special Educational Needs Code of Practice 2001; DfES publications, Ref: DfES 581/2001

Websites

www.bbc.co.uk/health – advice on a range of conditions and illnesses

www.cafamily.org.uk – national charity for families of disabled children

www.diseed.org.uk – national charity supporting the inclusion of disabled people in mainstream education, through the provision of training, consultancy and resources

www.direct.gov.uk – go to 'Special educational needs' for advice and support

www.everychildmatters.gov.uk

www.ncb.org.uk – National Parent Partnership Network, supporting parents and children

www.specialfamilies.org – national charity for families of disabled children

www.surestart.gov.uk – government programme to deliver the best start in life for every child

14 Support Individuals during Therapy Sessions

This unit is for those who support pupils in mainstream or special schools who have therapy sessions as part of their teaching and learning programmes. You will need to know how to support therapists and pupils best before, during and after therapy sessions. This may be for pupils who have needs such as speech and language therapy or physiotherapy and may take place on or off the school site.

You should be prepared to deal with some of the risks and effects of different areas of therapy and to speak to individuals and their advocates or interpreters about any concerns that arise. These may touch on practical or social and emotional areas.

You may need the support of an expert witness for this unit as some of the performance may be outside the area of your assessor's expertise. However, your assessor will make the final judgement about your competence based on testimony provided by the expert witness together with any other supporting evidence.

What you need to know and understand

For this unit, you need to know and understand:

Values

- Legal and organisational requirements on equality, diversity, discrimination and rights when supporting during therapy sessions

- How to provide active support and promote the individual's rights, choices and well-being when supporting them to take part in therapy sessions

Legislation and organisational policy and procedures

- Codes of practice and conduct; standards and guidance relevant to your own and the roles, responsibilities, accountability and duties of others when supporting individuals to take part in therapy sessions

- Current local, UK and European legislation, and organisational requirements, procedures and practices for:

    - a   accessing records

    - b   recording, reporting, confidentiality and sharing information, including data protection

    - c   health, safety, assessing and managing risks associated with supporting individuals prior to, during and after therapy sessions

    - d   supporting individuals prior to, during and after therapy sessions

Theory and practice

- Key changes that may occur to individuals with whom you work and actions to take in these circumstances

- The impact of stress and fear on behaviour and the individual's ability to take part in and use therapy sessions effectively

- The conditions and impairments that the therapy is addressing

- The benefits and problems that might occur prior to, during and after therapy sessions

- The outcomes that therapy sessions aim to achieve for individuals

- The best ways of supporting the individuals through therapy sessions

- How to form a supportive relationship with individuals to enable them to benefit as much as possible from the therapy

- How to observe and record observations to support therapy sessions

- The key signs of problems and difficulties that need to be reported to the therapist

- How to involve the individual in collecting information about their experience of the therapy and its outcomes

- How to deal with conflicts arising prior to, during and after therapy sessions

- The risks, dangers and difficulties associated with different equipment and materials and in relation to specific individuals

Legal and organisational requirements on equality, diversity, discrimination and rights

All pupils, whatever their needs and abilities, have an equal **right** to education and learning. Equal opportunities should include not only access to provision but also to facilities within and outside the school setting. Schools and other organisations that offer educational provision must by law ensure that all pupils have access to a broad and balanced curriculum. You need to find out about the organisational requirements for promoting equal opportunities and celebrating diversity within your school. If you are asked to work with a pupil during therapy sessions, make sure you know how to support them for the best and work with others to do this.

Provision may be affected if the school does not take active steps to make sure that barriers do not occur.

Barriers to inclusion include:

- **Physical barriers** – lack of access, equipment or resources
- **Organisational barriers** – school policies, lack of training, diversity within the curriculum
- **Barriers in attitudes of the school community** – staff, parents, other pupils.

It is important that schools:

- have high expectations of pupils and develop their attitudes of self-belief through appropriate challenges
- celebrate and value diversity, rather than fear it
- are aware that all pupils have more in common than is different
- encourage the participation of all pupils in the curriculum and social life of the school
- work to include all pupils in the main activities of the class wherever possible.

(For specific legislation and organisational policy, see K3, 'Codes of practice and conduct', page 204.)

How to provide active support and promote the individual's rights, choices and well-being

If you are supporting **individuals** during therapy sessions, you should be aware that they should be encouraged to do as much as possible for themselves and also to put forward their own thoughts and ideas. **Active support** is about encouraging pupils to be as independent as possible. You should take guidance from therapists about the level of support you should be giving individual pupils according to their needs. All pupils, even young children, should be asked about any individual preferences or concerns while they are participating in therapy sessions.

Key term

Rights – the rights that individuals have to:

- be respected and protected from harm
- be treated equally and not be discriminated against
- be treated as an individual
- be treated in a dignified way
- privacy
- be cared for in a way that meets their needs, takes account of their choices and protects them
- access information about themselves
- communicate using their preferred method of communication and language

Key term

Equality of access – Ensuring that discriminatory barriers to access are removed and that information about provision is accessible to all families in the community

Key terms

Individual – the person requiring health and care services. Where individuals use advocates and interpreters to enable them to express their views, wishes or feelings and to speak on their behalf, the term 'individual' is used in this unit to cover the individual and their advocate or interpreter

Active support – Support that encourages individuals to do as much for themselves as possible to maintain their independence and physical ability and encourages people with disabilities to maximise their own potential and independence

Case study

Promoting the rights and choices of individuals

Alex is 6 and has developmental dyspraxia. He has been referred to the occupational therapist for some support. He has difficulties with his motor skills and has become more anxious about this lately as he wants to play football with his peers, but says he is 'rubbish at it'. You have been asked to accompany him to his first therapy session and, although Alex is anxious, he is keen to go. During the session, the therapist asks you directly about areas Alex finds hard.

- What would you say to the therapist?
- Why is it important for all professionals to remember to promote the rights and choices of the individual?

Codes of practice and conduct

There have been many changes to legislation in the UK over recent years, which have affected educational provision for children who have disabilities and special educational (Additional Support for Learning (ASL)) needs. A very brief outline is listed below.

Education Act (Handicapped Children) 1970

Until this time, children with special educational needs were looked after by the health service. This act transferred the responsibility for their education to the local authority and as a result many special schools were built.

The Warnock Report 1978

This was a Report rather than an Act of legislation, but it had an impact on subsequent Acts of parliament as it was a study of the needs of children with special educational (Additional Support for Learning (ASL)) needs. It introduced a number of suggestions as to how children with these needs should be supported – through access to the curriculum, changes to the curriculum and changes to the environment. It influenced the Special Educational Needs (SEN) Code of Practice 2001 through its focus on inclusion.

Education Act 1981

This was based on the findings of the Warnock Report and gave additional legal responsibilities to local authorities as well as power to parents.

Education Reform Act 1988

This introduced the National Curriculum into all schools in England and Wales. Although this meant that all schools had to teach the same basic curriculum, it allowed schools to change or modify what was taught for pupils with special educational (ASL) needs if the basic curriculum was not appropriate for them.

Children Act 1989

The welfare of the child must be considered at all times and their rights and wishes should be taken into consideration. The Scottish equivalent is the Children (Scotland) Act 1995.

Education Act 1993

This required that a Code of Practice be introduced for guidance on the identification and provision of special educational needs. The role of the SENCo (Special Educational Needs Co-ordinator)(ASL teacher) was introduced in schools and parents were able to challenge local authorities about providing for pupils with special educational (ASL) needs.

Disability Discrimination Act 1995

This made it illegal for services such as shops and employers to discriminate against disabled people.

Carers and Disabled Children Act 2001

This was the first Act that recognised the needs of carers as well as those of children.

SENDA and Special Educational Needs Code of Practice 2001

The Special Educational Needs and Disability Act (SENDA) strengthens the rights of parents and children with special educational (ASL) needs to a mainstream education.

Every Child Matters 2005

This was put into place to ensure that all organisations and agencies involved with children between the ages of birth and 19 years should work together to ensure that children have the support needed to be healthy, stay safe, enjoy and achieve, make a positive contribution and achieve economic well-being. The acronym SHEEP can help you remember this:

| Stay safe | Healthy | Enjoy and achieve | Economic well-being | Positive contribution |

Standards and guidance

As well as teachers, there will be others both within and outside the school who will contribute to the support of pupils who require different forms of therapy. You may also have access to written information and reports from these people:

- SENCo (ASL teacher) – This member of school staff will be available to support the class teacher and teaching assistant in the development of Individual Education Plans (IEPs).
- Specialist teachers – These professionals may be available from different agencies such as the local Sensory Support Service to offer advice and equipment and to visit pupils from time to time in school.
- Physiotherapists/occupational therapists – They may be able to visit the school or pupils may have to go on a waiting list before they are able to see them. They will develop individual programmes for pupils to use at home, with advice for activities they can work on in school.
- Other professionals – They may be inside or outside the school, but may have experience of dealing with children who have physical or sensory impairment, or social and emotional development needs.

You will also periodically need to provide these people with information about the pupil's progress and participation in learning activities, whether these are cognitive, creative or physical. However if you are asked to do this, you should have some advice from the school as to the format that this should take. For example, if you are required to write a report, you should have some help on how to approach this.

Your school will also have its own special educational (ASL) needs policy, which will give you guidelines and organisational detail on how you should approach and manage your work with pupils. Local authorities may also produce their own guidance on issues such as the safe lifting and handling of pupils with physical disabilities.

Portfolio activity

Reflecting on standards and guidance

Write a reflective account about the standards and guidance relevant to the therapy work you do with pupils. Consider any organisational (i.e. school-based) standards and guidance, as well as any laid down by the local authority and any national guidance for specific therapies.

Legislation and procedures for accessing records

The main area of legislation to consider when accessing records is the Data Protection Act 1998. As a result of this all schools are required to have a policy on record-keeping so that staff know the correct procedures to use. This policy may have a title such as 'Assessment, Recording and Reporting Policy' and will give information and guidelines about recording within the school.

Most of the school's records may be kept on computer, so staff will need to be trained in how to use the system. You may have opportunities for training with other staff and this will be important if you are to help them to update records. Even if you are not expected to do this, it will be useful to see how records are used and how information is kept within the school.

Schools should also give guidelines for the use of personal information and make sure that systems and documentation are secure and only restricted to appropriate staff. There should be a policy for the storage and security of pupil records within the school and you should be familiar with this if you are dealing with pupil records.

Legislation and procedures for recording, reporting and sharing information

The Data Protection Act 1998 is also relevant in relation to recording, reporting and sharing information. When storing information on individuals, be aware that the information may consist of different levels of confidentiality. All information held on pupils comes under data protection guidelines, but you will be able to share some of it with colleagues as part of your day-to-day dealings with pupils. However, you may find that you are working with individuals who are a particular cause for concern. Unfortunately, sensitive issues regarding pupils do come to light in school and if you have any concerns or if a pupil confides in you, you may need to pass on sensitive information. This will usually be straight to the headteacher. You should not share this kind of information with others.

Although the main purpose of confidentiality legislation is to protect the individual's right to privacy, in some cases it may need to be shared without consent. The Data Protection Act 1998 is not intended to stop information being shared; it is often very important for different organisations to share information. As far as schools are concerned, information can legally be shared with other professionals who have a need to know it. In the case of pupils, parental consent needs to be given before information can be shared with other professionals. However, if there are any issues that indicate that a pupil is at risk from the parents or if there is a legal obligation placed on the school to disclose information, this should go ahead.

Legislation and procedures for health, safety and risk management

All organisations are required by the Health and Safety at Work Regulations 1992 to carry out risk assessments in order to minimise any risk that could cause harm to individuals. If you are supporting pupils with special educational (ASL) needs during therapy sessions, you need to be aware of the kinds of risks associated with what you are doing and act accordingly. Read any health and safety advice available in the centre where the activity takes place and speak to others who give support in this area. Risk assessments should have been carried out by your school to make sure that the facilities are safe and suitable for the activity prior to their use. Make sure that if you have any concerns, you have spoken to the appropriate person, for example your school's health and safety officer, before taking part.

Procedures for supporting individuals prior to, during and after therapy sessions

You need to have an awareness of any organisational requirements around the support of pupils during therapy sessions so that you can support pupils at all stages to ensure that they gain the maximum benefit from their therapy.

Before the therapy
You should speak to pupils about the targets or activities they have been given to work on since any previous sessions and about any concerns they may have about participating in the sessions. You should also work with others to identify what preparations need to be made before the therapy sessions. Finally, you should prepare the environment to ensure that it is appropriate and meets the requirements of the particular therapy.

During the therapy
You need to guide pupils through what they are expected to do and enable them to follow the requirements of the session according to their needs and abilities. If they are having particular difficulties, you need to inform the therapist and possibly stop the therapy session.

Following therapy
You may need to discuss any changes that need to be made with the therapist or the pupil to maximise the pupil's participation or to ensure the effectiveness of the therapy.

Key changes that may occur to individuals with whom you work and actions to take in these circumstances

You may find that, as you work closely with pupils, you become aware of changes that affect them. This in turn may affect the therapy you are doing with them. Some examples of such changes might be:

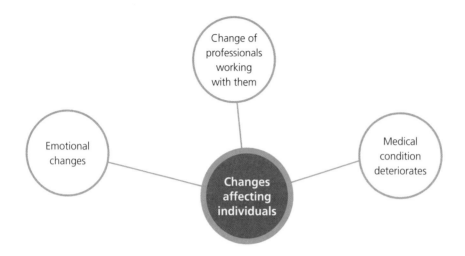

▲ **Figure 14.1** The key changes to individuals

Medical condition deteriorates

If the pupil's medical condition deteriorates, he/she may not be able to continue with therapy and the sessions will need to be suspended. In this situation, you should be supported by a range of other professionals, who will be able to guide you and the pupil and offer support in other areas.

Emotional changes

The pupil may be going through difficult emotional changes in his/her life caused by a range of factors such as family breakdown or difficulties associated with their condition. You need to be sensitive to this and to offer as much support as you can. If you feel at all concerned about a pupil, you must always refer to others. Depending on individual cases, you may need to refer to different people; for example, if you have a close working relationship with a class teacher, it might be that you discuss any issues like this on a regular basis and so you would report to them. In a secondary school, it may be more likely that you speak to the SENCo (ASL teacher) about your concerns. If you are not sure who to approach, your line manager should be able to advise you.

Change of professionals

The pupil may become used to working with certain individuals and be adversely affected if there is a change in therapist. If you notice that a pupil has been affected by a change, you may need to discuss this with teachers and with the therapist concerned.

Giving effective support through key changes

Hamid is in Year 8 (S2) and has cerebral palsy. He has just moved into the area and changed schools. You have been employed as his support assistant and are working with him closely to make sure that he settles into school and makes friends quickly. You are finding this difficult as Hamid is a quiet child and does not volunteer much information. He has the support of a range of professionals including a physiotherapist, although because he has moved quite a distance everything is very new to him.

- How might the changes have affected Hamid?
- What could you do to help Hamid further?

Impact of stress and fear on behaviour and the individual's ability to take part in and use therapy sessions effectively

You may find that the pupil with whom you are working becomes stressed or anxious either before or during therapy sessions. In this situation you should always speak to the pupil, teacher, therapist and, if possible, the pupil's parents about the reaction in order to have their opinion. Stress will affect the individual's ability to proceed with the therapy as it releases chemicals in the brain that may affect them in different ways:

- fight – the individual may become aggressive and confrontational
- flight – the individual may not attend the therapy session as they are too anxious to cope with it
- freeze – the individual may be unable to continue due to their anxiety
- flock – the individual might need the reassurance of having others around them.

Sometimes, if fears are confronted, it is possible to overcome them by showing the pupil that the fear is worse than the actual event. You may be able to reassure the pupil by giving them examples of your own experiences. However, if you are unable to reassure the pupil and the therapy is affected by their fear, it may be necessary to suspend it until such a time as they are able to continue.

Conditions and impairments that the therapy is addressing

You need to know about the condition or impairment that the therapy is designed to address. You should be given information by other professionals such as the SENCo (ASL teacher), teachers or the therapist. If the pupil has a rare condition or disorder, the parents or carers may have the most information when the pupil first comes into school.

K7 # Portfolio activity

Reflecting on particular conditions and impairments

Write a reflective account or speak to your assessor about the condition or impairment of the pupil you are supporting. Include a description of where you obtained information about this.

Benefits and problems that might occur prior to, during and after therapy sessions

When embarking on work with pupils and therapists, you should be prepared for what you are undertaking and have considered any potential problems that may arise so that you can prepare for them if possible. For example, if you know that a pupil has reacted adversely to therapy in the past, you may need to spend time with them before sessions to encourage them to discuss any worries they have. If you have a good knowledge of the particular therapy, it may help to explain what will take place in the session, or you may need to speak to the therapist beforehand to clarify this. You may also need to consider the likely benefits to the pupil if the sessions have been set up with their needs in mind; for example, you may know that a pupil works better if their parent is present. Potential problems and benefits can occur for physical, social or emotional reasons.

Outcomes that therapy sessions aim to achieve for individuals

Therapy sessions have different aims depending on the areas they are addressing. It is important that you have some guidance from others and are clear about exactly how a pupil will benefit from the particular therapy.

K9 # Case study

Identifying realistic outcomes of therapy

Charlotte is working closely with Amy, who is at a school for pupils with severe and complex needs. Amy, who is 8, has weak joints and is about to start hydrotherapy sessions, following the installation of a special hydrotherapy pool at the school. Charlotte has been invited to a meeting with the class teacher, physiotherapist, Amy and her parents to discuss the benefits of the hydrotherapy for Amy and what they are hoping to achieve.

- Do you think that it is essential for all of these people to know about the aim of the sessions?
- Why is it important for Amy that these outcomes are realistic?

Best ways of supporting individuals through therapy sessions

There are four main ways of effectively supporting individuals through therapy sessions:

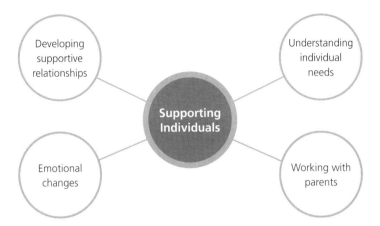

- Developing supportive relationships
- Understanding individual needs
- **Supporting Individuals**
- Emotional changes
- Working with parents

◀ **Figure 14.2** Supporting individuals in therapy

Developing supportive relationships

In order to maximise the benefits of therapy to the pupils with whom you work, you need to have good relationships with them so that they trust you. This is very important as they need to be able to work closely with you during their therapy sessions. (See also K11, page 212.)

Understanding individual needs

You should be very clear on the needs of the pupil and the purpose of the therapy. If you are working directly with one pupil all the time, you have more opportunity to get to know their needs and how best to support them. If you work with a range of pupils who are undergoing therapy, for example in a special school, you should have pupil profiles to refer to for further information.

▼ **Figure 14.3** Make sure the lessons are based around the pupil

Liaising with teachers and therapists

Make sure you speak to other professionals about pupils before and after sessions so that you keep all channels of communication open. Also make sure that you have access to written reports and any other available information.

Working with parents

You may find that parents want to speak to you regarding therapy sessions and you should encourage them to do this. You will then be able to support the individual's needs more effectively.

How to form a supportive relationship with individuals to enable them to benefit as much as possible from the therapy

As already mentioned, you need to get to know pupils with whom you are working so that you can maximise the support you give them. If you have a good relationship with individuals, it is more likely that you will be able to support them effectively.

Pupils with physical impairments or other conditions that require therapy may be less able to concentrate than their peers. They may tire easily or become frustrated if they are unable to complete tasks as quickly or as well as they would hope to. It is important that adults are able to reassure such pupils and give them encouragement to maintain their interest and enthusiasm. This can be done by praising them for their efforts and by giving them levels of assistance consistent with their abilities. If too much help is given, individuals will not experience a sense of achievement and independence, but if too little is given, they may become frustrated and lose interest. Inclusive education is important to ensure that these pupils do not lose confidence by being unable to participate in learning activities enjoyed by their peers.

How to observe and record observations to support therapy sessions

You may be asked by teachers or the SENCo (ASL teacher) to observe pupils specifically to support therapy sessions. Depending on the needs of the pupil and the therapy involved, this may involve observations of different aspects of their development. Make sure you are clear on the exact purpose of the observation and the type of recording you are required to use (see Unit 9, page 156 for examples of these).

Social skills

Pupils may be referred for behaviour therapy if their social and emotional development is such that they need to work on controlling their emotions and stepping back to think before acting impulsively. You may be asked to observe them in social situations during breaks and lunchtimes and in situations that require them to interact co-operatively with others.

Physical skills

You may need to observe in situations such as break times or PE lessons in order to record pupils' gross motor skills, such as throwing, catching, running and so on. Fine motor skills, such as holding a pencil or scissors, doing up laces or coats, holding a needle and thread, manipulating a computer mouse or using a keyboard, may also be observed.

It is possible that you may be working alongside the pupil while you are observing, in which case you may need to make notes and write up your observation following the session.

Key signs of problems and difficulties that need to be reported to the therapist

As well as informing the therapist if the pupil becomes stressed or anxious (see K6, page 209), you may need to inform them about signs of other problems. These could include:

- the pupil is not receiving support at home from parents or carers
- the pupil does not wish to take part in therapy in the home or school setting
- the pupil does not appear to be making progress despite therapy sessions and adhering to the programme.

It is important that therapists are informed about any disruption to the programme because this means that the pupil is unlikely to make progress. Where pupils are reluctant to take part, the therapist may decide to stop therapy and try to resume at a later date.

Case study K13

Identifying and acting on key signs of problems

Fraser is 8 years old and in Year 3 (P4). He is in mainstream school and has been under the speech therapist since he was 6, as he has a stutter. Fraser has had several blocks of therapy and now his mother tells you that he has been refusing to work on the programme set by the therapist. She is concerned because his behaviour has also been deteriorating at home lately.

- What would you say to her?
- Would you take any further action?

How to involve the individual in collecting information about their experience of the therapy and its outcomes

As far as possible, the pupil(s) you are supporting should be involved in gathering and reviewing information about their experience of the therapy and what has happened. This is because it is important that they are part of the process and that the therapy is not something that is being 'done' to them without their consent or involvement. Where possible, the pupil should be invited to review sessions in order to discuss their progress and therapy outcomes. They should be invited to think about and comment on their experiences and can do this in a variety of ways depending on their needs so that they can be involved in the development of further targets. A pupil with communication difficulties, for example, may be asked to think about the impact that their speech and language therapy is having on their learning. When pupils are invited to contribute they should always be given enough notice so that they have time to think about what they are going to say.

How to deal with conflicts arising prior to, during and after therapy sessions

You may have to deal with conflicts as part of your work with pupils around therapy sessions. This may be for a variety of reasons, some of which are given below.

Prior to sessions

If the pupil or parent is reluctant to take part, you need to speak to them and try to establish the cause of their reluctance. If it is anxiety, you may also need to ask the therapist to reassure them. However, if conflict has arisen around this point, it may be necessary to postpone the session and arrange a discussion meeting so that each individual can have the opportunity to put forward their point of view.

During sessions

The pupil may not wish to continue or there may be difficulties with the implementation of the therapy, which causes disagreement. In both these cases you may need to take the pupil out and talk through what has happened. It may be necessary to stop the session and resume at a later date when the area of conflict has been discussed.

After sessions

If the pupil or parent does not agree with advice given by the therapist, you may need to seek a third party to reassure the pupil or parent. This may mean making an appointment for them to speak to teachers or other therapists in order to discuss what has taken place.

Areas of conflict may also arise around poor communication or disagreements between individuals. In this situation you may find that you need to act as a mediator. If you are involved in a conflict situation due to a disagreement yourself, always remember to remain professional and to speak calmly to others. If you are concerned about areas of difficulty between individuals or if you are involved in a conflict yourself and are unable to reach a resolution, you need to ask others in the school for support.

◀ **Figure 14.4**
Defusing tension and arguments is a vital skill

Resolving conflicts around therapy

You have been asked to support Max, a child with a Statement of Special Educational Needs (Co-ordinated Support Plan), who is in Reception (P1) in a mainstream school. He has a variety of needs, which require occupational and physiotherapy for the development of his fine and gross motor skills. He has regular appointments to see the therapist outside school and is accompanied by his mother, although the occupational therapist has sent you a series of activities to carry out with Max in school to develop his handwriting and other skills. He is also required to carry out activities to develop his co-ordination during PE lessons.

His mother has come to see you and the class teacher because she is upset that Max is being given such a large programme of activities to do at home and school each day. She says that he is exhausted after being at school all day and she feels it is more important for him to settle into school and make friends than to have a list of physio- and occupational therapy exercises. She has not said anything to either of the therapists yet, but wants to stop the therapy for a while.

● How do you think you and the teacher should approach this?
● What other professionals might you involve to help you all to decide what is best for Max?

Risks, dangers and difficulties associated with different equipment and materials and in relation to specific individuals

Although some forms of therapy do not require the use of equipment, it is possible that you may need training in the use of specific items in order to support pupils. Always make sure that you seek training if it is required and that you are aware of any hazards that may be associated with the use of particular equipment.

In addition, a pupil whose behaviour is unpredictable may pose a hazard to themselves or others supporting them. In this situation make sure that you are not working on your own with the pupil and seek advice from other professionals about how you should best manage their needs for the safety of all.

For your portfolio...

Write a reflective account that includes a description of the needs of the pupil(s) you support for therapy sessions. This should include how the therapy is designed to support the condition, how long the therapy will continue and the kinds of benefits and problems you have noticed while working on the programme. You should also include any difficulties or issues you have needed to report to the therapist or other professionals, either relating to the therapy or to any equipment used.

Websites

www.bbc.co.uk/health – This website has advice for a range of conditions and illnesses

www.dca.gov.uk – Department for Constitutional Affairs

www.everychildmatters.gov.uk

www.ncb.org.uk – National organisation supporting parents and children

www.parentpartnership.org.uk – National Parent Partnership Network

www.opsi.gov.uk/ACTS/ – for the Data Protection Act 1998 and the Human Rights Act 1998

www.surestart.gov.uk – Sure Start, aiming to deliver the best start in life for children

15 Support Children and Young People's Play

This unit is for those who support or supervise children or young people's play activities. As well as being applicable to classroom environments, it will also be useful to those who support play in extended school situations and clubs. You may be supporting children in different age groups between the ages of 4 and 16. The unit is about being able to create, support and end play sessions effectively.

If you are planning on doing this unit for your S/NVQ, you will need to refer to your candidate handbook as you should plan to show that you have created a variety of play environments for children from two age groups and with a range of needs.

What you need to know and understand

For this unit, you need to know and understand:

■ The assumptions and values of playwork relevant to this unit

■ The importance of play to children and young people's development

■ Why children and young people's play should be self-directed

■ Why play opportunities should focus on children and young people's needs

■ Why it is important to ask children and young people about what they want in their play environments

■ How to identify children and young people's play needs

■ The types of play environment that stimulate children and young people's play and the role that you can play in helping to provide that environment

■ The importance of risk and challenge in children and young people's play and how to balance these against requirements for health and safety

■ Why children and young people need variety and choice in the play setting

■ The importance of planning play opportunities that are flexible and easily adapted by the children and young people to their own needs

■ Why children and young people should be involved in creating play environments and how to gain their involvement

■ The requirements of your organisation that are relevant to creating play environments

■ The basic requirements of relevant laws that you need to follow when creating play environments

■ Why it is important to offer play opportunities while respecting the children and young people's right to explore and adapt the opportunity to their own needs

■ Why it is important to involve children and young people in discussing and agreeing ground rules

■ Why it is important to encourage children and young people to explore, choose and adapt play opportunities for themselves

■ How to balance the rights of the child or young person to play in a self-directed way against the rights of others

■ The types of support that children and young people might need to adapt a play opportunity and how to provide this support without taking control

■ Why children and young people should extend themselves through play and how to encourage this

■ The dangers of pushing children and young people too far and undermining their confidence and self-esteem and the signs that this may be happening

- The types of support that children and young people may need during play

- How to identify when children and young people need support during a play opportunity

- Why it is important to provide support without undermining the children and young people's personal control of their play

- Children and young people's play cues and why it is important to respond to these sensitively

- Situations in which your own involvement in play could increase the children and young people's involvement and stimulation and situations where it could have the opposite effect

- How to bring a play session to an end in a way that respects the children and young people's needs and involvement but meets the requirements of your play setting

- Your organisation's procedures for tidying up the play setting and dealing with the resources

- Your organisation's procedures for children and young people's departure

- Your organisation's record-keeping procedures

Assumptions and values of playwork relevant to this unit

The national standards for playwork list a set of assumptions and values relevant to your work with pupils. They have been reproduced here in shortened form so that you can identify the key areas of importance when supporting opportunities for play. They are also reflected in the standards for this unit.

Assumptions

Children's play is freely chosen, personally directed behaviour, motivated from within. Through play, they explore the world and their relationship with it, all the while elaborating a flexible range of responses to the challenges they encounter. By playing, they learn and develop as individuals.

Whereas children may play without encouragement or help, adults can, through the provision of an appropriate human and physical environment, significantly enhance opportunities for them to play creatively and thus develop through play.

Values

Play opportunities are provided in a number of settings (e.g. local authority, voluntary or commercial) for children with a variety of needs, in a complex society diverse in culture and belief; nevertheless, competent playwork always has the following underlying values:

- the child must be the centre of the process
- play should empower the child and support their right to make choices
- adults should try not to control a child's play
- every child has a right to a play environment that is safe
- every child is an individual and should be respected
- consistent consideration should be given to all children and their families
- all children should be given equal opportunities
- play is a co-operative activity and children should be encouraged to be sensitive to the needs of others
- play opportunities should be provided within the current legislative framework
- every child has a right to a play environment.

Portfolio activity

Enriching play experiences through national standards

How do you think your setting takes account of these assumptions and values when planning play for children and young people? Give at least five examples and show how you have supported the school and the pupils in enriching their play experiences.

Importance of play to children and young people's development

Play is an important part of pupils' learning. Pupils of all ages, needs, backgrounds and cultures will benefit from having the opportunity to be creative and make choices about their play.

▲ **Figure 15.1** Play opportunities can come in a number of different ways

- **Promotes creativity and imagination** – Pupils need to use their imaginations and have different opportunities to do so. If left to their own devices, for example on playgrounds or in role-play situations, they will usually make up games and play with one another.
- **Develops social skills and builds friendships** – Play is an important part of developing pupils' social skills and learning about taking turns and sharing. They will also be making and developing friendships and co-operating with one another, as well as learning about one another's different backgrounds.
- **Encourages independence** – Play encourages pupils to experiment with their ideas and to have control over their environment in different situations.
- **Builds communication skills** – Through play, pupils develop their skills of communication and language, as well as their vocabulary.
- **Promotes decision-making** – Play enables pupils to be responsible and have control of different activities in the setting.

Why play opportunities should focus on pupils' needs and be self-directed

Pupils' play should be self-directed as much as possible because this encourages them to have ownership of their environment. In many school and home situations children and young people are told what they have to do; play gives them an outlet for their creativity and also enables them to have some control of their experiences.

Play opportunities also need to be appropriate for the age and needs of the pupils. Your setting should provide a range of different activities and resources that give pupils the chance to explore their environment in a spontaneous way through opportunities that are suitable for their different needs. These might be:

- **Pupils who have special educational (Additional Support for Learning (ASL)) needs** – Care should be taken to ensure that all pupils have access to the activities being offered.
- **Pupils who have a shorter or longer concentration span than others** – The more flexible the play opportunities, the greater likelihood that pupils will be able to explore them spontaneously and come and go as they would like.
- **Pupils who have a particular focus of interest** – Those who are keen to work on a particular area or skill can have the opportunity to do this in their own time, although care should be taken that they do not dominate or monopolise particular activities.
- **Pupils who are reluctant to contribute** – Pupils who are less confident will benefit from being able to select those activities that appeal to them in order to develop them. They could also be 'buddied' with others, if necessary, to give them more support.

Why it is important to ask pupils what they want in their play environments

Pupils are more likely to feel that they are part of the learning experience when they are given opportunities to contribute and put forward their ideas in different ways. This helps to harness their enthusiasm and further their learning opportunities. When you are planning play environments, it therefore makes sense to give them the chance to suggest the kinds of activities they would like to explore. You can do this through discussion, where you should make sure that everyone has the opportunity to contribute. In this situation make sure that those who are more confident or appear to have more ideas are not taking over the group or intimidating others. You may also wish to encourage pupils' input through other means, for example by having an open ideas box or policy of encouraging them to speak to adults about their ideas whenever they occur. It is important that if pupils are encouraged to do this, adults always respond to them appropriately, as they will be reluctant to make suggestions if they are not acted upon or discussed.

Case study

Involving pupils in decisions about play environments

As part of the plan for school development this year, St Saviour's Primary are rethinking the layout and facilities in the playground areas. At a whole staff meeting, the headteacher has asked the staff to think about how the budget could be used and the kinds of equipment, games and shelters they may be able to put on both the infant and junior playgrounds.

- What might you suggest to the rest of the staff?
- What would be the benefits of pupil involvement?

How to identify pupils' play needs

In order to identify pupils' play needs, it is important for staff to get to know the pupils and to discuss with them the kinds of environments they would like to explore (see also K4 and K5, page 221.) This can be done informally through speaking to pupils about the kinds of activities they enjoy and those they find less interesting. Your school may be in an area of high or low cultural mix – in either case, the kinds of play activities available to pupils should be representative of a wide range of cultures. You should also think about the age and stage of the pupils, as this will have a bearing on the kinds of activities that may or may not appeal to them. You may also glean information about individual pupils through speaking to parents and carers, or other professionals working with them.

Types of environment that stimulate pupils' play and your role in helping to provide that environment

You should be able to provide a range of activities and opportunities that enable pupils to get the most from play opportunities. Depending on the age and individual needs of pupils, they will find different environments stimulating. It is important to involve pupils and discuss ideas with them so that you can use scenarios and ideas that they find appealing. They may be particularly interested in creating an environment that enables them to provide their own input. You should consider the following factors.

Resources and materials available

There are many resources available on the market to stimulate children and young people's play and encourage them to participate in play activities. It is important that schools ensure that they have a wide range of, for example, toys that represent different cultures and resources that offer stimulation in different ways. Often, young children in particular improvise and make up some of their own play activities. You can also encourage them to do this through creating activities around their interests.

Indoor and outdoor environments and spaces available

Outdoor environments may include gardens, playgrounds and outdoor classrooms. Indoor environments may include role-play areas, shared areas of the school such as halls and open-plan spaces, and specific areas of the classroom available for activities such as construction or role play.

Ideas and themes that reflect pupils' current interests

You should ensure that you ask pupils for ideas around themes that are particularly interesting to them at the time. Older pupils may use forums such as school councils (in Scotland Pupil Councils) to request facilities or equipment, such as more facilities for a particular sport or a larger computer area.

Portfolio activity K7

Encouraging pupils in play opportunities

Devise a list of activities for pupils in *two* different age ranges to encourage them to take part in a range of play opportunities in different environments.

Importance of risk and challenge in play and how to balance these against requirements for health and safety

Children and young people need to learn how to assess circumstances that may pose a risk to themselves or others. This is particularly important in play situations where pupils may not have focused adult supervision. At a young age, children need adults to regularly discuss with them why there are rules and what kinds of risks may arise in different situations. As they grow older, they need to start to think about these issues for themselves, although in new environments adults should always remind them to think about safety (see also Unit 2, page 38). There should always be some adult supervision so that pupils can quickly access support if needed.

Keys to good practice

Managing risk and challenge

✓ Carry out risk assessments on all new learning environments.
✓ Ensure pupils have opportunities to think about safety and discuss ground rules when starting new activities (see also K15, page 227).
✓ Ensure there is adequate supervision if activities pose a higher risk.
✓ As pupils get older, give them more responsibilities so that they gradually get used to thinking about risk for themselves.

Why pupils need variety and choice in the play setting

In order for play to stimulate pupils, they need to have a choice of activities that will give them the chance to select those with most appeal. If they are routinely given a limited number of activities or if play opportunities are regularly repeated with no consideration given to the needs of the pupils, they will be less likely to be excited and motivated to use them.

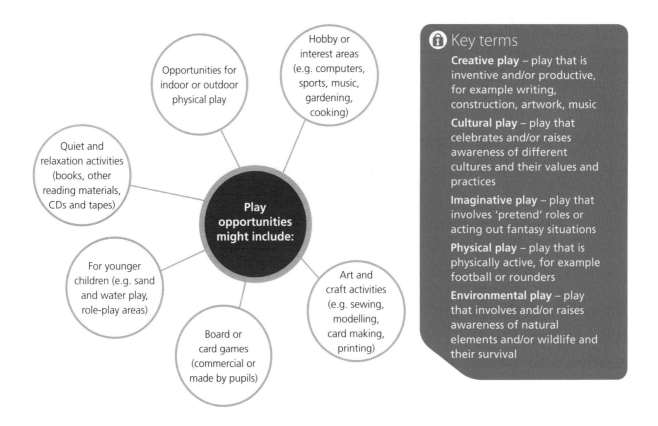

▲ **Figure 15.2** Can you find an opportunity to exploit all the benefits of play?

You should also monitor the use of different activities, because some may be more popular than others. If you notice that some areas are hardly used, you may wish to change or remove these.

Importance of planning play opportunities that are flexible and easily adapted by pupils to their own needs

It is important to ensure that some play opportunities are flexible enough for changes to be made by pupils as they see fit. This gives them further opportunities to take control of their environment and decide on how they are going to be used. An example of this might be an environment with a dressing-up box containing a variety of fabrics, clothes and hats for pupils to use as they want.

Why pupils should be involved in creating play environments and how to gain their involvement

As well as involving pupils in decisions about what they would like to have in their play environments, it is also beneficial for them to help to create them. Pupils take satisfaction from helping to create something based on their own ideas and through working with others to achieve this (see also K5, page 221). Some may spontaneously do this anyway, through the use of props or improvisation with materials or resources available in the environment. Others may need support to realise their ideas.

Encouraging pupils to create play environments

You have been working in Year 1 (P2) and the pupils have asked you if they can create a play environment around 'Dr Who' as many of them enjoy the television programme and regularly play games with this theme. After some discussion in your presence, they decide that they would like to make a large tardis, which they will keep in the role-play area of the classroom.

- How could you support the pupils further so that they are able to create their tardis?
- Can you think of examples of situations in which you have helped pupils to create play environments and how you involved them?

Requirements of your organisation that are relevant to creating play environments

You should ensure that when you are creating environments for pupils, you are aware of the particular requirements of your school. This means being mindful of issues such as timetabling, space, safety and the resources available. It is not sensible, for example, to plan to spend lots of money on resources or play opportunities if you have not checked whether this is available. You also need to ensure that staffing levels are adequate if pupils need to be supervised or supported during a particular activity.

Working within your school's requirements and resources

Cilem, a teaching assistant with a particular interest in art, has been approached by a group of Year 8 (S2) girls who have asked for an art and craft club to be set up at school. Cilem is keen to take on the idea and tells them that she will set one up as soon as possible.

- What should Cilem have said to the girls?
- Why is it important that she checks the organisation's requirements first?

Basic requirements of relevant laws that you need to follow when creating play environments

Children Act 1989 and Children (Scotland) Act of 1995

The Children Act protects individual children. Under its requirements, all children should be treated equally regardless of race, culture, ethnicity, age, language or religion. They should be treated fairly and consideration given to their different needs. Children also have the right to be kept safe and to have access to a broad and balanced curriculum (see also Unit 3, (page 49).

Health and Safety at Work Act 1974

Your responsibilities under this statute are that you must ensure that the learning environment is checked regularly for potential risks to health and safety. All staff need to be aware of hazards and to deal with or report any that they come across in the course of their work. This includes:

- checking any equipment for breakages and making sure that it is appropriate for the age of the pupils
- checking all learning environments, including outdoors, for any hazards and keeping them clean and tidy
- checking that security precautions are being observed by all staff (e.g. that doors are kept locked where required and that visitors are signed in and out)
- making sure that any dangerous items such as cleaning materials or sharp items are kept locked out of pupils' reach
- making sure that spillages and waste are dealt with promptly.

You should have seen a copy of your school's health and safety policy and know how your responsibilities relate to this.

Control of Substances Hazardous to Health (COSHH) Regulations

These regulations lead on from the health and safety requirements and include any substances that could cause harm or injury due to misuse. In schools, any such items should be stored well out of the reach of pupils and need to be appropriately labelled so that adults know what they are.

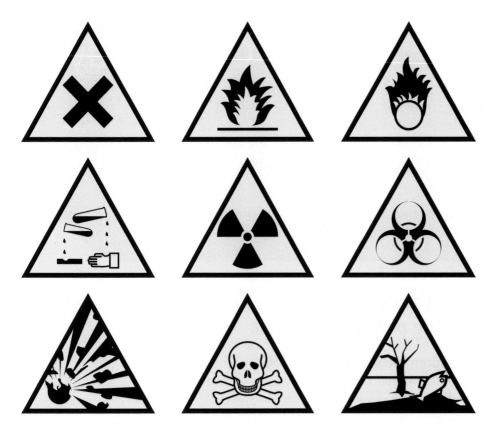

▲ **Figure 15.3** Accurate labelling is essential for dangerous materials

Familiarising yourself with legislation relating to play environments

List the legislation above and any other legislation you can find out about which might be relevant to the creation of play environments (e.g. look in the Manual Handling Operations Regulations 1992, Unit 3, page 51).

Respecting pupils' right to explore and adapt play opportunities to their own needs

It is important for pupils to have some say in how they use the learning environment and the kinds of activities on offer. This is because they present a chance for pupils to feel involved in what they are doing. You may do this through questioning pupils about the kinds of play resources and activities they would like and also through allowing them to adapt and change the play environment so that they gain maximum use from it (see also K16, page 228).

Why it is important to involve pupils in discussing and agreeing ground rules

Pupils benefit from having the opportunity to discuss and agree ground rules when starting play activities in different environments. This gives them further ownership of the activities and encourages them to think about safety and consider the needs of others in addition to their own.

In addition, the fact that pupils have discussed and agreed the ground rules means that if they are broken you can point out to them that they agreed to the rules before they started, and the reasons for your speaking to them will make more sense.

> **ⓘ Key term**
>
> **Ground rules** – agreed rules for a play opportunity; they usually cover issues such as behaviour, health and safety, co-operation, respect or other issues requested by the pupils

Case study K15

Recognising the importance of ground rules

You are working in an out-of-school dance club with a group of pupils of different ages. The club takes place in the school hall, which has a range of PE apparatus stored around the edges. This is the second time you have taken the group and their behaviour is quite excitable. You have not discussed ground rules with them. On this occasion, some of them have started to climb on the PE equipment just as you arrive.

- How would it have helped if you had agreed on some rules before you started?
- How would doing this first have helped you when pupils started to misbehave?

Encouraging pupils to explore, choose and adapt play opportunities

Most pupils enjoy the freedom of play because it gives them the chance to explore their environment and make their own choices about what they are doing. They should have some time available when they can select what they would like to do from a range of available activities. In both indoor and outdoor environments, they should also have the opportunity to adapt materials and equipment in order to develop their imaginations.

K14
K16

Case study

Encouraging pupils to adapt play opportunities

This week in Reception (P1) the class teacher has asked that predominantly 'boy' and 'girl' activities are monitored so that all pupils are being given equal opportunities to use different equipment and they are not taken over by groups. Deirdre, the teaching assistant, is happy to see that a mixed group of pupils are enjoying using construction equipment, as this is usually dominated by boys when there are free-choice activities. She also notices that a small group of boys are playing with the dolls' house and have been playing very well together for some time. She goes to see what they are doing and finds that they are using the small world play figures to go up and down the stairs. She asks them what they are doing and they tell her that they are playing 'Super Mario'.

- What do you think about the boys playing this game?
- Is this an effective play opportunity?
- Should Deirdre say anything else to the boys?

How to balance the rights of the pupil to play in a self-directed way against the rights of others

You may find that you are supervising pupils in a play situation that requires your intervention due to the behaviour of one or more individuals. This may be because they have become over boisterous and are interfering with what others are doing or because they are simply taking over an activity so that others are unable to play. Because it is important that all pupils should be able to play in a self-directed way, you need to ensure that quieter or more reticent pupils are not discouraged from joining in due to the enthusiasm of their peers. It is also important that those who have more confidence learn to have consideration for others and think about giving them the opportunity to join in.

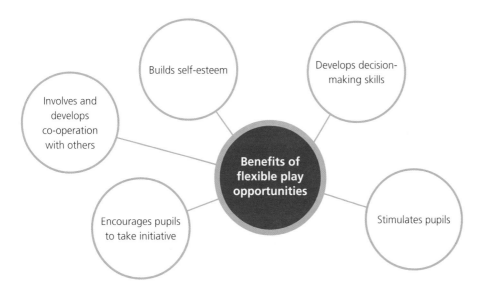

Benefits of flexible play opportunities

- Builds self-esteem
- Develops decision-making skills
- Involves and develops co-operation with others
- Stimulates pupils
- Encourages pupils to take initiative

▲ **Figure 15.4** Can you allow for flexible play opportunities?

Case study K17

Achieving a balance between different pupils' rights to play

You are supervising primary pupils from different classes during a nature club, which takes place in the school grounds. Several pupils are particularly interested in finding out about insect and animal homes and have decided to list all those they can find and think of. Although the pupils have started well and are very involved in what they are doing, Elisha is taking over the activity and says that she will be in charge of the lists and everyone should come to her to tell her what she should write down.

- Is there any harm in Elisha organising the group like this?
- Why might you need to speak to her?

Types of support that pupils might need to adapt a play opportunity

If you need to intervene in any play situation, remember that it is important that you do not take control of what pupils are doing. For example, pupils may ask for or need your help in order to continue with their play or if they need to move equipment or resources to support what they are doing. You should offer the help needed, inviting pupils to work with you to adapt the environment, and then check with pupils that they are able to continue without further support.

Why pupils should extend themselves through play

You should make sure that pupils have the opportunity to extend themselves through play because it gives them the chance to experiment without the fear of failure or being told what to do, in a non-threatening and relaxed environment. In play situations, pupils can try out new activities and ideas, which will develop their confidence and self-esteem. Your role is to encourage and support pupils so that they are given opportunities to extend their learning without feeling pressurised to do so.

Dangers of pushing pupils too far

If you are extending pupils' learning, you need to be careful that you do not push them too far. They should be able to carry out activities in their own time and at their own pace because rushing them may reduce their confidence and ability to try things out for themselves next time. They should be carrying out activities because they want to rather than because they are hoping to please adults.

K19 K20

Case study

Recognising the dangers of pushing too far

You are working outside with a group of pupils and two of them are learning to ride a bicycle without stabilisers. One of them, Said, has nearly mastered it and you have been encouraging him to keep trying. After some time, however, he says that he would like to stop and try again another day.

- Why is it important that you encouraged Said when he started to use the bicycle?
- What do you think would happen if you insisted that he continue when he wanted to stop?

Types of support that pupils may need during play

Pupils may need to have support in different areas while they are engaged in play activities. Although you should not be standing over them or giving them unsolicited help, make sure that you tell pupils where you will be if you are needed and give them any support they ask for during their play.

Prior to play activities

You need to ask pupils to think about the environment and how to work co-operatively with others, discuss safety and the equipment and resources they might need, tell them what to do if they need help and how much time they have to carry out the play activities.

During play activities

If you are supervising the play environment, ensure that you can see what different groups of pupils are doing. For example, if working with younger pupils in an outside area, you need to be able to see them so that you can intervene if required. Pupils may also ask you to take part in play activities with them and, if this is the case, you should be prepared to do so, You may also need to extend activities for pupils who are cautious about trying out new activities.

Following play activities

Ensure that pupils know when they need to stop and how to finish the session. This is sometimes difficult if they are engaged in their activities, so it is a good idea, particularly with older pupils, to tell them how much time they have at the start. At the end of the session you need to work with the group to ensure that the setting has been tidied up.

How to identify when pupils need support during a play opportunity

Pupils may seek your help or you might notice that it is needed, so it is important that you are able to see what is happening during play sessions so that you can intervene if required. Although older pupils need less support, you should still be on hand in case you are needed.

Pupils may actively seek your help for a number of reasons, for example because they have had some kind of disagreement and need a mediator to help discuss what they should do. Pupils may also need support with the use of resources or equipment, or if there may be safety issues that mean that you need to give assistance.

Why it is important to provide support without undermining pupils' control of their play

You need to be able to provide support sensitively so that pupils do not feel that their play is being undermined by an adult. This means that you should deal with the issue that needs addressing and then withdraw, if possible, so that play can continue. The support you give may be verbal (e.g. pupils may need to know something such as the rules for a particular game) or practical (e.g. showing them how to use a piece of equipment). You should also be careful that you do not intervene in such a way that any individual's credibility is damaged in front of others, especially when working with older pupils.

Pupils' play cues and why it is important to respond to these sensitively

As you get to know individual pupils, you should be able to respond to their play cues. Cues may mean that pupils would like to join in with activities or would like someone to join in with them. If you notice that a pupil appears to be very interested in joining a play activity, but seems reluctant or apprehensive about asking others directly, it may be appropriate for you to intervene and support them as they approach the group. However, you need to be careful that you do not do this too regularly with particular pupils because they need to develop their confidence through taking initiative. You may also need to support individuals if they have not realised that they are being invited to join in with play activities. However, if they do not want to play, they should not be pressured into doing so.

 Key term

Play cues – facial expressions, language or body language that communicates the pupil's wish to play or invite others to play

Case study K24

Responding to play cues sensitively

You are outside at playtime and notice a group of boys playing football. At the side by the wall is a pupil who you suspect would like to join in.

- What would you do first and why?
- Why is it important to be careful if you are intervening in this situation?

When to intervene in play activities and reasons for leaving pupils to their own devices

You need to look out for situations in which pupils need support in order to increase their involvement in play activities. As someone who works regularly with these pupils, you are in the best position to judge whether they are engaged in their activities or whether it is a good idea to intervene. The kinds of things you should look out for include:

- pupils who are not joining in with an activity
- pupils whose body language indicates that they do not want to participate
- pupils who are using equipment inappropriately or who are overexcited
- pupils who are putting themselves or others in danger.

You need to be careful how you respond if you judge that it is necessary to become involved. If you are unsure, it is a good idea to observe the situation for a little longer before intervening. However, it is important to intervene if a pupil does not appear to be enjoying the activity or if there is any danger to pupils' safety.

It is likely that pupils will make it clear to you if they no longer need your help and you will be able to tell if they are playing happily without you. In this situation, you should withdraw because otherwise there is a chance that you could inhibit what they are doing. It is important that you do not try to take over the activity as this means that it is no longer directed by the pupils. You may need to leave pupils gradually, particularly if they have sought your help, for example if they needed you to show them how to play a game. You should tell them that they are managing well and ask them if they still need you to stay with them.

Keys to good practice

Supporting play

✓ Ensure that any intervention is offered for a reason.
✓ Ask pupils what they would like you to do.
✓ Remember that you are there to support pupils' independence.
✓ Give support in such a way that pupils are encouraged to think for themselves.
✓ Do not take over activities or overexcite pupils.
✓ Leave pupils when they are ready for you to do so.

K25 Case study

Recognising how and when to get involved

Ramira is supervising a group of 11–15 year olds in an after-school club. There is a range of facilities for pupils to choose from. Ramira notices that there is a group of pupils around the table football and that the pupil who is about to have a turn is looking anxious. Ramira goes to the table and says, 'Come on, Chris, let's get them!' and starts to take over what is happening in order to encourage him to participate.

- Has Ramira done the right thing?
- Do you think that this action might encourage Chris or dissuade him from joining in?

How to bring a play session to an end

You should know and understand your school's requirements for bringing sessions to an end. If you are new to the environment, you need to check what you are required to do with others, to ensure that you follow normal procedures. These are likely to include telling the pupils when they have a limited time to finish what they are doing, giving them an opportunity to discuss their activities and making sure that you have put away materials and resources safely. Sometimes you may need to end play sessions quickly and without warning, for example, an outdoor activity when the weather changes. If pupils are unhappy about finishing play sessions, it is important to speak to them about how they are feeling and perhaps discuss with them when they might be able to resume the activity.

Your organisation's procedures for tidying up the play setting and dealing with the resources

It is likely that your school has requirements for tidying and putting away resources. You may have rotas so that all pupils are involved at different times or they may take collective responsibility on a daily basis. You should encourage and support pupils to help one another in this task.

Portfolio activity K26 K27

Ending a play session

Write a reflective account to show how you would end a play session in your setting for pupils from *two* different age groups. It needs to include how you would manage the pupils and the different ways in which you might end the session.

Your organisation's procedures for pupils' departure

Depending on the age of the pupils, your school will have different procedures for their departure and you need to know if the class, group or individuals you are working with have a particular procedure to follow.

If you are working with very young pupils, it is important that you know who is collecting them. Your school will keep records of contact details of parents and for younger children these may include who is going to collect them from school. It is particularly important to be forewarned of any changes to the day-to-day routine. In some Early Years classes or at after-school clubs, a book is kept by the door for parents to fill in if someone different will be collecting their child from the next session.

As pupils go through primary school, procedures will change, so if you are present when pupils leave, make sure that you know what you should do and whether you need to hand them over to a parent, carer or after-school club staff member.

At secondary level, it is likely that most pupils will leave the school without adult supervision or collection. However, you do need to check that this is the case if you are in a position of responsibility at the end of the school day.

Case study

Working within the school's procedures for departures

You are supervising a Year 1 (P2) class at the end of the day because the class teacher has an urgent appointment with a parent. The normal procedure is that you let pupils out when you recognise the parent or carer who is coming to collect them at the door. On this occasion, you notice that a pupil's grandmother has come to collect him although the school has not been notified of this and his mother usually comes. You know the lady in question and have met her several times.

- Outline what you would do in this situation.
- What are your own organisation's requirements for pupils' departure?

Your organisation's record-keeping procedures

After play activities are finished, it is likely that you will have to complete administrative tasks to comply with the requirements of your setting. These may be for a variety of purposes.

- **To record how pupils have managed different tasks** – You may need to fill in records if pupils have used play opportunities particularly well or if they have had difficulties.
- **Accident books or incident reports** – These need to be filled in following any incidents that have taken place during the day.
- **Attendance registers** – You must ensure that attendance for the session has been correctly recorded.
- **Planning and evaluation sheets** – You should keep a record of activities that have been popular or unpopular with pupils.
- **Notes or memos to others** – The end of the session may be the only time available to write and inform other staff about what has happened during the day if you will not be present the following day or if they need to be notified about something that has happened.

For your portfolio...

K3
K4
K5
K6
K7
K8
K10
K15
K16

You need to show how you have set up and managed play experiences for pupils, while encouraging them to maximise their ownership of different situations. You should write about or show your assessor at least two environments that you have set up in school, showing how you have included pupils' views in decisions about the selected activities. Check with your assessor when you have done this to make sure you have covered the knowledge points above.

Websites

www.4children.org.uk – support with children's centres, extended schools and play provision

www.playwork.org.uk/downloads/values – assumptions and values of playwork

17 Invigilate Tests and Examinations

This unit is designed for those who invigilate external examinations and tests in schools, such as module tests and practical and oral examinations. You may be involved in preparing for and running examinations as well as dealing with specific arrangements for individual pupils. It is also likely that you will be asked to manage collation and record-keeping of examinations and should know the procedures set by examination boards. You will also need to be aware of school requirements for emergency procedures and evacuation of the hall if necessary.

What you need to know and understand

For this unit, you need to know and understand:

- The centre's tests and examinations policy

- Procedures and regulations for the conduct of external examinations and any inspection procedures related to this

- Your own role in the test and examination process and how this relates to the role of others including the examinations officer, other invigilators and subject teachers

- The role of special educational needs staff and/or others in handling access arrangements

- What sorts of access arrangements may be required and the implications for invigilation of tests and examinations

- The correct procedures for setting up an examination room

- What stationery and equipment is authorised for use during tests and examinations and your responsibility for arranging supplies

- The health and safety arrangements for the examination room, e.g. location of fire extinguishers and emergency exits

- Any emergency communication system used by the school and how to use this

- What equipment and materials are not allowed to be brought into the examination room and how to ensure these are not brought in

- The procedure for dealing with candidates who are not on the test or examination attendance list

- The procedure for dealing with candidates who arrive late for a test or examination

- How to complete an attendance register including specific requirements for candidates who are withdrawn from the test or examination, not on the register, late or absent

- Your responsibilities and procedures for dealing with:

    - a   queries from candidates

    - b   any disruptive behaviour

    - c   any actual or suspected malpractice

    - d   candidates who wish or need to leave the examination room during a test or examination

    - e   any health, safety or security emergencies

- The importance of working within the boundaries of your role and competence and when you should refer to others

- The centre's behaviour management policy and how this applies to tests and examinations

- Where to seek medical assistance in an emergency

- The arrangements for escorting candidates who need to leave the examination room during a test or examination

- The arrangements for the emergency evacuation of the examination room

- How to end tests and examinations when:

  - a   all candidates are due to finish their test or examination at the same time

  - b   some candidates are still engaged in a test or examination

- Why a candidate may need to be supervised between tests and examinations and your role and responsibilities in relation to this

- The test and examination records that you need to complete and how to do this

Centre's tests and examinations policy

If you are asked to invigilate tests and exams, you should be familiar with your school's (the centre's) policy and your responsibilities. It is important that the policy sets out procedures for organising exams and that you are clear on what you are expected to do. The examinations procedure, at whatever stage, is intended to be a formal opportunity for pupils to demonstrate their knowledge and skills to the best of their ability. You should ensure that facilities and requirements provided by the school enable them all to do this.

Portfolio activity K1

Identifying responsibilities within the text and examinations policy

Make sure that you have obtained a copy of your school's test and examinations policy and are able to identify your responsibilities.

External requirements for how to run exams and any inspection procedures related to this

Each regulatory board that regulates the administration of exams provides a list of requirements to the school to ensure that the exams are being carried out in the specified manner. This usually comprises of guidelines for invigilators and examinations officers and may also include the following:

- the required number and positioning of desks
- display of notices
- seating plans
- clock
- centre number
- instructions for candidates
- attendance registers
- health and safety arrangements
- heating, lighting and ventilation.

The examinations board may require that the process is inspected by their representatives from time to time in order to show that the school's systems and procedures are running smoothly. If your school is likely to be inspected during the examinations process, you should be informed about this by the school examinations officer and told what to expect.

Your own role in the examinations process and how this relates to the role of others

If you are asked to **invigilate** exams, you will not be the only adult present. There will be a team of invigilators and teachers who will work together to make sure that the process runs smoothly. You should have opportunities before you first start to carry out examination invigilation to discuss the process and any specific candidate requirements such as those for pupils who have special educational (Additional Support for Learning (ASL)) needs. It should be clear to you what your role is and when you should seek advice from others. Your main point of contact for clarifying any concerns or for seeking advice should be the examinations officer.

Key term

Invigilate – conducting an examination session in the presence of the candidates

K3 Portfolio activity

Reflecting on your role as invigilator

If your job description contains information about your role as an invigilator and how it relates to that of others, you can highlight this and use for your portfolio. If not, you will need to write a reflective account stating this.

Role of special educational (ASL) needs staff and/or others in handling access arrangements

Depending on the needs of the pupils, there may be special educational (ASL) needs staff present at the examination to support those who have this entitlement. Examination boards need to be informed of any pupils who have special educational (ASL) needs and the nature of their requirements: this usually takes place through the submission of special arrangement request forms, and evidence is provided. Procedures for the administration of additional support should be found in your school's special educational (ASL) needs or examinations policy, and may take different forms. The school should be aware of the pupils' needs when registering them for the examination so that they have notice and can offer the correct provision. It is likely that if pupils have a Statement of Special Educational Needs (Co-ordinated Support Plan) they will be supported by the learning support assistant who is most familiar with their needs and this should be arranged between the school's SENCO (ASL teaching) and the examinations officer.

Key term

Access arrangements – the arrangements made by the school and agreed by the appropriate awarding body for candidates with additional needs, e.g. reading assistance, scribe, sign interpreter

What sorts of access arrangements may be required and the implications for invigilation

The kinds of access arrangements required by pupils will vary according to need, but they may include:

- **Allowing students extra time to complete the examination** – This may mean that the majority of students leave the examination hall prior to the SEN (ASL) pupils. In this case, these pupils may need to be seated separately so that there is less disturbance to them when others depart. Alternatively, they could carry out the examination in a separate room, if one is available, so that disruption is avoided.
- **Providing modified or enlarged examination papers** – For example, for candidates who have visual impairments. These pupils may also need additional time for rest breaks.
- **Providing a scribe or reader** – This has implications for noise levels within the examination room so your school may decide to provide alternative arrangements for these pupils such as a separate room.
- **Providing specialist computer software or additional equipment** – Pupils may need to have the use of a laptop or specific software to support their needs, although this should not be connected to any network and should be provided by the school. Care should be taken so that the computer or equipment does not disturb others. In some cases, candidates may need to arrive early to ensure that the computer is set up according to their needs.
- **Providing an interpreter or signer** – This may also mean that the pupil requires a separate room from other candidates.

Correct procedures for setting up an examination room

Procedures for setting up an examination room should be set by the examinations board and should include seating plans, health and safety arrangements, display of notices and so on (see also K2, page 237). As an invigilator, you should ensure that you are aware of the school and examination board requirements.

Keys to good practice

Setting up an examination room

✓ Make sure you have had invigilator training if you are required to invigilate.
✓ Allow plenty of time to arrive and ensure the room is set up appropriately.
✓ Familiarise yourself with health and safety arrangements (heating, lighting, noise levels and evacuation procedures).
✓ Ensure that you have checked the requirements set by the examinations board and those for the individual exam.
✓ Make sure that there is enough stationery such as additional sheets.
✓ Prepare access arrangements for any pupils who have special educational (ASL) needs.
✓ Check timings of exams and how many staff will be covering.

What stationery and equipment is authorised for use and your responsibility for arranging supplies

Candidates should only be authorised to use stationery and equipment that has been specified for use during examinations by awarding bodies. They should not be permitted to bring their own paper into exams. As an invigilator, you should ensure that there is adequate additional paper for the potential requirements of candidates and know where to obtain more if necessary. Additional equipment authorised for use in examinations is covered in K10, page 240.

Health and safety arrangements for the examination room

The health and safety arrangements for the examinations room come under the remit of your school's health and safety officer. However, as an invigilator you should be aware of procedures you would be required to follow during evacuation of the examination room or during an emergency. Candidates should also be informed of these at the start of the examination.

K8 Portfolio activity

Identifying the location of fire extinguishers and emergency exits

There should be a plan available of your examinations room. Take a copy of it and mark the location of fire extinguishers and emergency exits. If one is not available, you can show these to your assessor during one of your assessment visits.

Using an emergency communication system

Your school may have some system of communication for contacting others in an emergency, for example, if there is an incident in the examination room that cannot be resolved by those present. If you are the chief invigilator of an exam, make sure that you are aware of the correct procedure to use and what is accessible to you.

Equipment and materials not allowed in the examination room

Depending on the nature of the examination and the awarding body regulations, there should be a list available of the equipment and materials that are not allowed to be brought into the examination room. Candidates should be made aware of these before the exam so that invigilators and examination officers do not have to give this information out on the day. Examples of these guidelines might be:

Equipment which *must* be brought by candidates	pen, pencil, rubber, ruler
Equipment which *may* be brought in by candidates	small calculator where specified (without case), batteries, pencil sharpener, additional equipment such as laptops for SEN (ASL) pupils
Equipment which *must not* be brought in by candidates	mobile phones (can be switched off or on silent setting if left in candidates' bags), large calculators or instruction texts, programmable watches, personal stereo devices, electronic or radio communication devices, additional papers

As an invigilator, you are responsible for making sure that candidates have not brought any inappropriate equipment or materials into the examination room and to check during the exam that none are in evidence. It is likely that inspection of equipment will take place when candidates first enter the room and are checked against the attendance register. All equipment they have with them should be kept visible on their desks and any pencil cases used should be transparent.

Procedure for dealing with candidates who are not on the examination attendance list

If candidates who are not on the examination attendance list are present you should firstly report this to the examinations officer who may be able to help. Failing this, you should contact the head of the relevant department to confirm their non-entry. It may be possible for them to sit the exam if they have not been entered in error and can be added to the attendance list. However this will depend on individual awarding body regulations.

Sometimes it can also be assumed that pupils are to receive help during exams if they are on School Action or School Action Plus – this should always be checked with the SENCo before sending them to any learning supported area.

Procedure for dealing with candidates who arrive late for an exam

Candidates and invigilators should be aware of the procedure for those who arrive late for an exam. These may be specified by the school or the examinations board and will usually stipulate that late arrivals may be admitted up to a certain time (e.g. 15 minutes) after the start of the exam. It is unlikely that they will be granted any additional time to complete the exam.

How to complete an attendance register

It is likely that the examinations officer will be responsible for completing attendance registers for exams. However, as an invigilator, you may be asked to support them in doing this. The procedure as candidates come into the examinations room will usually be that they show a form of identification along with their candidate number so that they can be checked on the attendance list. They should then be shown their seats if there is a seating allocation. If there are specific circumstances, such as those who are not on the register, late or absent, these should be reported to the examinations officer (although see also K11 and K12 above). Withdrawn candidates should be marked accordingly on the attendance register.

Your responsibilities and procedures for dealing with incidents during the exam

Queries from candidates

Candidates should be instructed that if anyone has a query during an exam they should raise their hand. As an invigilator and in the first instance, you should go to them to find out the nature of their query. In most cases you should be able to resolve this, for example if they need more paper. However if you cannot deal with the query yourself you may need to refer it to the examinations officer.

Any disruptive behaviour (see also K16)

Disruptive behaviour should be dealt with immediately so as not to disturb other candidates. You should be absolutely clear what to do in this situation, but it is unlikely you would have to deal with it on your own. Candidates should be aware that disruptive behaviour may result in their being removed and disqualified from the examination.

Any actual or suspected malpractice

If you suspect or become aware that a candidate may have been cheating, either by copying others or bringing information into the exam, you must report this immediately. Make sure you are able to explain the grounds for your suspicions.

For responsibilities and procedures around candidates who wish or need to leave the examination room during an exam, see K18, page 243 and around any health, safety or security emergencies, see K8, page 240 and K17, page 243.

Importance of working within the boundaries of your role and competence

As an invigilator you should be aware of your own role and responsibilities while in the examination room. It should be clear to you when you are able to act and when you should refer to others before doing so. You should also know who to speak to in an examination situation if you need further advice. This is important as you and other invigilators should be seen to have confidence in what you are doing.

K15 Case study

Identifying the responsibilities of the invigilator's role

Carol is working as an invigilator in a secondary school. She has been doing this for two years and has mainly been involved with GCSE invigilation. This year her role has changed slightly and she has been asked to be the chief invigilator for some of the exams as the school has a reduced number of staff available. Carol has agreed to be chief invigilator but is unsure what is involved because the school has not been very forthcoming about telling her what she is required to do.

- What should Carol do?
- Why is it important that she finds out what her responsibilities are as soon as possible?

Centre's behaviour management policy and how this applies to exams

Your school (the centre) will have a behaviour management policy to which all staff should have access. This gives staff, students and parents guidelines about the expected behaviour both in school and when representing the school off-site. The behaviour policy may have separate sections outlining rules in different situations, for example on the playground, during swimming lessons, or during exams. If examination guidelines are not within the behaviour management policy, your school should provide a list of guidelines for candidates so that they are aware what is required of them.

K16 Portfolio activity

Identifying behaviour management policy for exams

Check your school's behaviour management policy to see whether it gives guidelines for exams. If so, you can photocopy or highlight these to show the behaviour expected of candidates in examination situations and use them as evidence for your portfolio. If it does not, your school should provide a list of guidelines for candidates such as the one above, which you can use as evidence instead.

Where to seek medical assistance in an emergency

While invigilating exams, there may be instances when you need to seek medical assistance for candidates or for other adults who are present. The school should have a first aider available on hand to assist with any accidents or emergencies. You are unlikely to be the only adult present in the examinations room and, if there is no first aider in the immediate vicinity, you should send for one through another adult if necessary. You should be aware of your own limitations and the importance of having first aid training when dealing with accidents and emergencies.

Case study K17

Dealing with a medical emergency

You are invigilating during Key Stage 3 SATS tests, which are taking place in your school sports hall. One of the girls close to the front of the hall puts up her hand and as you approach her you notice that she is having a severe nose bleed. She is in considerable distress and is calling out.

- Whose needs should you take into account first?
- What would you do and in what order?

Arrangements for escorting candidates who need to leave the examination room during an exam

You should follow your school policy, which will be based on awarding body requirements, if you are required to escort candidates from the examination room. If you have not been given clear instructions, check with another invigilator or the school's examinations officer. There may be specific rules for leaving the room, for example, that candidates may not do this within the first 30 minutes or in the final 15 minutes.

Arrangements for the emergency evacuation of the examination room

In the event of an emergency on school premises it is likely that candidates and other invigilators would be familiar with school procedures for the evacuation of buildings. They should leave the room quietly and in an orderly fashion by the nearest available exit and assemble at the required point. When leaving the examination room, all materials and papers should be left behind.

How to end an examination

When all candidates are due to finish their exam at the same time

When ending examinations, you will be required to follow the procedures of the school and examining body regulations. In most cases, the candidates will need to be given some prior notification that the examination is about to finish, for example about 15 minutes before the end. At the required time they should then be told to:

- stop writing
- ensure their name and candidate number are on all paperwork as required
- to ensure all paperwork is left in the examination room and not removed
- to remain in their seats until asked to leave.

When some candidates are still engaged in an examination

If some candidates are still engaged in an exam, the exam will usually finish as usual but those who leave the hall will be required to remain silent until they are away from the examination area. In this situation candidates must be informed what will happen at the beginning of the exam to avoid disruption.

Why a candidate may need to be supervised between exam and your role and responsibilities in relation to this

You may find that you are required to supervise a candidate in between exams. This may occur if candidates need to complete more than one exam during a session, but are permitted to take a break in between. It may also be due to timetable clashes, which mean that they need to do an exam at a different time from others on the same day. If you are supporting a pupil who has special educational (ASL) needs and needs longer to complete an exam, they may also require supervision. Your role is to ensure that they do not communicate with others between exams. This includes communicating via mobile phone or email. You should also ensure that they have some form of comfort break and access to meals or refreshments as required.

Examination records that you need to complete and how to do this

At the end of examinations, invigilators should make sure that papers are collected in exam number order. Following the collection of examination papers, you may be required to fill in examination records, although this is usually the responsibility of the examinations officer. This might include recording the number of scripts against attendance registers and checking that they are kept safely until being posted to the awarding body or examiners. They should be sent with a hall plan and an attendance list. If you have acted as a scribe for a pupil you must complete an amanuensis form, which you must sign and put with the relevant candidate's exam paper. For guidance on filling in examination records, you need to check the written requirements of individual exam boards.

For your portfolio...

K6
K7
K9
K13
K15
K17
K18
K20
K21

In order to gather evidence for this unit, you need to show that you act appropriately and according to your role and responsibilities when invigilating exams. It is unlikely that your assessor will be able to observe you doing this. You may therefore need to refer to an expert witness, for example your school's examinations officer, to provide a witness testimony stating that you are competent in invigilating exams. This may be written on school headed paper or through a conversation with your assessor and should aim to cover some of the performance criteria and knowledge points for this unit. Alternatively, in order to cover the knowledge points only, you can write a reflective account as described below.

Write an account of the procedures you follow in your school when preparing for and running exams. This should include your own duties in preparing and setting up the examinations room and the stationery requirements, and your responsibilities in relation to this. You must include how you would complete attendance registers and any problems arising from this. You should also outline the emergency procedures that you would need to follow, including where you would seek help if required. Show what procedures you would follow if you needed to escort a candidate from the exam or supervise them between exams. Finally explain the routines for ending exams and your role in relation to this, including procedures for candidates finishing later than others.

Activities to Accompany DVD Footage

Introduction

This edition of *S/NVQ Level 2 Teaching Assistant's Handbook* is designed to help you to gather further evidence for your portfolio through the use of DVD clips. The clips were filmed in primary settings, and show teaching assistants working in a variety of situations. They relate directly to knowledge aspects of the National Occupational Standards for Supporting Teaching and Learning in Schools at Level 2. The DVD can be played on a home, college or work computer, or on your home DVD player. It offers you the flexibility to pause and rewind, so that you can take things at your own pace.

By watching the DVD, you can see at first hand scenarios which you may not have experienced in your school, or you can use it to help you think about areas of practice which you may find more challenging. You should not aim to use all of the activities; you should dip into them to support your evidence gathering as an additional resource rather than working through them as a series of activities. This is because as much evidence as possible for your NVQ should be based on your own experiences and the observations which your assessor carries out.

You will be able to match the different clips to your portfolio through clear referencing in the activities. Although they mainly relate to the knowledge and understanding section, and help you gather evidence for this, they may also refer to performance criteria – and this will be indicated in the text through the symbols **K** for knowledge or **P** for performance. Remember, however, that performance indicators should mainly be observed by your assessor and that if you wish to use these as sole evidence, you should check with your assessor first.

The DVD clips have been taken from the *Interactive Tutor Resource File for Teaching Assistants* and the *Introduction to Child Development* DVD and tutor resource booklet. More information on these resources can be found at www.pearsonschoolsandfecolleges.co.uk (select FE & Vocational, then Childcare).

Understanding shape or measures

Activity

In this clip, the teaching assistant is working with a group of Year 1 pupils on an activity to encourage them to name and describe the properties of different 2D and 3D shapes.

1   While watching the clip, consider the following questions.

- What evidence is there in the video that the assistant has a clear plan for the activity?

- What positive teaching and learning strategies does she use throughout the task? Are there any negative aspects?

- How will the teaching assistant be able to assess whether the learning objective has been met?

Make notes on how you might carry out the activity differently if you were asked to work on it with pupils. **K5, K6, K8, K10, K12**

K

2   Look at the factors which promote effective learning on page 13 of this book. Which of these are evident from the clip?

3   What do you think about the method of feedback used in this clip? Trial this method with your class teacher if you have not done this already and use as evidence for your portfolio, including the teacher's signature to confirm this as performance evidence. Remember to remove the children's names. **Section 1.3: P1, P2, P3, P4** (if you have included all these aspects)

P

4   Watch DVD clip 8 (SEN [physical impairment]) and answer the same questions for the teaching assistant supporting the PE lesson.

Transcript of voiceover: Understanding shape or measures

These Year 1 children are working with a teaching assistant to assess whether they are able to name and describe the properties of different 2D and 3D shapes.

The teaching assistant has been asked to take particular note of those children who use the correct mathematical vocabulary when describing the shapes.

At the end of the session the teaching assistant writes down which children have achieved the learning objective and successfully described the properties of the shapes, and feeds back this information to the teacher.

Unit 2: Support children's development

Child development

Activity

1   Watch the short clip on child development which includes a brief narrative.

2   Write a case study on a child you support, and include:

  - age, sex, health, social background and position in family

  - friendships – do they have lots of friends, or one or two close friendships?

  - attitude to learning – are they eager to learn?

  - physical development – are they big or small for their age? Does this affect their relationships or their confidence?

  - whether they have any areas of special educational need.

3   Think about the four areas of development – physical, intellectual, social and emotional. How are the child's experiences in these areas influencing their behaviour and learning? Where would you refer any concerns you have about a child? **K3, K4, K6, K7, K8**

K

You may need to carry out a few observations on the child or note down some of their interactions as they occur. Include these work products as evidence **Section 2.1: P1, P2; Section 2.3: P1, P3, P5** Remember to speak to the class teacher and check your school's procedures before selecting your child. You should also check with the child's parent or carer, and change the child's name for the purpose of the study. (See also DVD clip 5 [Record keeping and observation] for more on carrying out child observations.)

P

Consider how your observations have helped you to assess the child and plan for their needs, and record how you will do this alongside the class teacher. Make sure you show it to your assessor so that you can use this as a work product to cover performance criteria if the class teacher signs it for you.
 Section 2.4: P1, P2, P3

P

Transcript of voiceover: Child development

All children follow a general path of development, but not every child will grow and develop in the same way or at the same rate. So, while the pattern is broadly the same for all children, it is important to keep in mind the uniqueness of each child. Some babies crawl for a long time, whereas other babies stand and walk without crawling much at all. Even twins grow and develop in different ways at different times. This holds true for all areas of development. You will learn just how children develop physically, from babies who are dependent on their parents or carers for all their needs, into young children who have learned how to control their own bodies and can perform many complex physical activities. You will also learn how children develop the ability to think, to reason and to use language to express themselves. This growing ability to think and to understand the way other people behave is closely linked with their emotions and with their family relationships and friendships. All children need to develop a sense of identity and self-worth. By understanding the all-round – or holistic – developmental stages which children pass through, you will be better able to promote their development and help them to reach their own potential.

Communicating with parents

Activity

In order to achieve your qualification, you will need to demonstrate that you are able to develop and maintain positive relationships both with adults and pupils in the school environment. This will include relationships with parents.

In this clip, the teaching assistant is liaising with parents in different school situations.

1   After watching it, write a brief outline to show how, as part of your role, you have communicated different kinds of information to parents and followed school policy. You can also ask a parent or staff member to write a witness testimony for your portfolio stating how you have shown positive relationships with parents or other adults in school over time, giving examples and stating any areas of difficulty which have occurred and how you have resolved them. **K9, K10, K13**

    This may also cover K6 and K8, and the performance criteria for sections 4.2 and 4.4 if it is in the form of a witness testimony. If you are at all unsure, you should speak with your assessor in order to map it to the standards.

K

Transcript of voiceover: Communicating with parents

Teaching assistants frequently come into contact with the parents and carers of the children they support and must be approachable, actively encourage positive relationships, and remain professional by following school procedure. It is important to note the concerns of parents and carers, and reassure them wherever possible. They can provide important information on the social and emotional welfare of their children, as well as any physical needs that need to be addressed.

Assistants often act as mediators. It is essential to remember to pass on all information to the relevant staff members.

Teaching assistants may occasionally be required to liaise formally with parents and carers during school open days or parents' evenings. Most of the time, however, they interact with parents and carers on a less formal basis at the beginning and end of the day, where it is important to update them on incidents that have occurred during the school day.

Unit 6: Support literacy and numeracy activities

Early literacy support

Activity

In this clip, the teaching assistant is working with a small group of Year 1 children out of class. She is following the Early Literacy Support programme and works regularly with the same group of children. Watch the clip and answer the following questions:

1 Does the teaching assistant demonstrate an awareness of the existing literacy skills of her group? Outline how you think this is evident.

2 What problems does the assistant face as she is working with the group and how does she overcome them? Would you have done this any differently? Outline how you would have run the session if so.

3 Think about the use of praise in the clip and how the assistant settles the group and ensures that they are on task. How does this affect the learning experience?

    You can also use your work on Unit 1 as evidence for the numeracy aspect of this unit. Answer the above questions again after watching the first clip of the assistant working with Reception on shapes (clip 1, Understanding shape or measures) and substituting the word 'literacy' for 'numeracy'. You can then use your work on both videos as evidence for **K2, K9, K10.** **K**

4 Compare the approaches by the two assistants. Which do you think is a more effective learning experience for the children, and why?

Transcript of voiceover: Early literacy support

The intervention sessions for the Early Literacy Support programme are led by an experienced teaching assistant and take place during the second term of Year 1.

The teaching assistant begins with the oral opener and looks at previous learning, goes over the outline and introduces the objectives for the session.

The second stage in an intervention session focuses on developing the phonic awareness of the individuals. Puppets are used to increase interest in the activity.

The third stage introduces activities to help enhance the children's reading or writing skills.

Each intervention session ends with a fast finisher where the teaching assistant recaps the learning intentions. The children may also be given work to take away with them to extend their learning.

Record keeping and observation

Activity

Watch the clip of an assistant carrying out a formal observation on a group of pupils using the free description method as a non-participant observer.

1   How has the observation been set up to ensure a minimum of disruption and distraction for those who are being observed? What sources of distractions might there have been during the art activity? **K4**   **K**

2   What do you need to be absolutely clear about before carrying out an observation? How can you ensure that you keep the observation reliable, subjective and valid?

3   Should you use pupil names when carrying out an observation? If so, how can you ensure that the records you make remain confidential while keeping track of whom they relate to?

4   Include an example of an observation which you have carried out on pupils. Make sure that for the purpose of your portfolio you remove any names, and state how you have maintained confidentiality.
    Section 9.2: P1, P2, P5, K9, K10, K11   **P** **K**

Transcript of voiceover: Record keeping and observation

Much of our observation of children is done on an 'informal' basis – we notice if a child does something which is unusual or makes unexpected progress. Occasionally teaching assistants are asked to carry out more formal observations on children.

Here the assistant is observing individual children working on an art activity. Children are observed in school for a variety of reasons. Teaching assistants need to be clear on the purpose of any observations they carry out.

This teaching assistant is using the 'free description' method of observation, but others may include checklists, 'target child', or time and event sampling.

It is important to make sure that any observations remain objective and the observer only records what is seen. Once observations have been made they need to be filed appropriately and confidentiality maintained.

Unit 10: Support children's play and learning

DVD 6

Creative play

Activity

If you are working in an early years classroom, you will need to be aware of the importance of play in children's learning and development. For this unit's performance criteria you will need to look at play in five different areas, one of which (10.2) is providing opportunities for children's drama and imaginative play. Watch the clip of the assistant playing alongside a group of children in the home corner.

1   Looking at your own classroom and thinking about your experience, list the kinds of opportunities which are available for children to initiate play opportunities themselves. How do staff encourage and promote this without being directly involved themselves? **K13** What are the advantages of this when considered alongside the experience of the children in the video? **K12**

    K

    K

2   Consider other aspects of creative play which may be found in an early years classroom (make sure you consider both indoor and outdoor opportunities). Why are all these kinds of play opportunities important for children? **K5, K9**

    K

If your class teacher is in agreement, take some photographs of displays or different areas of the learning environment if you have been involved in setting them up, and describe how and why you have done this. (Do **not** include photographs of children in your portfolio.) **K14, K24, K25**

    K

Transcript of voiceover: Creative play

'Home corners' in early years classrooms encourage pupils to participate in role-play activities and to play cooperatively in different situations. This home corner has been turned into a wolf's lair. The teaching assistant is working with the group and ensuring children are using the props that have been provided.

The assistant also leaves the home corner to give the children the opportunity to work without the direction of an adult, but remains close by to monitor their interactions and return if necessary.

Children need to be given different situations to work in, such as shops, services and homes, and these should always have a broad cultural base.

DVD 7 | **Supporting EAL pupils**

'EAL' is the term sometimes used for children who speak English as an additional language.

Activity

Watch the clip of an assistant working with a bilingual child.

1   Find an example of how the assistant models the correct language – in particular, if the child makes an error. Does she use any other helpful strategies? What do you think of her use of praise and of constructive feedback? **K4, K6**   **K**

2   Why is this sort of activity useful? What kinds of activities might you work on with bilingual or multilingual children in school? Give examples of work you have carried out with pupils and show how you work with the teacher to ensure a consistent approach. This should include both planning and feedback. **K8, K10, K12**   **K**

If you include work products which the teacher has signed you may wish to use these to cover performance criteria P9 (Section 11.1) and P8 (Section 11.2).
Section 11.1: P9; Section 11.2: P8   **P**

3   Show how you gather information about the bilingual pupils with whom you work. Why is it important to obtain recent and relevant information when you are working with these children? **K9**   **K**

Transcript of voiceover: Supporting EAL pupils

There are many effective strategies to help support EAL children in schools. The use of specific materials and equipment, such as dual-language books, allow EAL children to make comparisons between English and their first language.

Specific support methods such as modelling the language are also effective. Segmentation and sounding out help EAL children's understanding of phonetics.

Effective questioning helps EAL children develop their speaking and listening skills. These pupils may benefit from using visual cues and it is important to find opportunities for them to produce independent language.

Unit 12: Support a child with disabilities or special educational needs

DVD 8

SEN (physical impairment)

Activity

1   List some of the ways in which the teaching assistant supports the child throughout the lesson. How does she remove any barriers which exist to the child's learning? **K9**

    K

2   This lesson was filmed in a mainstream school where the child has been included fully with the rest of the class. Think about the kinds of benefits this will have for all of the children. Give examples of inclusion in your own setting and how this works. **K5**

    K

3   Sara, the teaching assistant in this clip, works closely both with parents and with the class teacher to ensure that the child she supports is able to participate in whole-class activities as much as possible. Which other professionals might be involved in supporting special needs provision in schools, and how might this help teaching assistants? **K6**

    K

Transcript of voiceover: SEN (physical impairment)

Physically impaired children with both fine and gross motor skill difficulties benefit during physical education lessons. Activities such as the ones here help children improve their agility, balance and develop their gross motor skills.

During indoor PE the acoustics in the hall may make it difficult for children with communication impairments to follow instructions. Teaching assistants may be required to repeat and clarify what the teacher says.

It is important to praise the efforts of the physically impaired individual, however basic the movements may seem. Teaching assistants should be aware of the child's limitations and use this knowledge to challenge the individual to their full potential.

Children with balance and coordination problems, or those who are unable to determine space effectively due to visual impairments, may need assistance on the apparatus. However, the teaching assistant should always encourage maximum independence.

Playground project

Activity

In this clip, the assistant is talking through some of the playground opportunities which are available during break times.

1   Why is play so important as part of children's development? **K2** What other play opportunities exist for different age groups in your school? Although it is important for play to be mainly self-directed, can you think of any cases when this may not always be positive? **K17**

  K

  K

2   Consider the different ways in which the school in the clip made sure that children's needs are met during playtime. What do you think of the types of environments which they have been given?

3   Give examples of the kinds of opportunities which the children have had to contribute to the discussion about their play and state why this is important. **K5, K6, K9, K11**

  K

4   In the clip there are some examples of situations where pupils may need additional support in play situations. Outline some areas where you have had to intervene when supporting play, and describe why you felt that adult intervention was important. Can you think of situations where your involvement has not been as beneficial as you had anticipated? **K21, K22, K25**

  K

Transcript of voiceover: Playground project

To overcome the problematic experiences reported by staff on playground duty, the Department for Education and Skills teamed with Nike and the Youth Support Trust to introduce a playground improvement project. Some schools have introduced their own versions of this playground project. In schools that have adopted the project, the playground is separated into three zones:

- The red zone is for those who wish to play the traditional games that once dominated the whole playground, such as basketball or football.
- The blue zone is a multi-activity area where games can be played individually, in pairs or as a team.
- The third zone, known as the yellow zone, is a quiet area where activities such as board games are available for quieter individuals.

Year 5 and 6 pupils are chosen to lead the activities and act as playground leaders or playground friends. These roles are excellent for the development of leadership, management, organisational and citizenship skills.

Playgrounds also have 'friendship stops' where a leader is located to talk to anyone who feels alone.

Index